CAPITAL FLIGHT AND THIRD WORLD DEBT

Capital Flight

DONALD R. LESSARD AND
JOHN WILLIAMSON

and Third World Debt

INSTITUTE FOR INTERNATIONAL ECONOMICS
Washington, DC 1987

Donald R. Lessard was a Visiting Fellow at the Institute and is currently Professor of International Management at the MIT Sloan School of Management. He has published extensively on various aspects of international finance including corporate finance, portfolio investment, and external financing for developing countries.

John Williamson is a Senior Fellow at the Institute for International Economics. He was formerly economics professor at Pontifícia Universade Católica do Rio de Janeiro, University of Warwick, Massachusetts Institute of Technology, University of York, and Princeton University; Advisor to the International Monetary Fund; and Economic Consultant to Her Majesty's Treasury. Williamson has published numerous studies on international monetary issues, including IMF Conditionality, The Exchange Rate System, The Failure of World Monetary Reform 1971–74, *and* Political Economy and International Money.

The authors gratefully acknowledge the many helpful comments of C. Fred Bergsten, José Diaz-Asper, Miguel A. F. Rodríguez, and the referees, and the dedicated typing of Debby McGuire.   D.R.L. *and* J.W.

INSTITUTE FOR INTERNATIONAL ECONOMICS
11 Dupont Circle, NW
Washington, DC 20036
(202) 328–9000 Telex: 248329 CEIP
Fax: (202) 328–5432

C. Fred Bergsten, *Director*
Kathleen A. Lynch, *Director of Publications*
Ann L. Beasley, *Production Manager*

The Institute for International Economics was created, and is principally funded, by the German Marshall Fund of the United States.

The views expressed in this publication are those of the authors. This publication is part of the overall program of the Institute, as endorsed by its Board of Directors, but does not necessarily reflect the views of individual members of the Board or the Advisory Committee.

Printed in the United States of America
91 90 89 88 87   5 4 3 2 1

Library of Congress Cataloging–in–Publication Data

Capital Flight and Third World debt.

References
1. Capital movements—Developing countries. 2. Debts, External—Developing countries. 3. Debts External—Latin America—Case studies. I. Williamson, John, 1937– . II. Lessard, Donald R. III. Institute for International Economics (U.S.) IV. Series.
HG3891.C267 1987 332'.042 87–17279
ISBN 0–88132–059–5

Contents

APPENDIX

TABLES

vi

FIGURE

Preface

Capital flight has become a topic of major policy concern in the context of Third World debt and development, especially in Latin America. The issue also raises questions about the interaction between economic policies in the industrial and developing countries, and regarding the role of international banks as both lenders to the Third World and depositaries for their capital exports. The Institute thus decided to conduct a comprehensive analysis of the issue, beginning with a conference in October 1986. This volume presents the proceedings of that conference together with the analytical findings and policy recommendations that resulted.

The Institute has previously conducted a number of studies of the debt problem: *International Debt and the Stability of the World Economy* (1983), *International Debt: Systemic Risk and Policy Response* (1984), and *Mobilizing Bank Lending to Debtor Countries* (1987), all by William R. Cline; *Financial Intermediation Beyond the Debt Crisis* (1985) by Donald R. Lessard and John Williamson; and *Bank Lending to Developing Countries: The Policy Alternatives* (1985) by C. Fred Bergsten, William R. Cline, and John Williamson. In addition, the overall problems of Latin America were addressed in *Toward Renewed Economic Growth in Latin America* (1986), by Bela Balassa, Gerardo M. Bueno, Pedro-Pablo Kuczynski, and Mario Henrique Simonsen. The present study seeks to extend those earlier analyses by appraising the problem of capital flight and suggesting possible responses to it. The concluding chapter of this volume was released separately as one of the Institute's Policy Analyses in International Economics.

The Institute for International Economics is a private nonprofit research institution for the study and discussion of international economic policy. Its purpose is to analyze important issues in that area, and to develop and communicate practical new approaches for dealing with them. The Institute is completely nonpartisan.

The Institute was created by a generous commitment of funds from the

German Marshall Fund of the United States in 1981, and continues to receive substantial support from that source. In addition, major institutional grants are now being received from the Ford Foundation, the William and Flora Hewlett Foundation, and the Alfred P. Sloan Foundation. A number of other foundations and private corporations are contributing to the increasing diversification of the Institute's financial resources.

The Board of Directors bears overall responsibility for the Institute and gives general guidance and approval to its research program—including identification of topics that are likely to become important to international economic policymakers over the medium run (generally, one to three years) and which thus should be addressed by the Institute. The Director, working closely with the staff and outside Advisory Committee, is responsible for the development of particular projects and makes the final decision to publish an individual study.

The Institute hopes that its studies and other activities will contribute to building a stronger foundation for international economic policy around the world. Comments as to how it can best do so are invited from readers of these publications.

C. FRED BERGSTEN
Director
October 1987

1

Introduction

Donald R. Lessard and John Williamson

Massive capital outflows from a number of developing countries, most notably Argentina, Mexico and Venezuela, have contributed to the foreign exchange scarcity that has arrested economic development in much of the Third World during the 1980s. Recently, commercial bankers have pleaded the occurrence of capital flight to justify their reluctance to increase their exposure in some debtor countries. A reversal of capital flight might therefore provide a double easing of the foreign exchange constraint.

So we wrote in the summer of 1986, in the opening paragraph of the background note to the October 1986 conference whose proceedings are reported in this volume. We hoped that the conference would confirm or refute our assertion as to just how critical the issue of capital flight has become. We hoped also that, unless the conference led us to conclude that the problem has been much exaggerated, it would point the way to a set of policy actions that might succeed in reversing capital flight. In the event, we were led to conclude that the size of the phenomenon but not the importance of the topic had been exaggerated, and hence we have done our best (in the concluding chapter) to distill the policy implications suggested by the conference.

Capital flight is hardly a novel phenomenon, as the initial paper in the collection, by the dean of international economic historians, Charles P. Kindleberger, makes clear. From the Huguenots of the seventeenth century to the problems of President François Mitterrand in the 1980s, Kindleberger describes the causes, magnitude, mechanisms and consequences of a dozen or more instances of capital flight.

Like many other papers in the conference, Kindleberger starts by reflecting on the slippery nature of the concept of "capital flight," but he does not subsequently appear troubled by any difficulty in identifying concrete instances of it. Nevertheless, even if capital flight is—like the proverbial elephant—easier to identify than to define, it seemed to us important to try

1

to pin down what is meant by the phrase. Is it just a pejorative term for foreign investment of which we disapprove? Or is there some operational way of distinguishing capital that is "fleeing" (Walter, ch. 5) or that "desires to run away" (an old Kindleberger phrase, cited by us in chapter 9) from that which moves abroad in the "normal" course of portfolio diversification?

These elusive issues are one of the two topics taken up by Robert Cumby and Richard Levich in chapter 3. They argue that the only satisfactory basis for distinguishing "capital flight" from "normal" capital outflows from an internationalist perspective is to limit the former to illegal transactions. Since this clearly does not capture the essence of the concern about capital flight (no laws were broken in the periods of major capital outflows from Argentina, Mexico, or Venezuela), it must be that the internationalist perspective is inappropriate. Definitions need to "be consistent with the . . . policy question under consideration"; since policy issues are being debated from a nationalistic point of view, a definition of capital flight should represent "a good proxy for the measure of national welfare loss." Capital flight is a capital outflow that is regarded as disadvantageous by the national authorities.

Few contributors to this volume have refrained from adding their input to this debate, and our concluding appraisal (ch. 9) is no exception. We reject the Cumby-Levich position in favor of the Kindleberger-Walter one, on the question of linguistic principle: words should be used to mean what normal use of the English language suggests they mean unless there is overwhelming precedent for a deviant technical use. Capital flight is distinguished by its motivation, not by its consequences. The Jewish capital that left Nazi Germany was still flight capital, even though we may approve of it. And the reason that capital flight is a problem in Latin America is not because we define it to be a problem, or that we perceive things from the nationalistic viewpoint of a Latin country, but because it has intensified the foreign-exchange constraint on those countries to a degree that has been damaging to the prosperity of the world as a whole, and even to the *collective* interest of the wealthy class that has bought foreign assets.

The other part of the Cumby-Levich paper is an extremely useful replication of several concepts of capital flight on leading definitions using a common data base, which provides both estimates of the magnitude of capital flight from six of the major debtor countries (Argentina, Brazil, Korea, Mexico, the Philippines, and Venezuela) and figures for the range of variation produced by different definitions and sources. It is supplemented by a note on the impact of trade misinvoicing on estimates of capital flight, by Sunil Gulati. Comparison of trade data from eight debtor countries with the corresponding data of partner (industrial) countries leads him to conclude that for most countries the underinvoicing of exports, presumably motivated by the desire to build up foreign assets, is actually outweighed by the underinvoicing of imports, presumably motivated by the desire to limit tariff payments or mitigate other trade controls. The surprising result is that many previous estimates have exaggerated the size of capital flight, sometimes by sizable amounts: it is noteworthy that Morgan Guaranty's (1986) estimate of $6 billion capital flight from Korea, which caused Korea to demand (and get) an official retraction, evaporates entirely.

The chapter also contains a comment on the Cumby-Levich paper by Michael Dooley, who argues that capital flight is better understood as a response to differences in the risks facing different groups of investors, notably residents versus nonresidents, than as a reflection of unfavorable aggregate investment opportunities. The chapter is concluded by a brief summary of conference discussion on issues of definition and magnitude of capital flight. (It is *not* intended to be a summary of the discussion that took place after the Cumby-Levich paper was presented, but rather a summary of discussion throughout the conference of the issues covered in the Cumby-Levich paper. The same principle was followed in summarizing discussion on other topics.)

Chapter 4 contains an econometric investigation of the causes of capital flight by John T. Cuddington. The factors that he pins down reasonably conclusively are overvaluation of the exchange rate, high interest rates in the industrial countries, and, in some cases, the magnitude of foreign borrowing. He recognizes that the limited number of observations may well preclude identification of other relevant variables, and mentions in particular the finding of Eduardo Conesa that a lack of growth in debtor countries contributes to capital flight. The chapter also contains a Comment focused principally on the Cuddington paper by Donald R. Lessard and a summary of conference discussion on the causes of capital outflow.

Chapter 5, by Ingo Walter, deals with the mechanisms of capital flight, meaning both the *conduits* through which money is shipped abroad and the *assets* in terms of which it is held once it arrives. Walter's description of these mechanisms is prefaced by an extension of the familiar portfolio-choice problem, defined over assets that vary with respect to risk and expected returns, to include a third variable that is highly relevant to much flight capital, namely secrecy. He uses this analysis to argue, *inter alia*, that abandonment of capital controls or a fiscal amnesty would reduce the advantages of secrecy and tend to shift investors toward assets with higher expected returns (and perhaps lower risk); these policies might in that way encourage repatriation.

Chapter 6, by Miguel Rodriguez of Venezuela, analyzes the impact of capital flight on the source countries. Rodriguez claims that this goes far beyond the effects analyzed by the two-gap model, namely a cutback in domestic output or in domestic investment or both as a result of a balance of payments crisis. There is also a perverse effect on income distribution, since the wealthy get subsidized foreign exchange before the crisis, which increases in value when devaluation finally occurs, and yields them tax-free income, while the poor bear most of the burden of servicing the public-sector debt that finances the capital flight and also increases in local currency value after devaluation. The magnitude of the strain on public-sector finances imposed by the increased burden of foreign-debt service—often reinforced by socialization of private debt—creates a structural budget deficit. The exportation of financial intermediation stunts development of the local capital market. And to the extent that investors move on from passive investment in financial assets to active investment in the corporate sector, not only are the prospects of capital repatriation diminished, but the local entrepreneurial class finds its interests and its energy divorced from the prosperity of the local economy. In sum, Rodriguez sees a thoroughly corrosive social process that jeopardizes the prospects of resuming development. His discussant, Rudiger Dornbusch, basically endorses this gloomy assessment. The chapter concludes with a summary of conference discussion on the consequences of capital flight.

Chapter 7 contains three case studies. Authors were asked to assess the extent and causes of capital flight in their country, and to describe the policies that have been adopted with a view to ending or reversing the outflow.

José Pablo Arellano and Joseph Ramos describe the experiences of Chile, a country that has had relatively little capital flight, although there was a short, sharp episode in 1982. Chile has vigorously pursued a program of debt-equity swaps, and one aim of the program is to attract the repatriation of Chilean money held abroad.

Rudolph Hommes describes events in Colombia, another country that has experienced relatively limited capital flight, which he attributes in part to avoidance of the worst excesses of macroeconomic policy witnessed elsewhere and in part to the maintenance of exchange control. He describes the launching of "whitener bonds" in New York intended to promote the return of funds held abroad by Colombians.

The chapter is completed by a study of the country that, by all accounts, has one of the largest volumes of flight capital of all: Mexico. Ernesto Zedillo of the Banco de Mexico argues that the numbers are probably somewhat exaggerated, particularly for recent years, but he does not minimize the seriousness of the problem that capital flight has posed to Mexico. He is skeptical as to whether exchange control could do much to resolve the problem, at least in the Mexican case, and argues rather that its resolution has to be sought in a combination of consistently sound macroeconomic policies in Mexico and more supportive policies in its northern neighbor. By this he means lower interest rates, an end to tax incentives, and abandonment by the private banking departments of the commercial banks of their solicitation of Mexican money.

Chapter 8 contains the panel discussion on appropriate policy responses. The panel consisted of Rimmer de Vries of Morgan Guaranty, Pedro-Pablo Kuczynski of First Boston International, and Miguel Urrutia of the Inter-American Development Bank, each of whom was asked to address the responsibilities of both source and haven countries. Their presentations are followed by an account of the conference discussion on policy responses. A comment describing Swiss views on bank confidentiality, by Aloys Schwie-tert of the Swiss Bank Corporation, rounds out the chapter.

The final chapter contains our concluding appraisal. Since this is also being published independently in the Institute's *Policy Analyses* series, some sections contain considerable material summarizing the preceding chapters of this volume. This is particularly true of the sections on the magnitude, causes, and consequences of capital flight (although even here we draw on material not included in the conference volume), rather less true of the discussion of definitions, and even less so of the final sections, on policy responses. Because the views of conference participants differed on most policy questions, the easy option of reporting the consensus of the discussion was not available. We hope that our conclusions will advance the public discussion.

2

A Historical Perspective

Charles P. Kindleberger

It is difficult—perhaps impossible—to make a rigorous definition of capital flight for the purpose of devising policies to cope with it. Do we restrict cases to domestic capital sent abroad, or should foreign capital precipitously pulled out of a country be included? What about the capital that emigrants take with them, or send ahead of them, especially when the people involved are being persecuted—Huguenots from France following the Revocation of the Edict of Nantes in 1685, noble *émigrés* after the French Revolution of 1789 and especially the Reign of Terror in 1793, German Jews or Jews in the countries neighboring Germany during the decade of National Socialism? Does it make a difference whether the emigration is likely to be permanent or temporary, to the extent that one can tell ex ante? And what about the cases where there is no net export of capital, but capital is sent abroad to be returned to the country as foreign investment: French investors buying bonds of the Chemin de Fer du Nord issued in London in the 1840s (Platt 1984, ch. 2), or Argentine investors buying their country's own securities issued in London both before 1914 and in the 1920s? Is there a valid distinction to be made between capital that is expatriated on a long-term basis for fear of confiscatory taxation, and domestic speculation against the national currency through buying foreign exchange that is ostensibly interested in short-term profits? The distinctions are elusive, and it is not clear how much they matter to the questions of how to prevent capital flight or to attract it back, except perhaps in the case of refugees escaping persecution who manage to take some or all of their capital with them.

The author is Ford International Professor of Economics, Emeritus, Massachusetts Institute of Technology, and Visiting Sachar Professor of Economics, Brandeis University. This paper was written when the author was a United Nations University scholar at WIDER in Helsinki. He expresses his gratitude to WIDER for the support, and to Carl-Ludwig Holtfrerich and Eric S. Schubert for helpful comments on a previous draft. Views expressed are those of the author alone.

In his article on capital flight at the depth of the Great Depression, Machlup (1932) left the inference that capital flight was unimportant provided that the monetary authorities pursued proper policies. If the authorities refused to accommodate the attempt to raise liquid funds at home, capital flight would raise interest rates, lower prices and start a transfer process automatically. Difficulty might be encountered if the funds were not invested abroad but hoarded, since transfer is assisted by expansion in the receiving country as well as contraction in the sending. Machlup recognized that the deflation in the sending country might have serious consequences in bank failures and the like, but at the time professed an Austrian view of macroeconomic policy that blamed the troubles of any bank in difficulty from falling prices on its own misuse of credit.[1]

I started to write this paper as a series of historical episodes, concentrating on the following cases:

France

☐ 1685 (and earlier) to 1700: revocation of the Edict of Nantes

☐ 1720: safeguarding the profits of the Mississippi bubble

☐ 1789–97: capital flight from the French Revolution, the assignats, and the Terror, and the return

☐ French purchases of French bonds issued in London in the 1840s

☐ the speculative attack against the franc in 1924 and the successful "squeeze"

☐ the 1926 Poincaré stabilization following the extreme depreciation of May–June 1926

☐ the 1936 middle-class strike against the Front Populaire

☐ the 1968 middle-class strike against the Accord de Grenelle

☐ the 1981–82 middle-class strike against the Mitterrand socialist campaign of nationalization.

----

1. For an analytical account of capital flight of a half century ago, see chapter 10 of my *International Short-Term Capital Movements* (1937), treating the literature by Machlup (1932), Iversen (1935), Nurkse (1935), and Fanno (1935). It covers all capital movements not based on normal income-induced flows, and includes such "abnormal" flows as reparations.

Italy

☐ 1866 and the onset of the "corso forzoso" that was finally halted in 1881

☐ foreign-exchange controls of the 1930s

☐ the 1961–63 flight of banknotes smuggled into Switzerland, representing a middle-class strike against the nationalization of the electricity industry.

Germany

☐ the outflow of German capital during the hyperinflation of 1919–23

☐ 1931 outflow leading to the Standstill Agreement

☐ foreign-exchange control with the death penalty for evasion in the 1930s.

Latin America

☐ some comments on international financial intermediation through Latino purchases of bonds issued abroad for Latin American account

☐ one or two comments on the present capital outflow.

After an extended false start, I changed to an analytical approach. Before presenting it in outline, I note that my background is in European financial history, and I lack all but the most superficial knowledge of Latin American capital flight. One should further observe that there are no English or Scandinavian episodes of an outstanding nature to draw on, despite speculation against the pound sterling at various times through leads and lags and the purchase of Kaffirs in London and their sale in Johannesburg.

The analytical outline conforms to taxonomies of the means of capital escaping a country on the one hand, and of measures to prevent it or entice it back, on the other. The outflow of flight capital can be financed by the following means:

☐ outflow of specie, especially important regarding the Huguenots, safe-guarding the profits on the Mississippi bubble, the émigrés of the French revolution, and in the outflow from Italy in 1866

☐ real transfer, through deflation; through the export and sale of valuables or in hyperinflation short-circuiting the exchange market by shipping goods abroad directly and retaining the proceeds; and through exchange depreciation, particularly relevant to France in the 1920s

▢ various types of countervailing inflow, including: governmental borrowing abroad (the case where domestic investors subscribe to foreign issues of their government or major domestic borrowers may not qualify as capital flight, but in any event arises from somewhat similar motivation); loss of foreign-exchange reserves; central-bank borrowing; monetary constriction at home to raise interest rates and attract a capital inflow; depreciation of the currency, leading to foreign speculative purchases betting on revaluation; dumping of currency in foreign markets purchased by foreigners for speculation or use.

While these various means of financing a capital outflow are analytically distinct, they may, of course, occur together, either simultaneously or in series. The price-specie-flow mechanism, for example, in principle starts with an outflow of specie that leads to deflation.

The taxonomy of measures to prevent capital flight or entice it back overlaps to some degree with the means of financing it. For example, deflation helps finance real transfer of capital exports, and at the same time, by making it more expensive, tends to cut it off. Again, the various measures are in many cases possible complements as well as substitutes.

The following alternatives are available to the country losing the capital:

▢ Ignore it. It sometimes pays to let a movement based upon a swing of sentiment burn out, holding various policies steady. This is especially relevant to the intermediation cases—the French buying bonds issued by French entities in London, or Argentine investors buying Argentine bonds issued abroad. The intermediary function of the foreign bond underwriter often leads, after learning, to direct dealing.

▢ Deflate through monetary and fiscal measures to the extent possible within political constraints, and lengthen the term structure of government debt to lock in possible flight capital and entice that abroad back through high yields. The French government's inability to refund at long-term the short *bons de le défense nationale* in the 1920s was the key weakness in its weaponry.

▢ Use exchange rate policy, including: holding the rate, with own funds or swaps, or both; devalue to a credible rate and exhibit determination to hold it; with own or borrowed funds run the rate up to "squeeze" those with a short position, as in the 1924 French operation and the US dollar action of October 1978; impose exchange control with prohibitions or a multiple exchange rate system, possibly with separate rates for the current and the capital accounts (though these are virtually impossible to operate even when backed by the death penalty, and certainly not without inspection of mail and regulation of credit terms on trade and service transactions that are difficult of public acceptance).

☐ Implement a monetary reform of sufficient scope and determination to win credibility, for example, the replacement of the mark by the Rentenmark and then the Reichsmark in 1923 and 1924.

Receiving countries have also sought to repel hot money from abroad by a variety of expedients.

☐ They may allow the currency to appreciate. The classic instance is the rise of the pound sterling to a high of well over $5.00 in 1936 to divert French capital from London to New York.

☐ They may set special reserve requirements against foreign bank deposits, a technique developed especially by Switzerland and the Federal Republic of Germany.

☐ They can threaten to report foreign owners of capital to their home governments. This is not only unattractive commercially, but is readily frustrated by the use of domestic nominees.

☐ The usual tactic is to ignore the influx and regard the problem as one for the authorities in the country from which the capital comes. In the "Golden Avalanche" of 1937, stimulated by the prospect of a reduction of the US gold price, the American authorities hung on, until the likelihood of a policy change vanished with the September recession.

☐ Other means of limiting inflows of capital through reporting mechanisms have been explored, especially in such cases as communications companies where foreign investment is limited by law (for example, ITT in the 1930s), or where the Securities and Exchange Commission (SEC) rules call for the identification of individual holders with more than 5 percent of the stock of a given company. Such regulations are difficult and probably impossible to apply generally.

Financing Capital Flight Mainly Through Specie

It is perhaps only of antiquarian interest to explore the three French cases of capital flight in the seventeenth and eighteenth centuries with a somewhat primitive monetary system, but some interesting points emerge. The Revocation of the Edict of Nantes, it will be recalled, took place in 1685 but was foreshadowed several years earlier by a policy of quartering dragoons on Protestants who refused to abjure and embrace Catholicism. A short, sharp outflow of capital took place, mainly in the form of coin, but also in jewelry and plate, wine, and bills of exchange bought from Catholic bankers in all large cities, from government agents in Paris and elsewhere, from the Swiss in Lyons and from foreign diplomatic representatives in France (Scoville 1960, p. 296). Scoville's chapter 9 on the "Effects of the Revocation on Finance and Agriculture" gives a great deal of anecdotal detail concerning individual escapes with and without valuables, but is unable to pin down an estimated loss between the extreme estimates of one billion livres (say £40 million) and a derisorily low figure of five million or 1.25 million livres, depending upon whether the emigrants amounted to 200,000 persons at 25 livres a head or 50,000 (ibid., p. 291). Other estimates are offered of 150 million livres, and by a scholar whom Scoville characterizes as less cautious, 360 million. Incidentally, Scoville accepts the estimate of approximately 200,000 emigrants out of a total of two million Protestants, divided roughly between 40,000 to 50,000 to England, 50,000 to 75,000 to Holland, and to Switzerland (largely Geneva) 60,000 gross and 25,000 net,[2] with others to Germany, Ireland and overseas (ibid., pp. 120–27). Louis XIV made an attempt to bring back the sailors among these numbers to strengthen the French navy, but I do not see that any systematic attempt was made to woo others. Many remained in close touch with their 1,800,000 coreligionists who had abjured, mostly insincerely.

Some evidence concerning the loss of specie is available in the receiving countries. The London mint is reported to have coined 960,000 louis d'or (of 23 livres or approximately one pound sterling each) as a consequence of the influx (ibid., pp. 292, 299). In the early eighteenth century, the Huguenots contributed some 10 percent of the wealth of Britain in the funded debt of England and Bank of England shares, having wider and deeper financial experience gained from dealing in *rentes* (Carter 1975, esp. ch. 7). The annual figures available for the Bank of Amsterdam for January 31 show an increase in deposits—for the most part specie—from 5.17 million guilders (approximately £465,000) in 1676 to 8.28 million guilders in 1681, 12.71 million guilders in 1689 and a peak of 16.75 million guilders in 1699. Assuming, for the sake of argument, that the Bank of Amsterdam's dealings with other customers than French cancelled out, and that the increase of 11.58 million guilders or over 23 million livres was entirely due to the

---

2. I presume that the difference between the gross and net of Huguenots going to Switzerland represents not a return to France but moves from Switzerland to other refuges.

Huguenots, the amount was about a million pounds sterling or roughly the same as the louis d'or minted in London (Van Dillen 1934, p. 119). In any event, refugee funds were said to inundate the Dutch market and led to financiers begging for borrowers at 2 percent (Scoville 1960, p. 292).

France was depressed for three decades at the end of the reign of Louis XIV, but neither Scoville nor other writers are ready to ascribe the major blame to the Revocation, citing, in addition, the two wars fought after 1685 against the British and bad harvests. In an early passage, Scoville states that the Revocation "may well have been responsible for the long depression" (ibid., p. 129). At the end of his intensive study, however, he notes that there is not enough evidence to estimate how much the loss of specie was responsible (ibid., p. 446) and concludes that it did much less harm than most historians of the nineteenth and twentieth centuries believed (ibid., p. 446). Another channel for harm, of course, was the loss of skilled artisans in glass, silk, and paper.

The Mississippi bubble was a "system" promoted by John Law to achieve prosperity in France through the issue of paper money that additionally bid up the price of the shares of the Compagnie d'Occident operating in the French colony of Louisiana through which the Mississippi River flowed, along with other places worldwide. The Compagnie, under John Law's aggressive push, also took over a series of monopolies in France. Initially, the *Banque générale* was restricted in note issue. In 1717 it gave way to the *Banque royale,* which was not. Frenzied speculation in shares of the Compagnie by French investors and by hordes of foreigners who flocked to Paris drove the price from an initial value of about 200 livres, when the moribund company was reformed, to 500 in early 1719, when Law offered to buy them at that price, to 1,000 in early September, and 5,000 later in the month, from which they rose to 10,000 in November, 15,000 at the end of the year, and nearly 20,000 at the peak early in 1720 (Carswell 1960, p. 93). These prices are, however, open to considerable question. Eric S. Schubert has compiled prices of Compagnie des Indes stock from the daily London press from October 1719 to April 1720 which show them rising from 1,000 percent of par (500 livres) or 5,000 livres to 2,000 percent or 10,000 livres on December 9, 1719, and again on April 9, 1720 (Schubert 1986, table 3.1, p. 131).

Major profit-taking by the "anti-system"—French merchants and bankers who were opposed to Law—began in the fall of 1719, although Chaussinand-Nogaret cites a company formed in July 1718 to transfer money to Cadiz by way of Amsterdam (1970, p. 143). Keeping profits in notes was risky because they were depreciating, and even buying real property in France—although many including John Law did—was dangerous since most financial troubles in France, and ends of reigns, had been followed by *Chambres de*

Justice in which excess profits—what we would perhaps call today "undue enrichment"—were examined and fined or confiscated. The problem was to get foreign assets or specie abroad. Lüthy notes that most complicated schemes with forward markets and the like proved illusory either because of the failure of the counter-parties, the cancellation of paper money and bank accounts, or the disastrous decline of the exchange for those who tried to shift their profits abroad late (Lüthy 1959, p. 347). The rate (ostensibly on Swiss francs) fell from 290 in March 1720 to between 1,200 and 1,300 at the end of September (ibid., p. 367). As an example of the difficulties faced by some, Swiss bankers and merchants in Lyon complained that they were "forced to receive in paper and pay in specie, a thing which one does not practice either at Tunis or Algiers" (ibid., p. 344).

Some did get specie out despite the facts that the Swiss frontier was closed for three months because of plague in Marseilles, and that silver, more readily available than gold, was too heavy. Various routes were used for shipment of specie, including Leghorn and Genoa, as a means of sending it to Amsterdam and London (ibid., p. 369). Lüthy tells of the triumphs of one Jacques Huber who won large profits speculating successively in the Mississippi bubble, the South Sea bubble and in the stock of the Dutch East India Company, each time telling his agents that he wanted to remit *espèces sonnantes* (money that would ring on the table [ibid., p. 369]). Mackay's colorful account of the Mississippi scheme has one Vermelet, a jobber, procuring gold and silver coin to the extent of nearly 1 million livres and taking it in a cart, covered with hay and cow dung, across the border into Belgium and ultimately Amsterdam, he dressed as a peasant (Mackay 1852, p. 29). On one unspecific report, there was said to be a sudden doubling of the creditors of the Bank (Chaussinand-Nogaret 1970, p. 172).

I can find no account of a return flow of capital to France after the liquidation of the Mississippi bubble. There was first a Chamber of Justice (called Visa II, Visa I having been the settlement after the death of Louis XIV) in which local ill-gotten gains were fined in whole or in part, although those with political protection, including a number who had used their profits to buy *offices*, were spared (Chaussinand-Nogaret 1970, pp. 138, 149). Economic recovery had been proceeding from 1717, with the inflationary impact of the Mississippi bubble offsetting any deflationary impact of the loss of specie. After the Visa, there was some gain in confidence, it would appear, from the slim evidence furnished by the decline in deposits of the Bank of Amsterdam, which fell from 28.89 million guilders on January 31, 1721, to 15.24 million in 1727. Of particular importance was the fixing of the price of gold in France in 1726, following the similar action of Britain in 1717. France remained on the bimetallic standard, with wartime interruptions, until 1885 when the shift was made to gold, but adjustments in the bimetallic ratio were made entirely in the silver price, and the gold price, officially, was unchanged until 1928. As a further remark, it may be noted that, unlike the Revocation, the Mississippi bubble did not involve extraordinary emigration.

The French Revolution

The French Revolution produced another flight of capital accompanied by emigration. Again for information it is necessary to look outside France. The class composition of some 87 percent of the 17,000 executed inside France has been studied by Greer (1935). Six and one-half percent were clergy, 8 percent were nobles, and 14 percent upper class according to a necessarily arbitrary categorization. The percentages of émigrés in these classes was doubtless much higher, as the peasants and laborers executed for their part in the counterrevolutionary movement in the Vendée, or the artisans of the uprising against the Revolution in Lyon, did not have significant émigré counterparts. The clergy did not bring much money with them, judging by their poverty in England, which required support from the British government, and the nobles spent what they took out freely until they too required subventions (Weiner 1960). But the movement of specie to Britain beginning in 1789 picked up with the assignats and the Reign of Terror. The mint that normally received £650,000 a year acquired £3¾ millions in 1793 and 1794 (Hawtrey 1919, p. 261).

Seen from England, the mass of refugee money pouring into the Bank of England from France between 1789 and 1791 led to a rapid increase in the number of note-issuing country banks, and financed the canal mania (Ashton 1959, p. 168). The panic of 1793 when the canal bubble collapsed occurred despite a continued inflow. But after the end of the Terror following the fall of Robespierre in July 1794 and the collapse of the assignats, a return movement of specie to France took place to provide some means of payment. The assignats survived somewhat longer in Paris than in the countryside, where they were refused. Even in Paris, however, prices began to be quoted in gold. Hawtrey notes that there was an enormous profit to be made on importing gold, as the premium on the louis d'or in the fall of 1795 was 20 percent higher than the premium on foreign bills (ibid., pp. 247–48). The Bank of England gold stock was also drained by British government expenditures during the war, and declined from £6¾ million in August 1794 to £2.5 million in December 1796 and £1 million in February 1797 (ibid., p. 258). With the panic engendered by a trivial military incident, the Bank of England suspended payment of its notes in coin—a suspension that lasted until 1819.

The Italian incident of 1866 was perhaps less capital flight by Italians than a halt to French lending and an attempt to repatriate advances to Italy that led to some Italian outflow and abandonment of the silver standard following a heavy outpouring of specie. Part of the occasion was the crisis in Northern Europe caused by Prussian mobilization against Austria, the Overend, Gurney crisis, and a French banking liquidity crisis caused by the collapse of cotton prices following the close of the Civil War. There had also been an internal Italian railroad and other public works boom, loosely financed. The outpouring of silver contributed to the troubles of that metal which ended in the abandonment of bimetallism everywhere. Of particular interest is that fiscal and monetary policy was orthodox, exchange depreciation moderate, and by 1881 the lira was reestablished at the old parity with a stabilization loan and a return flow of capital.

Real Transfer: Through Deflation

This is the therapy that Machlup (1932) prescribed for capital flight. Moreover, he and Viner thought that the success of the German payment of reparations after 1928 until breakdown in 1931 showed how malleable the balance of payments was in response to an "abnormal" capital transfer such as reparations or capital flight (Machlup 1950, p. 81n.; Viner 1952, p. 182). Machlup finally recanted on the ground that the political price—the breakdown of the Weimar Republic and the coming of National Socialism—was too high (Machlup 1980, pp. 128–31).

Deflation is strong medicine not only in terms of the possibility of political breakdown. It may be institutionally difficult or impossible. French fiscal policy was strongly contractionary insofar as the deficit was wiped out and replaced with a small surplus in the period to 1925, but it was impossible for the authorities to follow up with the appropriate debt policy. They were, that is, unable to lock in French capitalists with their short-term *bons de la défense nationale* by refunding them into long-term bonds that would halt the capital outflow by driving bond prices down, and interest rates up, every time wealth-holders tried to liquidate bonds to get money with which to buy foreign exchange. Each week a sizable amount of short-term bonds became due, and the market could insist on obtaining cash for these. A fiscal program of running substantial surpluses to pay off debt was impossible, given the widespread resistance to heavier taxes. The alternative was exchange depreciation, discussed below, which effected the real transfer of capital flight.

Deflation at home may also raise interest rates to such an extent that, given the appropriate expectations, flight capital is attracted back. In the process, some continuing capital flight may be transferred by a countervailing return flow, discussed below. The conditions to assure credibility are doubtless stringent: the establishment of confidence in the stability of money, the budget, the exchange rate, plus the possibility of the one-way option that the currency can only appreciate.

Deflation may be the orthodox neoclassical remedy. It is one, however, that calls for a great many necessary conditions and it is difficult to think of a clear-cut example of its implementation. The Poincaré stabilization of July 1926, for example, lowered taxes on the upper-income groups rather than raised them.

Real Transfer: Through Direct Export of Valuables or Other Merchandise

It was mentioned earlier in connection with the Huguenots and the émigrés that escapees took valuables with them, along with specie. Valuables may also be dumped at home to get currency for transfer through the exchanges: Tiffany's moved from selling paste jewelry to real diamonds when the price of the latter fell precipitously in Paris after the fall of the Orleanist monarchy in 1848.

The more interesting case, however, is that, when a currency is breaking down in hyperinflation and virtually infinite depreciation, the exchanges may be short-circuited by those exporting capital abroad. Goods are bought at home, shipped and sold abroad, with the proceeds retained in foreign currency. This was notably true of Germany in 1922 and 1923. The later development of foreign-exchange control, of course, tries to frustrate this method of escape by requiring exporters to turn in the receipts of foreign sales. Underinvoicing of exports and overinvoicing of imports provide one means of evading such control.

Real Transfer: Through Exchange Depreciation

Typically an attempt is made to prevent capital exports by letting the exchange rate go. This may lead to speculative purchases of the currency— a countervailing inflow, such as occurred in Germany before about June 1922. Or, if it does not, the depreciation as capital pushes abroad is apt to lead to undervaluation of the exchange rate and an export surplus, such as occurred after June 1922. (The statement rejects the McCloskey and Zecher [1976] notion that purchasing power parity is always automatically achieved.)

Other classic cases in point are the French depreciation of the 1920s, the capital flight of 1936 reacting against the Front Populaire of socialist Premier Blum, and the French outflow in the fall of 1968. Each of these was halted by devaluation to a lower level that provided profits to returning capital, requiring the rate to be set at levels, and accompanied by measures, that inspired confidence that the rate would be held. In the instant cases these were the Poincaré stabilization of July 1926, the Tripartite Monetary Agreement of September 1936, and the August 1969 devaluation agreed to by Germany.

Exchange depreciation raises the question of a possible squeeze to reverse the expectations of speculators and capital exporters. The classic instance is probably the squeeze engineered by Lazard Frères for the French government in March and April 1924, with the help of a stabilization loan from J.P. Morgan and Company in the amount of $100 million. The details have been written up by Phillippe (1931). Initially the squeeze was put into effect when the franc was 123 to the dollar. This rate was held with difficulty in the first week of the operation, after which the level was raised to 84.45 on March 19, 78.10 on March 24, and 61 at the end of April. At this last rate the authorities stopped buying francs and sold them to the badly beaten shorts—French, German, Dutch, and Austrian—who had to repay borrowed francs. The short-term gain was lost over time, however, as a left government won election in June 1924, and measures to stabilize the position judged adequate by the market were not taken. The rate sagged to between 80 and 85 in June, and the decline resumed thereafter until it reached a low of 249 in early July 1926 just before the Poincaré stabilization.

Other squeezes against short speculation on the part of investors, though perhaps not involving capital flight, have been put in place by Italy in 1964, the United Kingdom in 1976, and the United States on October 31, 1978.

Countervailing Inflow: Purchase of Local Bonds in Foreign Capital Markets

As already noted, this is not a net export of capital so much as a search for an intermediary in order to lend to one's own government or nationals. It can be a natural stage in the education of investors and the acquisition of trust in their national borrowers. Platt (1984), for example, observes that most estimates of United Kingdom nineteenth-century lending are too high because they fail to take account of the extent to which investors in the borrowing countries acquired bonds issued in London; while the investors wanted to invest at home, they wanted to do so by means of obligations that the local government or borrower would hold in higher esteem than those owed locally, and perhaps wanted the added liquidity that a bond traded on an international market would command. He noted initially that the bonds issued in London for the Chemin de Fer du Nord in the 1840s were largely bought by the French. It is well known that Argentine and Brazilian investors bought Argentine and Brazilian bonds, respectively, issued in London and Paris. As the New York market gradually started to issue bonds for European borrowers after World War II, substantial percentages of these were bought by investors in the issuing countries (Kindleberger 1971).

Platt makes the point that many borrowing countries have a lot of capital at home to invest at home but prefer to do it through the intermediation of investment bankers abroad. Whether this should be called capital flight depends, of course, on what happens next: whether it is followed, as in the French 1840 case, by the development of a French capital market which obviated the necessity for such intermediation, or whether distrust of domestic creditors grows and intermediation is followed by true capital flight.

Countervailing Inflow: Loss of Foreign-Exchange Reserves

The Revocation of the Edict of Nantes, the expatriation of Mississippi bubble profits, and the flight of capital during the French revolution occurred before central banks had been established on the Continent. After the establishment of central banks, capital flight could still be effected through gold losses, and in addition, where the central bank held foreign exchange in its reserves, with a loss of foreign exchange. It is perhaps stretching matters to call this a countervailing capital inflow, although technically such is the case. The issue is clearer where monetary authorities borrow abroad, a subject we are about to discuss, but it frequently happens that the loss of foreign exchange reserves or gold is an early means of accommodating capital flight, followed, after the flight has proceeded for some time, by borrowing.

Countervailing Inflow: Official Borrowing Abroad

The monetary authorities can borrow abroad in a variety of ways: through swaps in the case of the Group of 10 (G-10), through selling foreign exchange forward, through arranging for parastatal bodies to borrow abroad rather than at home and sell the proceeds to the authorities.

A classic swap case occurred in the Italian lira in 1963 following the nationalization of the electricity-generating industry and a middle-class strike that took the form of capital flight. The Italian authorities chose to meet the crisis not by depreciating the currency, which would have raised domestic prices in irreversible fashion, but by entering into swaps, primarily with the US government. This seems to me to have been wise. The irritation of the Italian capitalists did not last long when they learned that the Socialist terms for compensation were generous—overgenerous as a number of mainstream economists told me. By financing the outflow and hanging on, the position was restored—although again in the long run the inflation was not cured, and the exchange rate ultimately declined.

The French have gotten themselves into a bind, in my judgment, by holding on to their gold and borrowing foreign exchange through such parastatal bodies as Électricité de France to meet balance-of-payments losses and capital flight in 1968–69 and again as a response to the Mitterrand policy of nationalization in 1981. Gold is illiquid today if attempt be made to sell it in large amount. While the French dollar debt has been reduced in real terms by the fall of the dollar and the easing of interest rates, the overall position remains unstable.

Countervailing Inflow: Through Macroeconomic Policy

Deflation to attract private inflows through higher interest rates and depreciation to attract capital inflow through speculation may be discussed together since their possibilities of success turn on similar criteria. The relevant instances are provided by Germany. In the 1920s, exchange depreciation up to June 1922 encouraged a sufficient speculative capital inflow to finance reparation payments, the current account deficit, and some unestimated volume of capital flight. The inflow was based on inelastic expectations, the belief, that is, that the mark would one day return to par. There are many estimates of the amount of capital that flowed to Germany in 1919–23 and 1924–31 (Holtfrerich 1977, 1980, 1986; Schuker 1978), amounts said to be larger than American assistance to Germany under the Marshall Plan after World War II, but no reliable estimates of how much capital the Germans managed to export in the period before the Dawes plan. At French insistence, a committee parallel to the Dawes Committee had been appointed under McKenna to determine the amount of capital exported by Germany, just as, at the time of standstill in 1931, a Layton Committee was established alongside the Wiggin Standstill Committee for the same purpose. It is clear on theoretical grounds that after the shift in expectations from inelastic to elastic, usually ascribed to June 1922, when the American holders of marks and German securities tried to liquidate them, that German mark holders were on the same side of the market. But it is not readily estimated how much capital flight by Germans took place before that time. Schuker (1978, p. 350) says that German exporters left their foreign earnings abroad, just as Holtfrerich notes that the earlier movement in the other direction consisted partly of American exporters leaving the mark proceeds of sales in German banks waiting for the price to rise.

The central point is expectations. Higher interest rates and exchange depreciation will each attract foreign capital and help provide the counterpart of capital flight to the extent that they inspire confidence that the authorities are in full command and have every intention of restoring the position in the case of higher interest rates, and of appreciating the currency in the case of depreciation. Holtfrerich writes me that the return flow of German capital to Germany in the spring of 1924 was owing to tight money on the part of the Reichsbank. This forced business to repatriate hoarded exchange, especially after the establishment of the Golddiskontbank by Schacht strengthened confidence in the long-term stability of the currency, all this even before the adoption of the Dawes plan. He went on to say that the stringent requirements of the Dawes plan strengthened confidence still more and assisted that return movement. When such confidence is absent, however, and expectations are inelastic, raising interest rates leads to increased flight by foreigners and domestic holders alike, and the same is true in the case of depreciation.

Countervailing Inflow: Dumping of Currency Abroad

One method of capital flight is to buy foreign currency. In 1940 in Switzerland, I met a man who had arranged to receive five $100 bills from New York each week, which he sold for about $650. He then sent $500 back by draft each week and lived on the difference. A large capital inflow to the United States—outflow from Europe—took place through currency movements reported by banks, but more—much more—contributed to the residual debit in the US balance of payments through covert mail exports of US currency, and through purchases of currency through intermediaries in New York that were hidden in safe-deposit boxes. The counterpart of this US inflow, to the extent it was reported, was European capital flight, i.e., the increase in European holdings of US currency.

In addition to buying foreign currency at home, capital can be exported by selling domestic currency abroad. Various German, Italian, and especially Russian foreign-exchange controls were evaded by smuggling currency abroad and selling it—in Amsterdam and Zurich for the Reichsmark in the Nazi period, in Helsinki and Istanbul for the ruble. The countervailing party that bought the currency in the foreign market effected the capital outflow. If no one had bought it, the price would have gone to zero. There is, of course, no evidence on the point but the supposition is that most of it was bought to be smuggled back, for example to pay for German exports. One anecdotal suggestion is that the British secret service was a substantial demander of Reichsmark currency in Amsterdam.

A further anecdote is of interest because of the echoes it conveys of the export of the capital of Huguenots after the Revocation through "Catholic bankers, government agents in Paris. . .and foreign diplomatic representatives" (Scoville 1960, p. 296), the perfection of markets that made the prices of estates in London vary with South Sea stock at the time of the South Sea and Mississippi bubbles (Carswell 1960, p. 159), and of real estate in Geneva move in consonance with the notes of the Banque Royale (Lüthy, vol 1, 1959, p. 364). In (I believe) 1937, on a train from Amsterdam to Paris, Emile Despres fell into conversation with a man who said his business had been getting capital out of Germany. There were, he said, three methods: one could buy a Reichsbank official and get sterling in London; this was expensive but sure. Or one could bribe a bank clerk to get currency for deposits in large amounts, and get it out of Germany through the pouches of diplomatic officers of a number of small states. Or one could smuggle it out by train. The risk-return payoffs by each method were related, and what was especially notable was that when there was a coup by the German authorities that temporarily blocked one method, the cost of using the others rose. An analagous result materialized in the Italian export of capital to Switzerland in 1963: highway robbers gathered along the main road from Milan to Lugano to prey on those exporting capital in bundles of bank notes disguised as packages of butter (*Die Zeit,* October 15, 1963). Some part of the countervailing reflow of these notes to Italy, according to a tax accountant I interviewed in Milan in 1972, came from Italian companies repatriating "black cash" accumulated abroad through overinvoicing to get it back on their books to make good losses. These appeared as foreign purchases of the company's newly issued shares.

Means to Contain Capital Flight or to Entice it Back

Only a few loose ends remain to cover the list set forth above, since many of the options have already been covered in connection with the means of financing the outflow, notably: ignoring, deflating, depreciating, stabilizing at a devalued rate, operating a squeeze with or without stabilization loans, and, implicitly, monetary reform. A word or two may be useful, however, on forward operations, foreign-exchange control, and steps that might be taken abroad. I happen not to be sanguine about any of them.

It has been suggested by Keynes and others, notably John Spraos (1959), that central banks need not lose gold or foreign exchange, since they can create the equivalent by selling foreign exchange forward, roll the contract over as it matures, and keep going virtually to infinity. A domestic holder of, say, sterling, who wants protection against depreciation, can in capital flight either demand dollars—I write as if the system were one of a moveable peg—or be content with a contract to be provided with dollars against sterling at a set price in the future. The subject merits extensive exposition for which space is lacking. In short, however, it may be said that when the market believes that the authorities' commitments to deliver foreign exchange are likely to exceed their available reserves, the market may be unwilling to renew its forward engagements by rolling them forward, but demand fulfillment (Spraos 1969). This is broadly what happened in Britain in 1967. Again, the question turns on credibility.

Exchange control is another subject deserving extended treatment. Systems differ markedly in their approaches, whether they use prohibitions and enforced collection, differentiation by price, or some combination. All are porous to greater or lesser degree, depending to a considerable extent on the elusive concept of national character. Thus Britain in the 1950s managed to develop a wide spread between ordinary sterling and security sterling, whereas in France and Belgium the spread between current-account and capital-account foreign exchange never diverged beyond a few percent before being contained by arbitrage. As the Despres anecdote in the last section indicates, moreover, even the death penalty in Germany—an efficient country in policing transactions—failed to make the system of control tight. As a rough guess, I have suggested that at one extreme Germany might restrain 95 percent of the attempts to evade foreign-exchange controls whereas a typical Latin country might achieve success only in the range of 60 percent to 75 percent. In times of war or other national emergency that pulls a country together, the ratio rises.

The point of exchange control, of course, is to prevent the public from buying in the cheapest market and selling in the dearest. It attempts to override basic economic incentives.

A particularly instructive example of the futility of halfhearted exchange control is US experience in the 1960s with the interest equalization tax, Gore Amendment, Voluntary Credit Restraint Program, and Mandatory Control Program. The administration tried to prevent capital outflow one conduit at a time, when the US capital market was tied to markets abroad through many. As each link was cut off, the flow was diverted to others.

In the postwar period, Switzerland and Germany have at various times tried to keep out foreign funds by requiring banks to maintain special reserves against foreign deposits. The best known example is the German *bardepot*. I am not a deep student of the experience, but I think it was, on the whole, only partially successful. Nominees can be used to disguise foreign ownership, although there are risks that the fiduciary will fail to live up to commitments.

My own rather thin files from the period when I was working at the Federal Reserve Bank of New York include two memoranda addressed to Mr. Sproul, one of June 28, 1937, with E. Despres, entitled "Would American and British support for the franc bring French capital home?" and one with E.G. Collado, dated April 18, 1938, on "Hot Money." The first is a little bizarre, as the purpose of inducing capital repatriation to France was to induce the French authorities to buy gold and relieve some of the pressure on the United States from the "Golden Avalanche." The critical issue, it was stated, was whether French capital abroad was primarily a hedge against further depreciation or restrictions, or was held chiefly because of fear of expropriation. The conclusion was that the former was the primary motive, and that a US-UK announcement of an intention to stabilize the French currency would be effective in inducing capital repatriation.

The Kindleberger-Collado memorandum explored the possibility of limiting the capital inflow to the United States by taxation, thought to be unenforceable, and various means of limiting the inflow through short-term banking funds, such as a requirement of 80 percent to 100 percent reserves, taxes, widening of the gold points, and a lowering of the gold price. All but some widening of the gold points were rejected. A new method was proposed, simple in theory but deemed complex in practice, to limit foreign purchases of US securities, so as to create two prices after the limit was reached, one for foreign-held shares, and another lower one for those in American hands. The proposal came from recognition that this had already happened to ITT stock, because of limitations on foreign ownership of US communications. As I reread the memorandum now, however, I have the feeling that youthful optimism won out over practicality.

The Crucial Condition for Capital Repatriation

The historical record indicates that the crucial aspect inducing repatriation after capital flight is a return of confidence—confidence in the capacity of the country to maintain the exchange rate, in the safety of capital, in economic recovery. This criterion makes it unlikely, in my judgment, that capital repatriation will take place gradually over a long period of time, as contemplated, for example, in the 1986 report of the Inter-American Dialogue, *Rebuilding Cooperation in the Americas*. This report argues (p. 12) that Latin American recovery depends on an inflow of $20 billion a year, made up of $12 billion a year from the commercial banks, $4 billion from the multilateral agencies, $1 billion to $1.5 billion each from foreign direct investment and bilateral lending, and $1 billion to $2 billion in recaptured flight capital. This estimate of the return of flight capital, which the report considers "a reasonable goal" is too little if confidence is restored, and algebraically far too high if it is not, since the capital flight will continue. If I may quote once more from my files, a contribution of January 12, 1937 to a Federal Reserve Bank of New York Research Department collection, on

"Some General Implications of Recent Currency Developments," laid heavy emphasis on the restoration of confidence. Such restoration, it was thought, might precede or follow renewed domestic investment and economic recovery (in France), but excluded further depreciation of the franc. The same conclusion is central to Michael Bruno's (1985, p. 868) judgment about stabilization of the monies of the Latin American Southern Cone, i.e., the necessity of building "credible expectations." This essentially means that short-run measures in the foreign-exchange market, such as a stabilization or a squeeze, must be buttressed by long-run macroeconomic stabilization that is seen to be politically supportable. It is quite an order.

References

Ashton, T.S. 1959. *Economic Fluctuations in England, 1700–1800.* Oxford, England: Clarendon Press.

Bruno, Michael. 1985. "The Reforms and Macroeconomic Adjustments: Introduction." *World Development*, vol. 13, no. 8 (August), pp. 867–69.

Carswell, John. 1960. *The South Sea Bubble.* London: Cresset Press.

Carter, Anne Clare. 1975. *Getting, Spending and Investing in Early Modern Times: Essays on Dutch, English and Huguenot Economic History.* Assen, the Netherlands: Van Gorcum & Co.

Chaussinand-Nogaret, Guy. 1970. *Les financiers de Languedoc au XVIII siècle.* Paris: SEVPEN.

Fanno, Marco. 1935. *Abnormal and Normal Capital Transfers.* Minneapolis: University of Minnesota Press (Italian original 1935).

Greer, Donald. 1935. *The Incidence of the Terror During the French Revolution: A Statistical Interpretation.* Cambridge, Mass.: Harvard University Press.

Hawtrey, Ralph G. 1919. *Currency and Credit.* London: Longmans, Green.

Holtfrerich, Carl-Ludwig. 1977. "Internationale Verteilungsfolgen der deutschen Inflation, 1918–1923." *Kyklos*, vol. 30, pp. 271–92.

———. 1980. *Die deutsche Inflation, 1914–23.* Berlin: de Gruyter. Now in translation as *The German Inflation, 1914–1923.* New York, NY: de Gruyter, 1986.

———. 1986. "U.S. Capital Exports to Germany 1919–23 Compared to 1924–29." *Explorations in Economic History*, vol. 23, pp. 1–32.

Inter-American Dialogue. 1986. *Rebuilding Cooperation in the Americas.* Washington: Inter-American Dialogue.

Iversen, Carl. 1935. *Aspects of the Theory of International Capital Movements.* London.

Kindleberger, Charles P. 1937. *International Short-term Capital Movements.* New York, NY: Columbia University Press.

———. 1971. "The Pros and Cons of an International Capital Market." In Kindleberger, *International Money*, London: George Allen & Unwin, pp. 225–42.

Lüthy, Hubert. 1959. *La banque protestante en France de la révocation de l'édit de Nantes à la révolution*, vol. 1, *Dispersion et regroupement (1685–1730)*. Paris: SEVPEN.

Machlup, Fritz. 1932. "Theorie des Kapitalflucht," *Weltwirtschaftliches Archiv*, vol. 36, pp. 512–29.

———. 1950. "Three Concepts of So-Called Dollar Shortage." *Economic Journal.* In Machlup, *International Payments, Debts and Gold*, New York, NY: Scribner's, pp. 110–35.

————. 1980. "My Early Work in International Monetary Problems." Banca Nazionale del Lavoro *Quarterly Review*, no. 133, pp. 113–46.

Mackay, Charles. 1852. *Extraordinary Popular Delusions and the Madness of Crowds*. New York, NY: Harmony Books, 1980.

McCloskey, Donald N., and J. Richard Zecher. 1976. "How the Gold Standard Worked, 1880–1913." In *The Monetary Approach to the Balance of Payments*, edited by J.A. Frenkel and H.G. Johnson. Toronto: University of Toronto Press.

Nurkse, Ragnar. 1935. *Internationale Kapitalbewegungen*, Vienna.

Phillippe, Raymond. 1931. *Le drame financier de 1924–1938*. Paris: Gallimard.

Platt, D.C.M. 1984. *Foreign Finance in Continental Europe and the USA, 1815–1870: Quantities, Origins, Functions and Distribution*. London: George Allen & Unwin.

Schubert, Eric S. 1986. "The Ties that Bound: Market Behavior in Foreign Exchange in Western Europe during the Eighteenth Century." Dissertation submitted for the Ph.D. degree, University of Illinois at Urbana-Champaign.

Schuker, Stephen A. 1978. "Finance and Foreign Policy in the Era of the German Inflation: British, French and German Strategies for Economic Reconstruction after the First World War." In *Historische Processe der deutsche Inflation, 1914 bis 1924*. Edited by Otto Busch and Gerald D. Feldman. Berlin: Colloquium Verlag.

Scoville, Warren C. 1960. *The Persecution of Huguenots and French Economic Development, 1680–1720*. Los Angeles: University of California Press.

Spraos, John. 1959. "Speculation, Arbitrage and Sterling," *Economic Journal*, vol. 69, no. 1 (March), pp. 1–21.

————. 1969. "Some Aspects of Sterling in the Decade 1957–66." In *The International Market for Foreign Exchange*, edited by Robert Z. Aliber. New York, NY: Praeger.

Van Dillen, J.G. 1934. "The Bank of Amsterdam." In *History of the Principal Public Banks*. Edited by J.G. van Dillen. London: Frank Cass, 1964, pp. 79–124.

Viner, Jacob. 1952. *International Economics*. Glencoe, Ill.: The Free Press.

Weiner, Margery. 1960. *The French Exiles, 1789–1815*, London: John Murray.

3

Definitions and Magnitudes

On the Definition and Magnitude of Recent Capital Flight
Robert Cumby and Richard Levich

The economic performance of the world's developing countries (LDCs) is now a key factor affecting the future of the international financial system. Key to LDC performance is their ability to channel capital funds (from foreign loans, foreign equity, and domestic sources) into domestic investments, while meeting their commitments on existing external debt. It is curious that until recently the disposition of domestic funds (in particular, the possibility of large domestic capital outflows, or "capital flight") was not considered seriously within the context of LDC performance. Perhaps this oversight was aided by the ready availability of foreign funds or the inadequacy of data on domestic capital outflows. But even taking the philosophical stance that private citizens ought to retain the right to invest their funds globally, it still remains that a country's macroeconomic performance could be severely affected by a sudden or prolonged outflow of domestic capital.

Several studies that we review suggest that LDC private capital outflows over the last ten years were at least $50 billion and perhaps $200 billion or higher. Estimates of this magnitude support the view that if LDC capital outflows could be reduced or reversed, the adjustment burden on LDCs would be eased substantially. Furthermore, the magnitude of LDC capital outflows has been observed by commercial bankers and cited in order to justify a reduction in further lending to some developing countries. Thus, LDC capital outflows may impose a double cost if foreign sources of funds are cut off.

The authors are professors of economics in the Graduate School of Business Administration of New York University and Research Associates of the National Bureau of Economic Research. They acknowledge the dedicated research assistance of Julapa Rungkasiri and helpful comments on an earlier draft by John Cuddington, Alain Ize, Don Lessard, and John Williamson. The research reported here is part of the research program in International Studies of the National Bureau of Economic Research.

The purpose of this paper is to survey and analyze the various definitions and measures of capital flight that have been offered in the recent literature. Our approach is twofold. First, at the conceptual level, we discuss the basis for classifying particular domestic capital outflows as "capital flight" rather than as "normal" flows. It has been pointed out in other papers that selection of a particular definition for capital flight ought to be made with regard to the type of research question under examination. We explore this issue further, asking whether any of the definitions proposed so far is adequate to guide the decisions facing bankers and government officials.

The second part of our approach is empirical. We first discuss how to operationalize the various definitions of capital flight. Our objective here is to recompute alternative estimates of capital flight, using a common data base. Some researchers have adopted an accounting framework for measuring capital flight that includes only a designated subset of domestic capital outflows. Recent papers by Dooley (1986) and Khan and Ul Haque (1987) use a more indirect approach, measuring capital flight as the difference between all external claims and those external claims that generate receipts captured in the balance of payments accounts. We replicate these measurements on a common data base for standard time periods to show the dispersion in estimates of capital flight brought about by alternative definitions.

The empirical analysis also reviews the sources of estimation error that may affect our estimates of capital flight. Evidence on the extent of overinvoicing of imports and underinvoicing of exports using comparisons of partner-country trade data is discussed.

The plan of the paper is as follows. The second section, Alternative Measures of Capital Flight, contains our discussion of the conceptual issues related to the measurement of capital flight, and a review of the definitions of capital flight that have been adopted in the literature. Our empirical results and a comparison of alternative capital flight estimates are presented in the third section. The final section offers the policy implications of our findings and other concluding remarks.

The major conclusions we reach can be summarized simply. The empirical evidence suggests that for an individual country among our sample the range of estimates (high − low) of capital flight resulting from the various definitions is usually about $10 billion but sometimes greater than $20 billion. That there is considerable dispersion in the estimates should be neither surprising nor discouraging since theory does not offer a unique definition of capital flight. An appropriate definition will be one that is consistent with the kinds of economic questions under consideration. In theory, capital flight should be viewed within the context of a complete (i.e., general equilibrium) economic model. Without such a model, we can only guess whether additional lending to LDCs will foster more capital flight, or whether the same lending might signal an improvement in the prospects for better economic performance and trigger a reversal of capital flight.

Alternative Measures of Capital Flight

Economic principles do not guide us to a unique or natural definition of the term "capital flight."

Conceptual Issues Regarding Capital Outflows

Domestic residents in an open economy engage in international transactions. Some of these transactions lead domestic residents to acquire financial claims against nonresidents. Which of these transactions ought to be classified as domestic capital flight rather than normal capital outflows? The list might include all foreign assets (both reported and unreported, including financial assets, direct foreign investments, and real estate) acquired by the banking and nonbank private sectors as well as the public sector, or it could be only a subset of this complete list.[1] Alternatively, one might attempt to distinguish among flows by the circumstances or nature of the investment.

This classification problem is similar to the dilemma of computing the balance of payments under a pegged exchange rate regime. How did economists distinguish between "autonomous" and "accommodating" international transactions? In practice, some arbitrary decisions were made to classify the motives behind anonymous accounting entries.[2] Assuming that the classification was done correctly, the policy relevance of such a balance of payments estimate would be primarily as a *signal*. Policy making is carried

---

1. Cuddington (1986) reminds us that human capital could be included in a measure of capital fight. Indeed, in the 1960s, some observers considered the "brain drain" a serious detriment to the economic development of some countries. During that debate, "nationalists" (for example, Patinkin 1968) stressed the distributional effects of capital movements, thereby rejecting "the world" as the appropriate unit for welfare maximization. "Internationalists" (for example, Johnson 1968) argued that the brain drain was largely a symptom of other source-country policies, exacerbated by the increasing integration of labor markets and the mobility of well-educated people. The current debate on capital flight echoes many of the arguments used regarding the brain drain.

2. In a slightly different situation, the theoretical construct may be well-defined (for example the money supply, the labor supply, the price level), but there is no easy way to operationalize the concept. Here the solution may be to pick a proxy variable (for example, M2, or men and women above the age of 16 who are actively seeking employment, or a sample of prices of consumer goods and services) which the policymaker can influence or about which he collects data.

out ex ante to affect future outcomes, while the balance of payments figure reflects ex post events. To enhance its relevance for policy, the balance of payments definition would need to be imbedded within a complete (i.e., general equilibrium) model to determine how current and prospective economic policies might influence the future balance of payments and national welfare.

The analogy to the problem of estimating the magnitude of capital flight and determining the impact of capital flight on welfare is clear. Classifying capital transactions to arrive at an estimate of capital flight will require a certain number of arbitrary distinctions. Absent a complete model, it can not be clear how future policies will affect capital flight or how capital flight affects welfare. And even if capital flight reduces domestic welfare, the optimal amount of capital flight will not be zero as long as there are costs to preventing it.

Alternative Classification Measures

To approach the distinction between "capital flight" and "normal" capital outflows, one obvious dichotomy is the division between legal and illegal transactions. It seems fair to say that all illegal transactions are not "normal." However, illegal transactions need not be motivated by a desire to avoid domestic financial markets, per se. The primary motivation for certain current account transactions may be the evasion of tariffs, quotas, or laws regarding trade in illegal drugs or other activities, and these transactions necessarily generate a capital account dimension. However, illegal transactions are not reported, so it is difficult to determine how much they contribute to capital flight. Evidence presented in Gulati (this volume) and in the third section, on partner-country trade data, provides some indication of which countries are engaged in overinvoicing imports and underinvoicing exports, perhaps to effect capital flight.

Within the category of legal international capital transactions, our bias would be to classify all freely organized transactions as "normal." Assuming that domestic investors are risk-averse utility maximizers, portfolio theory strongly suggests that investors will hold a well-diversified portfolio of financial assets that maximizes real returns for a given level of risk. For investors from small countries with poorly developed capital markets, there will be a natural demand for assets in other countries with more developed capital markets. Where inflation has eroded real returns or real wealth, it is normal to expect investors to seek other markets or units of account that preserve purchasing power. When substantial exchange rate changes are expected (in larger industrial countries or poorer developing countries), we expect to find investors positioning themselves in advance to make the best of the situation. Whenever markets are highly integrated and transaction costs are low, private individuals will have strong incentives to circumvent what appear to be arbitrary barriers to their own utility maximization.[3]

Our bias for classifying all freely organized legal transactions as "normal" may seem in opposition to the notion that "flight capital is capital that flees" advanced by Ingo Walter elsewhere in this volume and earlier by Charles Kindleberger. In a market paradigm, the decisions of investors concerning whether to invest funds at home or abroad depend on relative returns suitably adjusted for rates of inflation, expected exchange rate changes, taxes, and risk factors. If, for example, this return differential favors the United States over Mexico, on what basis can we conclude that capital is fleeing from Mexico rather than being drawn into the United States? In general, economic models presume that private domestic investors are scanning the environment in search of higher expected returns and that capital movements are motivated by self-interest. In order to justify a negative connotation ("capital flight") for a subset of capital movements, there must be a derogation from the market paradigm, such as a deviation between private and social welfare.

Capital Flight and Nationalism

The notion that capital flight represents a source of disutility focuses on a nationalistic measure of social utility. In a variety of cases, it can be argued that domestic capital outflows might reduce domestic social welfare, even though they increase the private welfare of both domestic and foreign residents who participate in the capital transfer. Cuddington (1986) outlines several such cases, for example:

☐ hot money flows may destabilize financial markets

☐ social returns on domestic projects may exceed private domestic returns

☐ by raising a country's gross borrowing needs, capital flight raises the marginal cost of foreign debt

☐ once capital leaves it never returns, resulting in lower domestic investment and a lower domestic tax base.

As Cuddington suggests, in each of these cases one needs to ask whether policies to restrict capital flight would be second best, even if they could be

---

3. US policies to stem capital outflows in the 1960s such as the interest-rate equalization tax (1963) and the voluntary foreign credit restraint program (1968) were not viewed as highly successful. The Eurocurrency and Eurobond markets quickly developed over this period to expedite capital outflows and satisfy the offshore demand for funds.

made effective. Regarding the first, it is certainly a possibility that underlying macroeconomic policies and market fundamentals, rather than capital flight, were responsible for financial market volatility. Regarding the second, the first-best policy would be to attack a distortion of this sort directly by providing additional incentives to the private rate of return on capital. And regarding the last, reversals of capital flight have indeed occurred; but even if they had not, it is an exaggeration to claim that flight capital is "lost to the country," and there is no certainty that the alternative placement of flight capital would be in domestic investment.

As noted earlier, any definition of capital flight may seem to reflect arbitrary distinctions. One way to reduce these is to link a definition of capital flight to its impact on national utility.

Under the assumption that funds committed to capital flight would have been used for domestic investment, then the total buildup of foreign assets scales the magnitude of national disutility from capital flight. This assumption suggests that an expansive definition of capital flight that captures the reported and unreported increase in foreign assets for both the private and public sectors would be appropriate. Defining capital flight as the total buildup of foreign assets implies that:

□ foreign assets, even the working capital balances of source country multinational firms, never yield higher national utility than domestic assets

□ a buildup of domestic assets, rather than consumption of foreign goods or wasteful domestic spending, was the alternative to capital flight.

Both Erbe (1985) and the World Bank (1985) use such an expansive measure of capital flight.

Dooley (1986) proposes that the stock of claims held on nonresidents that *do not generate investment income* reported in the balance of payments be taken as a measure of capital flight. The presumption here is that the interest earned on legal and normal capital outflows would be reported in the balance of payments. Interest earned on illegal capital outflows, or outflows motivated by tax avoidance or the demand for secrecy, are assumed to go unreported. Capital flight can be approximated by capitalizing the stream of *reported* investment income and subtracting this from total external claims.

In one sense, this technique could be viewed as a novel approach for measuring the stock of unreported external claims, i.e., capital flight. But the definition implies that if all capital outflows and the investment income on them were reported, then there would be *zero* capital flight. This suggests that the loss of national utility from capital flight comes not from the diversion of domestic capital to offshore investments, but rather from the loss of foreign-exchange receipts upon repatriation of offshore earnings and the loss of taxing power over these offshore earnings. Even this is somewhat of an overstatement, since domestic residents could reinvest (and report) their offshore earnings without producing any foreign-exchange earnings for the domestic economy. With Dooley's definition, the disutility of capital flight seems to correspond to the inability of a country to generate foreign investment receipts sufficient to service its own external debt. However, if individuals have transferred funds offshore at lower yields (reflecting their demand for secrecy, stability, or safe haven), then the country could still have a debt-servicing problem even if all investment income is reported.

Measuring Capital Flight

The definitions of capital flight found in the previous literature can be usefully grouped into two types. The first type does not distinguish between "normal" capital flows and capital flight and seeks to measure the acquisition of net foreign assets, or some subset of these claims, by the private sector. The second type attempts to make the distinction between "normal" capital and flight capital by measuring the stock of foreign claims that does not generate income that is reported in the balance of payments accounts.

The broadest definition of capital flight has been employed by the World Bank (1985) and by Erbe (1985). This measure takes inflows of capital in the form of increases in external debt and net foreign direct investment and subtracts from these inflows the current account deficit and the increase in official reserves. The difference between these inflows and the extent to which they are used to finance the current account deficit and an increase in reserves is taken to reflect an increase in net foreign claims by the private sector. This increase in net foreign assets is the measure of capital flight they adopt.

The capital flight definition adopted by Morgan Guaranty (1986) also measures capital flight as a residual. In addition to the current account deficit and the increase in official reserves, Morgan Guaranty (1986) also subtracts the increase in short-term foreign assets of the banking system from total capital inflows. The Morgan definition then does not consider acquisition of foreign assets by banks to be capital flight, while acquisition of foreign assets by other agents is considered to be capital flight.

Cline (1986) critiques the capital-flight definition adopted by Morgan and discusses adjustments to the Morgan calculations. He argues that income from tourism and border transactions should be excluded from current account earnings since these earnings are beyond the control of foreign-exchange-control authorities, and thus should not be counted when calculating capital flight. In addition, he argues that reinvested investment income should not be considered capital flight since this income is also beyond the control of the authorities and that if residents do not repatriate income from capital held abroad, this should not be considered additional flight of capital.

What is the justification for these exclusions from the broad measure of capital flight? Morgan Guaranty (1986) offers no justification for treating the banking system differently from other firms and individuals. None will be given here. The question that Cline wishes to address regards the extent to which future inflows of funds will result in additional capital flight. He wishes to determine "the 'marginal propensity' of capital to leave the country" and argues that "the presence of a tourism surplus not garnered by the government, and of nonrepatriated private interest earnings abroad, have little to do with the issue of how new capital is used when obtained."

One aspect of determining how likely capital flight will be in the future is the extent to which capital controls are effective in preventing acquisition of foreign assets by the private sector. The adjustments suggested by Cline may be relevant to determining the extent to which the private sector has been able to circumvent exchange controls in the past.[4] If, after making these adjustments, the degree of capital flight is greatly reduced, the evidence would suggest that capital controls have been somewhat successful in restricting movements of funds abroad. On the other hand, if we are interested in the extent to which a country is likely to experience capital flight in the future, then we should examine how macroeconomic conditions and government policies underlying capital outflows have changed rather than attempting to identify particular items that should or should not be counted as income that is subject to capital flight.

Cuddington (1986) takes a different approach to measuring capital flight. His focus is on short-term capital flows, which he believes to be the typical meaning of capital flight, rather than all private-sector acquisition of external claims. Capital flight, defined to consist of acquisition of short-term external assets by the nonbank private sector, is calculated by adding the errors and omissions to selected short-term capital items that are chosen individually for each country he considers.

Why should the focus be on short-term capital movements rather than both short-term and long-term capital? Cuddington (1986) chooses to consider only short-term capital since he is examining "hot money," funds that respond quickly to changes in expected returns or to changes in risk. Presumably, these are also the funds that potentially will be the quickest to return to the country when conditions change. There are a couple of problems with measuring capital flight in this way, however. First, as Cuddington (1986) notes, the errors and omissions do not consist only of unreported

---

4. Indeed, it is in the context of discussing the degree of capital flight in Mexico after the imposition of exchange controls that Cline suggests these adjustments.

short-term capital. Second, the case for considering only short-term funds is less than compelling. An investor, reacting to unfavorable conditions at home (such as an anticipated devaluation), may acquire stocks, long-term bonds, or deposits with more than a year to maturity, or "real" assets, as well as short-term financial assets. The motivation for all such acquisitions will be identical, as will their effect on the investor's home country. In addition, it is difficult to make the case that short-term funds are more likely to react quickly either in leaving the investor's home country or in returning. In today's international financial markets there is very little loss of liquidity associated with acquiring long-term bonds (especially US government bonds, corporate bonds traded on US markets, or Eurobonds) or equities.[5] Thus, whether one wishes to measure private-sector acquisition of foreign assets or the component of these assets that can flow and reflow quickly, it seems best to look beyond short-term capital flows.

An alternative (not pursued in any previous attempts to measure capital flight) is to combine private-sector external borrowing with government and government-guaranteed external borrowing and measure the acquisition of gross rather than net private-sector external assets. The reason for doing so is that should a balance of payments crisis arise, the government may, as has happened in a number of cases, take on the obligation of servicing this private debt. If so, the private external borrowing may be considered a contingent liability of the government.[6] One might also include foreign-exchange-value guaranties provided to holders of foreign-currency denominated accounts and any forward market intervention that the authorities have undertaken.

Dooley (1986) and Khan and Ul Haque (1987) define capital flight as those external assets held by the private sector that *do not* generate income recorded in the balance of payments accounts of the country.

Dooley (1986) measures the stock of external claims by summing identified capital flows in the balance of payments accounts and making two adjustments to capture unreported capital flows. The first of these is to add the errors and omissions. The second adjustment Dooley carries out is based on a comparison of the World Bank data on the stock of external debt and external borrowing reported in the balance of payments accounts. If both sources report borrowing accurately, one ought to be able to match closely the change in the stock of debt reported by the World Bank with the net flows of new borrowing reported in the balance of payments accounts. This is frequently not the case, however. In several countries, the annual change

---

5. Some "real" assets, like real estate, are considerably less liquid, however, and funds invested in these are less likely to respond quickly to changes in conditions in the investor's home country.

6. We are indebted to Alain Ize and Don Lessard for suggesting this point.

in the stock of external debt as reported by the World Bank is considerably larger than flows reported in the balance of payments accounts, suggesting that part of the increase in external debt goes unrecorded in the balance of payments accounts. In the cases where a discrepancy arises, the unrecorded increase in external liabilities must correspond to an underestimate of balancing transactions. Dooley (1986) assumes that all of the underestimated balancing transactions consist of private-sector acquisition of foreign assets. He therefore adds the difference between each year's change in external debt as reported by the World Bank and the increase as recorded by the balance of payments accounts to his estimate of the increase in private-sector foreign assets. He then computes a market interest rate for each country's assets and calculates the stock of external assets that would give rise to the level of investment income recorded in the balance of payments accounts at this market interest rate. The difference between the two measures of external assets is his measure of capital flight.

Unlike any of the studies discussed above, Dooley (1986) and Khan and Ul Haque (1987) attempt to distinguish capital flight from "normal" capital flows that correspond to ordinary portfolio diversification and business activities of domestic residents. Both point out that looking only at the gross increase in external assets as a measure of capital flight may give misleading results since, in many countries that are generally recognized *not* to be experiencing capital flight, domestic residents acquire both foreign assets and foreign liabilities. That is, there are generally two-way capital flows between countries, and to identify one side of these flows as capital flight would be seriously misleading. Their solution is to identify foreign assets that do not generate reported income as capital flight because the presumption is that if the income is unrecorded, the motive of the investor is to place funds beyond the control of the authorities. Both claim that such capital is "lost to the country" and is identified as flight capital.

The problem of distinguishing "normal capital flows" from "capital flight" was discussed earlier. Does the solution adopted by Dooley (1986) and Khan and Ul Haque (1987) succeed in making this distinction? If this capital is "lost to the country" while owned by residents of the country, it must be that these foreign assets represent a welfare loss and should be distinguished from those that do not. If the problem associated with capital flight involves an externality of the sort described above (in which the social rate of return on capital invested domestically exceeds the private rate of return on such investments or in which there is a shadow value of foreign exchange that exceeds the market price), it seems that any movement of funds abroad that otherwise would have been invested at home should be considered in a measure of capital flight. The same would be true if the nature of the distortion is the absence of credibility on the part of the policymaker. In each of these cases, whether or not the income from foreign investments is reported seems irrelevant. One may wish to distinguish repatriated investment income from reinvested income on these grounds, as noted earlier, however. If, on the other hand, the problem addressed is the erosion of the domestic tax base and the need to levy taxes on other reported income that has less desirable allocative or distributional effects, their definition seems to be the natural one.

An alternative means of distinguishing capital flight from "normal" capital flows might be to examine the extent to which private-sector capital flows are two-way flows or one-way flows. In a situation in which private-sector capital account credits greatly exceed private-sector capital account debits, one might judge that capital is fleeing and that the "normal" two-way flow of funds is not occurring. While this means of distinguishing flight capital from "normal" capital flows might be conceptually useful in devising a measure of capital flight corresponding to Walter's in chapter 5 of this volume, it is difficult to see how it could be implemented in view of data problems.

Empirical Results

In this section we present estimates of capital flight based on a common data base and a standard time period and obtained using the definitions and methods discussed above. We do this with several goals in mind. First, we will be able to show in a concise way the range of estimates of capital flight implied by the alternative definitions that have been offered. Second, by comparing our estimates with those reported in previous work we will be able to determine the extent to which the estimates of capital flight are sensitive to differences in data sources. Finally, we will be able to determine if the different definitions adopted by the World Bank (1985), Erbe (1985), Morgan Guaranty (1986), and Cline (1986) give rise to significantly different estimates of capital flight.

Our results show that, in some cases, important differences arise when we compare our estimates of capital flight to those obtained by others when using the same definitions but somewhat different data sources. On the other hand, the differences in definitions adopted by previous authors make only marginal differences in most cases. We also consider adjustments to the capital flight estimates to reflect capital flight in the form of misinvoicing of trade flows and valuation changes on external debt due to exchange rate changes.

Tables 3.1 through 3.6 present summary measures of changes in external debt and some balance of payments aggregates for six countries from 1976 to 1984. The six countries considered are Argentina, Brazil, Korea, Mexico, the Philippines, and Venezuela. In addition, these tables present several

Table 3.1 Argentina: external debt, balance of payments, and capital flight
(billion dollars)

	1976–82	1976–84
A. Current account surplus	− 8.6	− 13.6
Excluded items	6.1	7.7
B. Net foreign direct investment	2.7	3.1
C. Private short-term capital	− 14.9	− 14.7
D. Portfolio investment: bonds and equities	0.0	0.0
E. Banking system foreign assets (minus signifies increase)	0.3	− 0.3
F. Change in reserves (minus signifies increase)	− 2.8	− 0.5
G. Errors and omissions	− 0.8	− 1.2
H. Change in debt	34.1	36.3

CAPITAL FLIGHT ESTIMATES	Authors' estimates using consistent data set		Previous estimates
Estimation method	1976–82	1976–84	1976–82
World Bank (H + B + A + F)	22.4[a]	n.a.	19.2[a]
Erbe (H + B + A + F)	25.3	25.3	32.2
Morgan (H + B + A + E + F)	25.5	25.0	27.0
Cline (Morgan, less excluded items in A)	19.4	17.3	n.a.
Cuddington (− G − C)	15.6	16.0	15.2
Dooley method	24.1	23.9	n.a.

n.a. not available.
Source: See statistical annexes.
a. Estimates for 1979–82 are given rather than 1976–82.

estimates of capital flight obtained using a single consistent data set and several definitions of capital flight described previously.[7] We have adopted the sign convention used in the balance of payments accounts. To facilitate comparisons across the various estimates, we present totals for 1976 to 1982 as well as for 1976 to 1984.[8]

7. A description of the data sources and tables containing the detailed data used to generate these tables are found in the appendix. The adjustments to the Morgan–World Bank–Erbe estimates suggested by Cline are not relevant for all countries and are presented here only for the purpose of comparison. We will discuss the importance of his adjustments when we turn to a discussion of Mexico.

8. As noted in the footnotes to the tables, the World Bank numbers are for 1979–82 rather than for 1976–82. As Cuddington (chapter 4) points out, when calculating these totals we ignore the effect of possible interest compounding, and hence the total probably understates the increase in the value of assets held abroad.

Table 3.2 Brazil: external debt, balance of payments, and capital flight
(billion dollars)

	1976–82	1976–84
A. Current account surplus	−70.0	−76.8
Excluded items	3.6	4.8
B. Net foreign direct investment	13.6	16.5
C. Private short-term capital	n.a.	n.a.
D. Portfolio investment: bonds and equities	n.a.	n.a.
E. Banking system foreign assets	1.2	1.3
F. Change in reserves	3.2	−0.3
G. Errors and omissions	0.3	0.1
H. Change in debt	65.9	79.3

CAPITAL FLIGHT ESTIMATES	Authors' estimates using consistent data set		Previous estimates
Estimation method	1976–82	1976–84	1976–82
World Bank (H + B + A + F)	5.8[a]	18.7	3.5[a]
Erbe (H + B + A + F)	12.6	18.7	7.8
Morgan (H + B + A + E + F)	11.5	17.3	3.0
Cline (Morgan, less excluded items in A)	7.9	12.5	n.a.
Cuddington (−G − C)	−0.3	−0.1	−0.3
Dooley	−4.6	12.3	n.a.

n.a. not available.
Source: See statistical annexes.
a. Estimates for 1979–82 are given rather than 1976–82.

Several conclusions emerge immediately from these tables. First, the extent of capital flight according to all measures is greater for Argentina, Mexico, and Venezuela than for the other three countries, with Mexico leading the list. In these three countries, the estimates of capital flight are large not only in absolute terms but also in relation to the increase in external debt accumulated over the period considered. The estimated degree of capital flight from Korea and the Philippines is very small. Regardless of the definition employed, countries estimated to have experienced considerable capital flight are those in which the increase in external debt greatly exceeds the cumulative current account deficits. Second, the smallest estimate of capital flight is generally obtained using Cuddington's definition. This is not surprising since he considers only short-term capital flows. Third, there is generally very little difference between the estimates obtained using the Morgan definition and those obtained using that of the World Bank and

Table 3.3 Korea: external debt, balance of payments, and capital flight
(billion dollars)

	1976–82	1976–84
A. Current account surplus	− 18.2	− 21.1
Excluded items	4.1	6.2
B. Net foreign direct investment	0.2	0.2
C. Private short-term capital	1.8	1.9
D. Portfolio investment: bonds and equities	0.0	0.0
E. Banking system foreign assets	− 3.4	− 4.1
F. Change in reserves	− 4.3	− 4.7
G. Errors and omissions	− 2.9	− 4.8
H. Change in debt	28.4	33.2

CAPITAL FLIGHT ESTIMATES	Authors' estimates using consistent data set		Previous estimates
Estimation method	1976–82	1976–84	1976–82
World Bank (H + B + A + F)	3.3[a]	7.6	0.9[a]
Erbe (H + B + A + F)	6.1	7.6	− 6.0
Morgan (H + B + A + E + F)	2.8	3.5	6.0
Cline (Morgan, less excluded items in A)	− 1.4	− 2.7	n.a.
Cuddington (− G − C)	1.1	2.8	1.1
Dooley	n.a.	n.a.	n.a.

n.a. not available.
Source: See statistical annexes.
a. Estimates for 1979–82 are given rather than 1976–82.

Erbe.[9] Fourth, the estimates of capital flight calculated using the method proposed by Dooley show that, in most cases, not only has the private sector acquired a substantial volume of foreign assets, but also a substantial fraction of these assets does not generate income that is reported in the balance of payments accounts. Finally, in many cases the estimates presented here are very close to the estimates presented by other authors.

The most striking exception to this last point is found when Erbe's reported capital flight estimates are compared to our estimates based on her

---

9. The only exception to this is found in the case of Korea, where the estimates of capital flight are reduced from $6.1 billion to $2.8 billion and $7.6 billion to $3.5 billion when the banking system's acquisition of foreign assets is excluded. A slight but noticeable reduction is also found in the case of the Philippines.

Table 3.4   Mexico: external debt, balance of payments, and capital flight
(billion dollars)

	1976–82	1976–84
A. Current account surplus	− 42.1	− 32.9
Excluded items	22.0	27.8
B. Net foreign direct investment	9.7	10.6
C. Private short-term capital: other assets	− 9.8	− 15.8
D. Portfolio investment: bonds and equities	0.1	0.2
E. Banking system foreign assets	0.5	0.2
F. Change in reserves	0.6	− 3.5
G. Errors and omissions	− 19.6	− 20.8
H. Change in debt	67.9	79.4

CAPITAL FLIGHT ESTIMATES	Authors' estimates using consistent data set		Previous estimates
Estimation method	1976–82	1976–84	1976–82
World Bank (H + B + A + F)	25.3[a]	53.6	26.5[a]
Erbe (H + B + A + F)	36.1	53.6	35.6
Morgan (H + B + A + E + F)	35.7	53.4	36.0
Cline (Morgan, less excluded items in A)	13.7	25.6	n.a.
Cuddington (− G − C)	29.3	36.2	30.1
Dooley	25.2	37.5	n.a.

n.a. not available.
Source: See statistical annexes.
a. Estimates for 1979–82 are given rather than 1976–82.

definition. The bulk of the difference can be traced to differences in estimates of the increase in external debt.[10] A fairly sizable difference can also be found between the Morgan estimates of capital flight from Brazil and our estimate based on the Morgan definition. The source of this difference seems to be in different estimates of the change in reserves and foreign assets of the banking system. These differences suggest that the estimates of capital flight are sensitive to the data sources employed and are especially sensitive to differences in estimates of external debt.

A few remarks about individual countries are in order. Argentina experienced substantial capital flight between 1976 and 1982 according to all measures. However, the data also show that no additional capital flight

---

10. Erbe (1985) uses OECD estimates of external debt, while World Bank estimates are used here.

Table 3.5 Philippines: external debt, balance of payments, and capital flight
(billion dollars)

	1976–82	1976–84
A. Current account surplus	−11.7	−15.7
Excluded items	2.3	3.7
B. Net foreign direct investment	0.5	0.6
C. Private short-term capital: other assets	−3.3	−3.1
D. Portfolio investment: bonds and equities	n.a.	n.a.
E. Banking system foreign assets	−1.3	−1.4
F. Change in reserves	−1.1	0.7
G. Errors and omissions	−0.3	−0.6
H. Change in debt	19.2	19.4

CAPITAL FLIGHT ESTIMATES	Authors' estimates using consistent data set		Previous estimates
Estimation method	1976–82	1976–84	1976–82
World Bank (H + B + A + F)	4.5[a]	5.0	n.a.
Erbe (H + B + A + F)	7.0	5.0	−3.0
Morgan (H + B + A + E + F)	5.6	3.7	7.0
Cline (Morgan, less excluded items in A)	3.3	0.0	n.a.
Cuddington (−G − C)	3.7	3.7	n.a.
Dooley	7.4	3.7	n.a.

n.a. not available.
Source: See statistical annexes.
a. Estimates for 1979–82 are given rather than 1976–82.

occurred in 1983 and 1984. The estimates of capital flight from Brazil, while considerably smaller than for the other Latin American countries, show substantial variation across definitions. All estimates except those based on Cuddington's definition point to a much smaller volume of capital flight between 1976 and 1982 than between 1976 and 1984 and indicate that capital flight of approximately $6 billion occurred in 1983 and 1984. Venezuela, like Mexico, is estimated to have experienced sizable capital flight both between 1976 and 1982 and during 1983 and 1984. Interestingly, the estimates of capital flight during 1983 and 1984, based on all definitions except Cline's and Cuddington's, indicate that capital flight during those two years exceeded the increase in external debt by a factor of approximately four.

Table 3.6 Venezuela: external debt, balance of payments, and capital flight
(billion dollars)

	1976–82	1976–84
A. Current account surplus	−3.8	5.6
Excluded items	4.4	6.8
B. Net foreign direct investment	−0.2	−0.1
C. Private short-term capital: other assets	−11.2	−13.3
D. Portfolio investment: bonds and equities	−0.9	−0.9
E. Banking system foreign assets	−0.3	−0.9
F. Change in reserves	−1.8	−3.7
G. Errors and omissions	0.9	1.0
H. Change in debt	26.3	28.7

CAPITAL FLIGHT ESTIMATES	Authors' estimates using consistent data set		Previous estimates
Estimation method	1976–82	1976–84	1976–82
World Bank (H + B + A + F)	20.7[a]	30.5	22.0[a]
Erbe (H + B + A + F)	20.5	30.5	11.0
Morgan (H + B + A + E + F)	20.2	29.6	25.0
Cline (Morgan, less excluded items in A)	15.7	22.8	n.a.
Cuddington (−G − C)	11.2	13.1	10.4
Dooley	11.0	24.6	n.a.

n.a. not available.
Source: See statistical annexes.
a. Estimates for 1979–82.

The most interesting case presented here is that of Mexico. In addition to the large volume of capital flight experienced by Mexico, the estimated increase in 1983 and 1984 is also striking. The adjustments to the Morgan definition of capital flight proposed by Cline lead to a substantial downward revision of the degree of capital flight both over the entire period and over the 1976–82 period. However, since the idea behind these adjustments is to determine the extent to which exchange controls have been effective, it would be useful to concentrate on the estimated capital flight during 1983 and 1984. While these adjustments reduce the degree of capital flight by approximately $6 billion for 1983 and 1984, capital flight of approximately $12 billion is estimated to have occurred during this period even if the Cline adjustments are used.

One possible source of error in the capital flight estimates stems from the use of changes in the dollar value of external debt. If a significant fraction of external debt is denominated in currencies other than the US dollar, then the dollar value of that debt will change as exchange rates change. For example, if part of a country's external debt is denominated in deutsche marks and the US dollar appreciates relative to the DM, the dollar value of the debt will fall. As a result, the capital-flight estimates derived from changes in the dollar value of the debt will be understated when the dollar appreciates, as it did from 1980 through 1984. Similarly, these valuation changes will overstate the extent of capital flight when the dollar depreciates. How quantitatively important are these valuation changes? It is difficult to determine the precise magnitude of these valuation changes since data on the currency composition of external debt are not readily available. To shed some light on the potential magnitude of these valuation changes, we have calculated some hypothetical valuation changes assuming that 10 percent of debt is denominated in DM or yen.

The hypothetical valuation changes in external debt are presented in table 3.7. As can be seen in table 3.7, if 10 percent of external debt is DM-denominated, the increase in the dollar value of the debt understates slightly the level of new borrowing undertaken by the country. The capital flight estimates based on these figures will then also be slightly underestimated. The calculations reported in table 3.7 indicate that the size of valuation changes that result if 10 percent of external debt is yen-denominated are even smaller than in the case of DM. In neither case is the size of valuation changes sufficient to result in substantial underestimates or serious over-estimates of capital flight, except in the unlikely case that a very large fraction of external debt is denominated in currencies other than the US dollar.

A comparison of partner-country data on trade flows can be used to consider two additional potential sources of mismeasurement of capital flight. The first of these possibilities is that balance of payments data are of such dubious quality as to warrant a broad degree of skepticism about any particular number that is derived from them. The second of the possibilities is that additional capital flight occurs through systematic misinvoicing of imports and exports. Gulati (this chapter, following) presents estimates of the degree to which capital flight estimates might need to be adjusted to reflect misinvoicing of trade flows.[11]

There are several reasons for differences in partner-country data on trade flows, quite apart from any systematic falsification of invoices. One of these,

---

11. Partner-country trade data have been used to examine the accuracy of balance of payments data by Morgenstern (1974) and to infer the extent of capital flight effected through misinvoicing by Bhagwati (1974), Naya and Morgan (1974), and Bhagwati, Krueger, and Wibulswasdi (1974). Gulati provides updated estimates.

Table 3.7 Potential valuation changes on external debt
(billion dollars)

	With 10 percent of debt denominated in DM	
Country	1976–82	1976–85
Argentina	−0.3	−1.5
Brazil	−0.4	−2.8
Korea	−0.3	−1.3
Mexico	−0.5	−2.8
Philippines	−0.2	−0.8
Venezuela	−0.5	−1.3
	With 10 percent of debt denominated in yen	
Country	1976–82	1976–85
Argentina	0.2	−0.1
Brazil	0.9	0.2
Korea	0.3	0.0
Mexico	0.5	−0.1
Philippines	0.1	−0.3
Venezuela	0.1	−0.2

Source: See statistical annexes.

problems arising from timing lags due to transit, can produce differences for two reasons. First, goods shipped and recorded by the exporting country in one year may not arrive and get recorded by the importing country until the following year. Second, when a country records these trade data in local currency, timing lags may result in their conversion into dollars at different exchange rates in the importing and exporting countries. The other major source of differences in partner-country reports of trade flows arises from mistaken allocation of the destination of exports or the origin of imports. Such mistakes can arise quite easily due to transit trading, reexport, or the participation of third country merchants.

In order to attempt to sort out the extent to which the discrepancies in partner-country trade data are due to systematic falsification of invoices and to poor quality data, we have carried out a number of calculations that can be compared to those reported in Gulati's paper. In table 3.8, we examine trade between the United States and four industrial countries, Canada, France, Germany, and the United Kingdom.[12] As can be seen, reported

12. The trade data are taken from IMF *Direction of Trade Yearbook*. Since exports are reported f.o.b. while imports are reported c.i.f., the import data are adjusted using each country's c.i.f./f.o.b. ratio reported in *International Financial Statistics* so that both imports and exports are f.o.b. for the purpose of the analysis undertaken here.

Table 3.8   United States: partner-country trade data comparisons

	Ratios of reported exports to reported US imports								
	1976	1977	1978	1979	1980	1981	1982	1983	1984
Canada	1.01	1.00	1.00	1.02	1.02	1.04	1.04	1.07	1.04
France	1.00	1.07	1.04	0.99	0.93	0.95	0.94	0.95	0.93
Germany	1.02	0.99	1.01	1.03	1.01	1.01	1.01	1.01	0.97
United Kingdom	1.03	1.04	0.87	1.06	1.08	0.98	1.01	1.03	0.95
	Ratios of reported imports to reported US exports								
	1976	1977	1978	1979	1980	1981	1982	1983	1984
Canada	1.05	1.05	1.06	1.13	1.13	1.11	1.11	1.12	1.11
France	1.30	1.34	1.38	1.40	1.39	1.29	1.23	1.31	1.28
Germany	1.18	1.10	1.21	1.26	1.25	1.19	1.22	1.21	1.17
United Kingdom	1.07	1.04	1.02	0.92	1.02	0.92	1.03	1.01	0.97

Source: IMF, *Direction of Trade Yearbook* and *International Financial Statistics.*

exports of these countries to the United States correspond very closely to reported US imports from these countries. The ratios of these reported magnitudes are generally much closer to one than is found in Gulati's study. On the other hand, sizable differences are found between reported French and German imports from the United States and reported US exports to these countries. These differences suggest either systematic overinvoicing of imports by these countries or, perhaps, may simply indicate that the destination of shipments from the US to the European Community (EC) countries may not be accurately ascribed to the proper country. In any event, the size of these differences is striking and raises questions about the general quality of the data.

A second set of comparisons is found in table 3.9, where trade data for five European countries with Germany are examined. Intra-European trade data provide an interesting benchmark comparison since the data problems described earlier should be minimized due to short transport time, relatively stable intra-European exchange rates, and the absence of intra-EC trade restrictions. A fairly close correspondence between partner-country reports is found in table 3.9, with the exception of French-German trade since approximately 1980. There is evidence of underinvoicing of exports, perhaps indicating capital flight from France. On the other hand, this apparent underinvoicing of exports corresponds to apparent underinvoicing of imports during the same period. Since the ratios in both reported exports and imports are nearly always less than one, either a systematic bias may be present in the German partner-country trade data, or the c.i.f.-f.o.b. adjust-

Table 3.9 Germany: partner-country trade data comparisons

	Ratios of reported exports to reported German imports								
	1976	1977	1978	1979	1980	1981	1982	1983	1984
Denmark	1.03	1.03	1.04	1.05	1.05	1.05	1.02	1.05	1.06
France	0.97	0.95	0.97	0.96	0.91	0.87	0.80	0.84	0.87
Netherlands	1.06	1.05	1.04	1.02	1.06	1.07	1.06	1.08	1.08
United Kingdom	1.00	0.89	0.86	0.98	0.97	0.94	0.87	0.89	0.87
Switzerland	0.89	0.89	0.93	0.93	0.90	0.91	0.92	0.96	0.95
	Ratios of reported imports to reported German exports								
	1976	1977	1978	1979	1980	1981	1982	1983	1984
Denmark	0.93	0.95	0.92	0.92	0.92	0.92	0.94	0.91	0.91
France	0.88	0.86	0.86	0.85	0.82	0.80	0.75	0.78	0.76
Netherlands	0.92	0.90	0.90	0.90	0.88	0.88	0.88	0.86	0.87
United Kingdom	0.95	0.82	0.91	1.00	0.96	0.95	0.94	0.99	0.98
Switzerland	0.90	0.91	0.93	0.91	0.88	0.91	0.92	0.92	0.91

Source: IMF, *Direction of Trade Yearbook* and *International Financial Statistics.*

ment—which uses average ratios for each country—overstates the corrections that need to be made to intra-European trade.

The final set of comparisons is found in table 3.10, where we examine partner-country trade flows between some developing countries. The first of these comparisons is between Mexico and Brazil. No striking differences are found between the partner-country reports in this case, especially when compared to the size of the differences found in the Mexico-United States and Mexico-industrial countries comparisons reported by Gulati. This would suggest that systematic falsification of invoices rather than other data problems accounts for the differences found by Gulati for Mexico. Next, consider the Venezuela-Brazil comparison and the Argentina-Brazil comparison. In the first of these, we find a relatively close correspondence between the partner-country reports, except in 1980 and 1981, when reported Brazilian exports fall considerably short of reported Venezuelan imports, and in 1978, when reported Venezuelan exports fall short of reported Brazilian imports. On the other hand, large differences are found between the partner-country reports for Argentina and Brazil. Here we find that, in several years, reported Argentine exports to Brazil fall considerably short of reported Brazilian imports from Argentina, while the correspondence is relatively close in other years. We also find that reported Argentine imports from Brazil fall short of reported Brazilian exports to Argentina, although the difference is smaller.

Table 3.10 Developing countries: partner-country trade data comparisons

	Ratios of reported first-country exports to reported second-country imports								
	1976	1977	1978	1979	1980	1981	1982	1983	1984
Mexico-Brazil	0.99	1.02	1.07	0.98	0.99	1.11	1.13	1.13	1.05
Venezuela-Brazil	1.04	0.95	0.82	1.03	1.23	1.05	n.a.	n.a.	n.a.
Argentina-Brazil	0.94	0.73	0.57	0.60	0.94	1.06	1.00	0.99	0.97
Philippines-Hong Kong	1.05	1.16	1.20	1.20	1.14	1.21	1.40	1.07	1.07
Korea-Hong Kong	1.06	1.04	1.11	1.16	1.17	1.30	1.33	1.30	1.51
	Ratios of reported first-country imports to reported second-country exports								
	1976	1977	1978	1979	1980	1981	1982	1983	1984
Mexico-Brazil	1.01	0.91	0.89	0.83	0.87	0.91	0.96	0.92	0.89
Venezuela-Brazil	1.00	1.14	0.97	0.95	0.73	0.56	n.a.	n.a.	n.a.
Argentina-Brazil	0.80	0.96	0.68	0.87	0.85	0.82	0.93	0.67	0.64
Philippines-Hong Kong	0.52	0.51	0.57	0.55	0.58	0.56	0.54	0.66	0.68
Korea-Hong Kong	0.35	0.29	0.31	0.40	0.40	0.65	0.71	0.54	0.88

n.a. not available, because Venezuela uses partner-country data after 1981.
Source: IMF, *Direction of Trade Yearbook* and *International Financial Statistics*.

It seems then that both data problems and systematic falsification of invoices account for differences in partner-country reports of trade flows. The differences reflect, at least in part, capital flight that is not included in the estimates discussed above. To the extent that the differences point to underreported trade flows, they must also reflect underrecorded balancing items. If we assume that the underrecorded balancing items are increases in private sector foreign assets, then the capital flight estimates discussed above will be underestimates. If we add import overinvoicing and export underinvoicing, and assume that the differences reflect capital flight rather than other data problems, then, as Gulati shows, the estimates of capital flight are generally *reduced* since import underinvoicing dominates export underinvoicing.

Policy Implications and Concluding Remarks

Our objective in this paper has been to survey the alternative definitions of capital flight that have been offered in the recent literature. At the conceptual level, we have noted that the definition of capital flight requires a somewhat arbitrary distinction between normal capital outflows and those labeled as capital flight. Any specification of capital flight ought to be consistent with the economic or policy question under consideration. Most current policy issues presume a nationalistic point of view in which capital flight reduces national welfare. Policy decisions will be aided to the extent that a definition of capital flight represents a good proxy for the measure of national welfare loss.

At the empirical level, we have attempted to replicate several of the leading definitions of capital flight using a common data base. Doing so illustrates the range of estimates of capital flight that are possible, and how alternative definitions and data bases contribute to the dispersion of estimates. Our results show that, for some countries, differences in definitions or data bases may be substantial, causing some estimates of capital flight to be positive and others negative. The change in a country's external debt position plays a major role in several definitions of capital flight. Our results suggest that revisions in external debt figures and differences across data sources may account for up to $5 billion to $10 billion of the difference in capital flight estimates.

The evidence suggests that capital flight is often a large absolute number. It is sometimes large relative to the stock of external debt. Capital flight is probably always small relative to the stock of domestic assets or other measures of net national wealth. What, then, is the relevance of these capital-flight estimates for policymakers?

In balance of payments analysis, international transactions are known to be interdependent. Consequently, to take the current US case as an example, it is unreasonable to hope that if the United States imposed a tariff and reduced its imports from Japan by $10 billion, that the US current account balance would improve by $10 billion. Because the US current account surplus equals the sum of net private US savings plus the US fiscal surplus, we need to know the impact of the tariff on these variables to determine its net effect on the current account. To make this calculation requires a general equilibrium model of the economy.

Policy making vis-à-vis capital flight is much the same. It is unreasonable to claim that if $10 billion in capital flight could be reversed, then the country's external debt needs would be reduced by $10 billion.[13] At a minimum, this conclusion would assume that the alternative use of the $10 billion was toward domestic investment. But if underlying forces in the economy were unchanged, domestic residents might be inclined to spend their $10 billion on foreign imports, or to convert these funds into gold or other commodities to preserve purchasing power.

---

13. Perhaps this claim is reasonable in the case of official misconduct, when public funds are moved offshore rather than recycled into the domestic economy. See Erbe (1985, p. 268) for an example.

From these examples it seems clear that capital flight is best thought of as a *symptom* of underlying economic forces rather than a *cause* of national welfare losses. To understand the role of capital flight, its impact on the national economy and the welfare gains from reversing it, an appropriate definition of capital flight must be imbedded in a complete model of the economy.

A current issue of concern is the impact that capital flight might have on the willingness of commercial banks to increase their lending to LDCs. Surely if domestic residents are unwilling to invest in their own countries, the argument goes, then commercial banks should be unwilling also. And the argument can be bolstered by the statistical relationship between new borrowings over the last several years and increases in capital flight.

But this argument can be easily refuted.[14] First, we would expect domestic residents to hold a diversified portfolio of international investments, even during normal times. As transaction costs decline, we would expect domestic residents to reduce their exposure to country-specific disturbances. Extreme risk aversion or market uncertainty would enhance the attractiveness of offshore investments. During a crisis, an expected discontinuity in financial policy could lead to a run on international reserves to engage in capital flight.

Second, commercial banks might be modeled as well-diversified professional lenders. In a corporate reorganization, banks have the power to force a change in management policies, to set covenants to protect their self-interest, to take an equity participation for enhancing returns, and to base their decisions on information that may not be available to the general public.

Thus, commercial banks might be in a more desirable situation than individual investors—there is a possibility that the interest rate needed to draw in additional bank lending is insufficient to retain the marginal domestic investor. We could easily envisage a model in which additional bank lending, perhaps accompanied by an IMF program, was taken as a signal that banks had reappraised economic conditions and had extracted certain pledges regarding the conduct of monetary and fiscal policy. In such a case, fresh bank lending might be accompanied by a reversal of capital flight.

The estimates of capital flight presented in this paper confirm that world capital markets are becoming more highly integrated. In the human capital

---

14. An analytical model by Diwan (1986) leads to a similar argument. Diwan posits that a country may be engaged in very high risk projects, and so domestic residents will acquire foreign assets to spread their risk. If external funding is less than adequate, a demand for insurance services is still present which domestic residents attempt to satisfy by placing funds offshore. The model predicts that increased commercial bank lending to LDCs should lead to a reduction in capital flight.

literature, it was argued that, given the mobility of factors, human capital would migrate if it did not receive a competitive market wage. Now the analogy is that financial transactions and financial capital will migrate also if domestic depositors and investors are not offered financial services with competitive risks and returns. In this environment, capital flight ought to be viewed as a symptom of underlying economic problems, rather than as the source of the problem.

References

Bhagwati, Jagdish N., Anne O. Krueger and Chaiyawat Wibulswasdi. 1974. "Capital Flight from LDCs: A Statistical Analysis." In *Illegal Transactions in International Trade,* edited by J.N. Bhagwati. Amsterdam: North-Holland Publishing.

Bhagwati, Jagdish N. 1964. "On the Underinvoicing of Imports," *Bulletin of the Oxford University Institute of Statistics,* November. Reprinted in J.N. Bhagwati (ed.) *Illegal Transactions in International Trade,* Amsterdam: North-Holland Publishing.

Cline, William R. 1986. Unpublished estimates.

Cuddington, John T. 1986. "Capital Flight: Estimates, Issues, and Explanations." *Studies in International Finance,* no. 58. Princeton, NJ, Department of Economics, Princeton University.

Diwan, Ishac. 1986. "LDC's Debt, Potential Repudiation and Capital Flight." Unpublished manuscript, New York University Graduate School of Business Administration, September.

Dooley, Michael P. 1986. "Country-Specific Risk Premiums, Capital Flight, and Net Investment Income Payments in Selected Developing Countries." International Monetary Fund Departmental Memorandum 86/17, Washington.

Dooley, Michael P.; William Helkie; Ralph Tryon; and John Underwood. 1983. "An Analysis of External Debt Positions of Eight Developing Countries Through 1990." *Journal of Development Economics* (May).

Erbe, Susanne. 1985. "The Flight of Capital from Developing Countries," *Intereconomics,* (November/December) pp. 268–75.

International Monetary Fund (IMF). 1985. *Balance of Payments Yearbook,* Washington.

Johnson, Harry G. 1968. "An 'Internationalist' Model." In *The Brain Drain,* edited by Walter Adams. New York, NY: Macmillan, pp. 69–91.

Khan, Mohsin S., and Nadeem Ul Haque. 1987. "Capital Flight from Developing Countries." *Finance and Development* (March).

Morgan Guaranty Trust Company. 1986. "LDC Capital Flight," *World Financial Markets* (March).

Morgenstern, Oskar. 1974. "On the Accuracy of Economic Observations: Foreign Trade Statistics." In *Illegal Transactions in International Trade,* edited by J.N. Bhagwati. Amsterdam: North-Holland Publishing.

Naya, Seiji, and Theodore Morgan. 1974. "The Accuracy of International Trade Data: The Case of Southeast Asian Countries," in J.N. Bhagwati (ed.) *Illegal Transactions in International Trade,* Amsterdam: North-Holland Publishing.

Patinkin, Don. 1968. "A 'Nationalist' Model." In *The Brain Drain,* edited by Walter Adams. New York, NY: Macmillan, pp. 92–108.

World Development Report. 1985. Washington: World Bank.

Statistical Annex A

The sources and methods used for calculation of the balance of payments and capital flight figures found in the tables in appendix A are as follows:

A. Current account surplus: IMF (1985).

B. Net foreign direct investment: IMF (1985).

C. Non-bank private short-term capital: IMF (1985). Items identified as "Other short-term capital of other sectors."

D. Portfolio investment: bonds and corporate equities: IMF (1985). Items identified as "Other bonds, assets" and "Corporate equities."

E. Banking system foreign assets: IMF, *International Financial Statistics.*

Table 3A.1   Argentina: capital flight estimates
(million dollars)

	1976	1977	1978
A. Current account surplus	653	1,131	1,870
1. Travel (credit)	180	212	280
2. Reinvested FDI income	0	0	0
3. Other investment income (credit)	50	127	316
B. Net foreign direct investment	0	145	273
C. Nonbank private short-term capital	−45	482	−1,510
1. Other assets	0	0	0
2. Loans extended	662	−1	29
3. Loans received	−708	−290	−755
4. Other liabilities	2	773	−784
D. Portfolio investment: bonds and corporate equities	0	0	0
E. Banking system foreign assets	n.a.	n.a.	n.a.
F. Change in reserves	−921	−1,837	−2,191
G. Net errors and omissions	−221	135	13
H. Change in debt	400	1,500	1,900
CAPITAL FLIGHT ESTIMATES			
World Bank, WDR; Erbe (H + B + A + F)	132	940	1,852
Morgan (H + B + A + E + F)	132	940	1,852
Cline (Morgan excluding 1–3 in A)	−98	600	1,256
Cuddington (−G − C)	266	−618	1,497

n.a. not available; WDR   *World Development Report.*

Calculated as the change in line 7ad (multiplied by -1 for consistency with the balance of payments sign convention).

F. Change in reserves: IMF (1985).

G. Net errors and omissions: IMF (1985).

H. Change in debt: data from 1978 to 1984 are World Bank data. Data for 1976 and 1977 are from Dooley et al. (1986).

Items A, B, C, D, F, and G are reported in million special drawing rights (SDRs). Conversion into US dollars is made using the period average SDR/dollar exchange rate (*IFS* line sb).

Capital flight estimates are obtained from these items using the formulae in the following tables.

1979	1980	1981	1982	1983	1984
− 500	− 4,783	− 4,635	− 2,379	− 2,439	− 2,542
267	344	413	611	452	440
0	0	0	0	0	0
680	1,227	882	523	441	264
262	791	930	254	182	269
1,450	− 1,991	− 8,466	− 4,808	− 1,513	1,687
0	0	0	0	0	0
846	− 36	− 1,487	− 511	291	706
1,965	2,927	− 2,211	− 2,675	− 1,242	13
− 1,360	− 4,881	− 4,767	− 1,622	− 561	968
0	0	0	0	0	0
n.a.	n.a.	n.a.	254	− 466	− 79
− 4,234	2,628	3,058	680	2,473	− 144
243	− 310	− 213	− 402	− 443	− 52
7,600	6,400	6,400	9,900	2,400	− 200
3,128	5,036	5,751	8,455	2,615	− 2,617
3,128	5,036	5,751	8,709	2,149	− 2,696
2,181	3,465	4,457	7,575	1,255	− 3,400
− 1,693	2,301	8,680	5,210	1,955	− 1,635

Table 3A.2   Brazil: capital flight estimates
(million dollars)

	1976	1977	1978
A. Current account surplus	−6,551	−5,106	−7,031
1. Travel (credit)	57	55	68
2. Reinvested FDI income	0	0	0
3. Other investment income (credit)	282	358	640
B. Net foreign direct investment	1,372	1,684	1,874
C. Nonbank private short-term capital	1,091	298	−126
1. Other assets	−21	187	46
2. Loans extended	0	0	0
3. Loans received	880	−42	50
4. Other liabilities	231	154	−224
D. Portfolio investment: bonds and corporate equities	n.a.	n.a.	n.a.
E. Banking system foreign assets	−246	−39	−829
F. Change in reserves	−2,683	−495	−4,559
G. Net errors and omissions	496	−618	299
H. Change in debt	7,800	8,200	12,300
CAPITAL FLIGHT ESTIMATES			
World Bank, WDR; Erbe (H + B + A + F)	−62	4,283	2,584
Morgan (H + B + A + E + F)	−308	4,244	1,755
Cline (Morgan excluding 1–3 in A)	−647	3,831	1,048
Cuddington (−G)	−496	618	−299

n.a. not available; WDR   *World Development Report.*

1979	1980	1981	1982	1983	1984
− 10,468	− 12,793	− 11,763	− 16,332	− 6,810	53
75	126	236	66	38	66
0	0	0	0	0	0
245	314	355	696	492	660
2,220	1,544	2,317	2,551	1,374	1,555
26	1,994	111	− 287	− 358	− 3,883
32	47	58	75	15	− 3,514
− 3	0	0	0	0	0
− 8	1,939	48	− 363	− 373	− 357
3	8	4	1	1	− 12
n.a.	n.a.	n.a.	n.a.	n.a.	n.a.
226	328	− 599	− 11	175	− 350
2,907	3,462	− 674	5,255	1,873	− 5,410
1,227	− 351	− 390	− 379	− 617	406
6,700	9,900	9,900	11,100	4,500	8,900
1,359	2,113	− 221	2,575	937	5,098
1,585	2,441	− 820	2,564	1,112	4,748
1,264	2,001	− 1,410	1,802	582	4,023
− 1,227	351	390	379	617	− 406

Table 3A.3 Korea: capital flight estimates
(million dollars)

	1976	1977	1978
A. Current account surplus	−307	9	−1,062
1. Travel (credit)	275	370	408
2. Reinvested FDI income	0	0	0
3. Other investment income (credit)	25	46	99
B. Net foreign direct investment	75	72	61
C. Nonbank private short-term capital	354	23	−1,198
1. Other assets	−83	−306	−255
2. Loans extended	0	0	0
3. Loans received	97	−15	−289
4. Other liabilities	339	346	−652
D. Portfolio investment: bonds and corporate equities	0	0	0
E. Banking system foreign assets	−222	−347	−810
F. Change in reserves	−1,314	−1,371	−709
G. Net errors and omissions	−242	−35	−326
H. Change in debt	2,000	2,400	3,000
CAPITAL FLIGHT ESTIMATES			
World Bank, WDR; Erbe (H + B + A + F)	454	1,111	1,291
Morgan (H + B + A + E + F)	232	764	481
Cline (Morgan excluding 1–3 in A)	−68	348	−26
Cuddington (−G − C)	−112	12	1,524

WDR *World Development Report.*

1979	1980	1981	1982	1983	1984
− 4,156	− 5,323	− 4,641	− 2,679	− 1,578	− 1,344
327	370	448	502	595	675
0	0	0	0	0	0
137	303	443	374	347	457
17	− 5	59	− 78	− 57	75
844	1,938	− 136	3	895	− 774
− 371	− 90	12	50	102	117
0	0	0	0	0	0
26	− 47	− 14	12	16	− 2
1,187	2,076	− 132	− 59	777	− 890
0	0	77	0	0	52
− 575	− 897.2	− 560.4	29	− 384	− 334
− 873	− 297	304	− 44	202	− 589
− 328	− 331	− 360	− 1,288	− 951	− 918
5,500	6,500	4,900	4,100	2,100	2,700
487	875	622	1,298	668	842
− 88	− 22	62	1,327	284	508
− 552	− 695	− 830	450	− 659	− 625
− 516	− 1,607	495	1,285	57	1,692

Table 3A.4 Mexico: capital flight estimates
(million dollars)

	1976	1977	1978
A. Current account surplus	−3,410	−1,849	−3,163
1. Border Travel (credit)	1,398	1,255	2,085
2. Reinvested FDI income	0	0	0
3. Other investment income (credit)	124	168	403
B. Net foreign direct investment	628	556	829
C. Nonbank private short-term capital	−405	−1,657	−538
1. Other assets	−708	−863	−441
2. Loans received	302	−794	−98
a. Government-owned enterprises	38	−198	−187
b. Private enterprises	264	−595	−89
D. Portfolio investment: bonds and corporate equities	−53	−32	1
E. Banking system foreign assets	0	0	−115
F. Change in reserves	172	−321	−388
G. Net errors and omissions	−2,623	6	−130
H. Change in debt	6,600	6,600	4,600
CAPITAL FLIGHT ESTIMATES			
World Bank, WDR; Erbe (H + B + A + F)	3,990	4,985	1,878
Morgan (H + B + A + E + F)	3,990	4,985	1,763
Cline (Morgan excluding 1–3 in A)	2,468	3,562	−725
Cuddington (−G − C.1)	3,331	857	571

WDR *World Development Report.*

1979	1980	1981	1982	1983	1984
− 5,452	− 8,162	− 14,020	− 6,051	− 5,323	− 3,905
2,742	3,573	4,593	1,236	1,103	1,331
0	0	0	0	0	0
694	1,023	1,389	1,320	1,282	2,054
1,335	2,184	2,541	1,644	454	392
− 1,115	2,800	3,978	− 2,222	− 6,231	− 4,506
− 1,755	− 892	− 2,592	− 2,458	− 3,368	− 2,346
640	3,691	6,570	235	− 2,862	− 2,159
− 97	267	4,784	− 639	12	− 23
736	3,424	1,786	873	− 2,875	− 2,136
− 52	− 131	− 12	300	106	− 192
− 296	− 610	336	204	50	259
− 317	− 959	− 1,097	3,546	− 2,020	− 2,134
647	− 3,776	− 8,318	− 5,399	− 946	− 238
7,100	14,300	20,800	7,900	7,900	3,600
2,666	7,363	8,224	7,039	11,656	5,763
2,370	6,753	8,560	7,243	11,706	6,022
− 1,066	2,157	2,578	4,686	9,322	2,636
1,107	4,667	10,910	7,856	4,314	2,584

Table 3A.5   Philippines: capital flight estimates
(million dollars)

	1976	1977	1978
A. Current account surplus	−1,101	−754	−1,093
1. Travel (credit)	92	145	210
2. Reinvested FDI income	0	0	0
3. Other investment income (credit)	15	30	29
B. Net foreign direct investment	126	209	101
C. Nonbank private short-term capital	−98	−167	−79
1. Other assets	−312	−337	−342
2. Loans extended	0	0	0
3. Loans received	214	169	263
4. Other liabilities	0	0	0
D. Portfolio investment: bonds and corporate equities	n.a.	n.a.	n.a.
E. Banking system foreign assets	405	77	−394
F. Change in reserves	57	29	−878
G. Net errors and omissions	−148	210	115
H. Change in debt	1,500	1,600	2,700
CAPITAL FLIGHT ESTIMATES			
World Bank, WDR; Erbe (H + B + A + F)	581	1,084	831
Morgan (H + B + A + E + F)	986	1,161	437
Cline (Morgan excluding 1–3 in A)	879	986	198
Cuddington (−G − C.1)	459	127	227

n.a. not available.

1979	1980	1981	1982	1983	1984
−1,496	−1,913	−2,125	−3,210	−2,753	−1,241
238	320	343	449	465	367
0	0	0	0	0	0
37	86	180	159	221	286
8	−107	172	15	105	−6
−596	319	11	95	−646	545
−889	−389	−702	−361	99	99
0	0	0	0	0	0
293	708	712	456	−744	446
0	0	0	0	0	0
n.a.	n.a.	n.a.	n.a.	n.a.	n.a.
−403	−816	29	−207	71	−122
−376	−961	348	703	2,044	−262
245	122	−504	−373	−347	96
2,500	4,100	3,400	3,400	−300	500
636	1,119	1,795	908	−904	−1,010
233	303	1,824	701	−833	−1,132
−43	−103	1,301	93	−1,509	−1,785
643	267	1,205	734	248	−196

Table 3A.6 Venezuela: capital flight estimates
(million dollars)

	1976	1977	1978
A. Current account surplus	254	−3,179	−5,735
1. Travel (credit)	109	168	205
2. Reinvested FDI income	0	0	0
3. Other investment income (credit)	163	128	260
B. Net foreign direct investment	−889	−4	68
C. Nonbank private short-term capital	−1,449	−453	−316
1. Other assets	−859	−221	−417
2. Loans extended	0	0	0
3. Loans received	−686	−216	29
a. Private enterprises	40	72	66
b. Public enterprises	−726	−288	−38
4. Other liabilities	96	−16	73
D. Portfolio investment: bonds and corporate equities	−192	−107	−239
E. Banking system foreign assets	4	−113	−199
F. Change in reserves	−2,343	−801	1,064
G. Net errors and omissions	2,024	2,278	1,489
H. Change in debt	−1,200	6,400	6,100
CAPITAL FLIGHT ESTIMATES			
World Bank, WDR; Erbe (H + B + A + F)	−4,178	2,416	1,496
Morgan (H + B + A + E + F)	−4,174	2,303	1,297
Cline (Morgan excluding 1–3 in A)	−4,445	2,007	832
Cuddington (−G − C.1 − D)	−973	−1,950	−833

1979	1980	1981	1982	1983	1984
350	4,728	4,000	− 4,246	4,427	4,972
178	243	187	309	310	358
0	0	0	0	0	0
322	521	1,009	631	629	1,078
88	55	184	253	86	58
1,876	− 1,971	− 2,760	− 5,773	− 3,493	− 3,017
− 640	− 1,446	− 2,609	− 4,951	− 723	− 1,313
0	0	0	0	0	0
2,568	− 570	− 262	− 838	− 2,798	− 1,666
413	85	− 38	168	− 1,835	− 132
2,155	− 655	− 224	− 1,006	− 962	− 1,533
− 53	46	111	17	27	− 38
6	− 263	− 118	− 10	− 7	− 1
− 156	8	59	99	− 686	102
− 4,098	− 3,764	21	8,165	− 336	− 1,568
497	− 1,128	− 2,139	− 2,161	7	104
7,300	5,500	2,300	− 100	500	1,900
3,640	6,519	6,505	4,072	4,677	5,362
3,484	6,527	6,564	4,171	3,991	5,464
2,984	5,763	5,367	3,230	3,052	4,028
136	2,837	4,866	7,122	723	1,211

Statistical Annex B

The sources and methods used for calculation of the capital flight figures found in the tables in annex B are as follows:

A. Cumulative non-FDI balance of payments claims: IMF, *Balance of Payments Yearbook,* as reported in Dooley (1986). The figures are the cumulated sums of lines 62–64, 69–71, 77–79, 84, 85, 89, 93, 94, 98–109. An estimated value for a base year is made by Dooley. The base years vary between 1964 and 1967 for the countries reported here.

B. Stock of external debt: data from 1976 to 1984 are World Bank data from *World Debt Tables.* Data for 1975 and 1976 are from Dooley et al. (1986).

C. Cumulative balance of payments liabilities: IMF, *Balance of Payments Yearbook,* as reported in Dooley (1986). The figures are the cumulated sums of lines 53–

Table 3B.1 Argentina: estimated capital flight, Dooley method
(billion dollars)

	1975	1976	1977
A. Cumulative non-FDI balance of payments claims	0.5	1.6	3.5
B. Stock of external debt	9.5	9.9	11.4
C. Cumulative balance of payments liabilities	2.4	2.8	3.5
D. Unrecorded claims (B − C)	7.1	7.1	7.9
E. Total external claims (A + D)	7.6	8.7	11.4
F. Reported non-FDI income	0.1	0.0	0.1
G. U.S. Treasury bill rate	5.8	5.0	5.3
H. Capitalized non-FDI income (F/G)	0.9	0.0	2.4
I. Stock of flight capital (E − H)	6.7	8.7	9.0

Table 3B.2 Brazil: estimated capital flight, Dooley method
(billion dollars)

	1975	1976	1977
A. Cumulative non-FDI balance of payments claims	5.5	8.2	9.6
B. Stock of external debt	25.1	32.9	41.1
C. Cumulative balance of payments liabilities	26.0	33.9	38.7
D. Unrecorded claims (B − C)	− 0.9	− 1.0	2.4
E. Total external claims (A + D)	4.6	7.2	12.0
F. Reported non-FDI income	0.4	0.3	0.4
G. U.S. Treasury bill rate	5.8	5.0	5.3
H. Capitalized non-FDI income (F/G)	6.3	5.6	6.8
I. Stock of flight capital (E − H)	− 1.7	1.6	5.2

61, 65–68, 72–76, 80–83, 86–88, 90–92, 95–97, 110, and 111. An adjustment for a base-year value is made by Dooley. The base years vary between 1964 and 1967 for the countries reported here.

F. Reported non-FDI income: IMF, *Balance of Payments Yearbook,* lines 15, 17, and 19.

G. US Treasury bill rate: IMF, *International Financial Statistics,* line 60c.

Items A, B, C, and F are reported in millions of SDRs. Conversion into US dollars is made using the period average dollar/SDR exchange rate (*IFS* line sb).

Items D, E, H, and I are computed using the formulae in the following tables.

1978	1979	1980	1981	1982	1983	1984
5.3	8.8	7.0	5.7	6.0	5.6	6.0
13.3	20.9	27.3	33.7	43.6	46.0	45.8
3.2	6.9	9.0	11.5	13.9	15.7	18.4
10.1	14.0	18.3	22.2	29.7	30.3	27.4
15.4	22.8	25.3	27.9	35.7	35.9	33.4
0.3	0.7	1.2	0.9	0.5	0.4	0.3
7.2	10.0	11.6	14.1	10.7	8.6	9.6
4.4	6.8	10.6	6.3	4.9	5.1	2.8
11.0	16.0	14.7	21.6	30.8	30.8	30.6

1978	1979	1980	1981	1982	1983	1984
14.5	10.4	7.7	10.1	6.4	6.9	17.0
53.4	60.1	70.0	79.9	91.0	95.5	104.4
48.8	52.9	61.4	73.3	83.3	89.3	97.8
4.6	7.2	8.6	6.6	7.7	6.2	6.6
19.1	17.6	16.3	16.7	14.1	13.1	23.6
0.6	1.2	1.1	1.1	1.2	0.7	1.3
7.2	10.0	11.6	14.1	10.7	8.6	9.6
8.9	11.6	9.9	8.1	11.2	8.2	13.0
10.2	6.0	6.4	8.6	2.9	4.9	10.6

Table 3B.3 Mexico: estimated capital flight, Dooley method
(billion dollars)

	1975	1976	1977
A. Cumulative non-FDI balance of payments claims	4.4	8.0	9.3
B. Stock of external debt	17.9	24.5	31.1
C. Cumulative balance of payments liabilities	17.7	24.1	26.7
D. Unrecorded claims (B − C)	0.2	0.4	4.4
E. Total external claims (A + D)	4.6	8.4	13.7
F. Reported non-FDI income	0.1	0.1	0.2
G. U.S. Treasury bill rate	5.8	5.0	5.3
H. Capitalized non-FDI income (F/G)	2.0	2.5	3.2
I. Stock of flight capital (E − H)	2.6	5.9	10.5

Table 3B.4 Philippines: estimated capital flight, Dooley method
(billion dollars)

	1975	1976	1977
A. Cumulative non-FDI balance of payments claims	2.9	3.2	3.4
B. Stock of external debt	5.0	6.5	8.1
C. Cumulative balance of payments liabilities	4.4	5.7	6.4
D. Unrecorded claims (B − C)	0.6	0.8	1.7
E. Total external claims (A + D)	3.5	4.0	5.1
F. Reported non-FDI income	0.2	0.1	0.1
G. U.S. Treasury bill rate	5.8	5.0	5.3
H. Capitalized non-FDI income (F/G)	2.7	2.5	2.6
I. Stock of flight capital (E − H)	0.8	1.5	2.5

Table 3B.5 Venezuela: estimated capital flight, Dooley method
(billion dollars)

	1975	1976	1977
A. Cumulative non-FDI balance of payments claims	10.7	12.2	11.4
B. Stock of external debt	5.5	4.3	10.7
C. Cumulative balance of payments liabilities	2.1	4.3	6.7
D. Unrecorded claims (B − C)	3.4	0.0	4.0
E. Total external claims (A + D)	14.1	12.2	15.4
F. Reported non-FDI income	0.7	0.7	0.8
G. U.S. Treasury bill rate	5.8	5.0	5.3
H. Capitalized non-FDI income (F/G)	12.8	13.9	14.8
I. Stock of flight capital (E − H)	1.3	− 1.7	0.6

1978	1979	1980	1981	1982	1983	1984
10.1	11.3	16.8	29.2	33.9	41.4	47.3
35.7	42.8	57.1	77.9	85.8	93.7	97.3
29.8	35.2	46.6	70.5	79.6	81.3	83.0
5.9	7.6	10.5	7.4	6.2	12.4	14.3
16.0	18.9	27.3	36.6	40.1	53.8	61.6
0.4	0.7	1.0	1.4	1.3	1.3	2.1
7.2	10.0	11.6	14.1	10.7	8.6	9.6
5.6	6.9	8.8	9.9	12.3	14.9	21.5
10.4	12.0	18.5	26.7	27.8	38.9	40.1

1978	1979	1980	1981	1982	1983	1984
4.5	5.6	7.1	8.1	8.1	6.4	6.4
10.8	13.3	17.4	20.8	24.2	23.9	24.4
8.5	11.1	14.6	17.5	20.7	21.7	22.9
2.3	2.2	2.8	3.3	3.5	2.2	1.5
6.8	7.8	9.9	11.4	11.6	8.6	7.9
0.2	0.2	0.3	0.5	0.4	0.4	0.3
7.2	10.0	11.6	14.1	10.7	8.6	9.6
2.5	2.0	2.9	3.7	3.4	4.3	3.4
4.3	5.8	7.0	7.7	8.2	4.3	4.5

1978	1979	1980	1981	1982	1983	1984
9.8	14.4	21.1	26.2	25.4	27.2	29.1
16.8	24.1	29.6	31.9	31.8	32.3	34.2
10.8	15.0	16.9	17.8	20.9	18.2	14.8
6.0	9.1	12.7	14.1	10.9	14.1	19.4
15.8	23.5	33.8	40.3	36.3	41.3	48.5
1.1	1.3	2.3	3.6	2.6	1.5	2.2
7.2	10.0	11.6	14.1	10.7	8.6	9.6
14.6	13.4	19.5	25.4	24.0	17.4	22.6
1.2	10.1	14.3	14.9	12.3	23.9	25.9

A Note on Trade Misinvoicing
Sunil K. Gulati

Most measurements of capital flight are based either on recorded short-term capital movements or on payments flows that do not show up directly in the recorded statistics and are thereby included in the balancing line of the balance of payments, "errors and omissions." A further mechanism for capital flight, which is, in essence, effected through the current account, has been discussed infrequently or only tangentially in the recent work on capital flight. It is this latter method of capital flight, involving the under-invoicing of exports and overinvoicing of imports, that we investigate here. We show that its inclusion, contrary to the general presumption, often reduces estimates of capital flight.

Current Measures and Estimates

While far from an exact science, the measurement of capital flight has been greatly enhanced through the recent work of Dooley, Helkie, Tryon, and Underwood (1986), Cuddington (1986), and Dooley (1986). If one "adjusts" the estimates generated in these recent studies using the technique introduced by Bhagwati (1964) and further used to advantage by Bhagwati, Krueger, and Wibulswasdi (1974), these calculations become much more complete.[1] After a brief review of the estimation procedure used in these three studies, we turn to this adjustment.

Dooley, Helkie, Tryon, and Underwood (1983), henceforth D-H-T-U, develop a methodology to estimate capital flight that has been used in a number of recent studies.[2] In essence the methodology consists of contrasting the "financing needs" of a country with the "financial inflows" available to it during a given year. The differences are then considered capital flight,

The author is a graduate student at Columbia University. He wishes to thank Professor Jagdish Bhagwati for extremely valuable comments and encouragement, and Professor Arnold Collery, John Cuddington, and Michael Dooley for helpful discussions.

1. Morgenstern (1950) in his classic work, *On the Accuracy of Economic Observations,* does indeed note the discrepancies that arise between partners in partner-country trade data. He attributes this to a number of reasons, many of which can be taken into account by an f.o.b.-c.i.f. adjustment. Bhagwati (1964), however, uses the partner-country technique to test for incentives-generated trade-invoice faking.

2. Four sets of recent estimates in particular use the methodology (in some cases with minor changes) developed in the D-H-T-U paper. These are Dornbusch (1985), *World Development Report* (1984), Diaz-Alejandro (1984), and the widely cited figures published by Morgan Guaranty Bank in *World Financial Markets* in April, 1986.

although the authors use the terminology "implicit capital outflows" or "increase in private claims on non-residents."[3] In this methodology, "financing needs" consist of current account imbalances (deficits) and changes in the reserves of the central bank and the assets of the commercial banking sector, while "financing inflows" consist of increases in external debt, which in this study include direct investment inflows. Though the evidence[4] for private accumulation of external claims varies over the eight countries analyzed, it is clear that in some cases capital flight estimates are large relative to, say, external debt figures.

Cuddington (1986) analyzes the capital accounts for eight heavily-indebted countries for the period 1974–82, defining capital flight as short-term speculative capital outflows. With this definition, the measure of capital flight used is primarily the "errors and omissions" line of the balance of payments, long considered to conceal unrecorded capital flows. In six of the eight countries analyzed, Cuddington adds to the short-term capital outflows that are recorded in the balance of payments statistics the "errors and omissions" figure; the exact line items vary by country, being based on descriptive footnotes to the International Monetary Fund's *Balance of Payments Yearbook*. Cuddington notes that by this measure the level of capital flight was increasing for most of the sample countries in the late 1970s and early 1980s, although the level of such outflows varies greatly across sample countries.

The final major study of capital flight through the capital account is that of Dooley (1986), who uses a different definition and estimation methodology than the previous studies in analyzing capital outflows in eight debtor countries. Defining capital flight as "the stock of claims on nonresidents that do not generate investment income receipts in the creditor country's balance of payments data," Dooley arrives at estimates that are in general larger than in the above studies (though not of the wider measures considered in the preceding paper in this volume). Capital flight is essentially calculated by subtracting the stock of claims implied by investment income (from balance of payments data) from the total stock of claims on nonresidents as calculated from World Bank debt tables and balance of payments data. Thus, as Dooley notes, estimates of capital flight calculated in this way could change even without a change in the total stock of claims on nonresidents if earnings on some of the existing claims came within the reach of the domestic authorities.

All three studies rely on balance of payments statistics and thus either explicitly (D-H-T-U) or implicitly (Cuddington and Dooley) on the current

3. The studies noted above, which use the D-H-T-U methodology, have, however, explicitly called the results of these calculations capital flight.

4. We discuss below the actual estimates for all three studies as well as the "adjustment" that should be made for over- and underinvoicing.

account balance in generating capital flight estimates. If the current account balance is itself subject to error because of systematic faking of trade invoices, these capital flight estimates will be affected.

Adjusting for Over- and Underinvoicing

Systematic over- and underinvoicing of exports or imports or both can be detected through the use of partner-country trade analysis as introduced by Bhagwati (1964). The conclusion reached in Bhagwati, Krueger, and Wibulswasdi (1974), using 1966 trade data, was that underinvoicing of exports seemed to be used as a mechanism for capital flight while overinvoicing of imports was much less prevalent. This was confirmed for the 1977–83 period by Gulati (1985). In that statistical note, I found that many developing countries were underinvoicers of exports and were simultaneously underinvoicers of imports, the latter phenomenon presumably being due to the stronger weight of the opposing incentives caused by tariffs, quotas, and other trade restrictions.

For purposes of studying capital flight, the expectation is that exporters (importers) will systematically underinvoice (overinvoice) and thereby gain foreign exchange that is outside the control of the central bank or exchange authority. In this note, we analyze eight debtor countries for the period 1970–85 and use the partner-country analysis to test for over- and underinvoicing. The estimates are generated by examining the partner-country trade statistics of these eight countries with the industrial countries. The industrial countries are used rather than the world because partner-country analysis relies on accurate reporting by one partner. If both countries fake trade invoices it becomes impossible to sort out under- and overinvoicing.

By using direction of trade statistics with the industrial countries as a partner and adjusting exports and imports for a f.o.b.-c.i.f. factor,[5] we can obtain a measure of invoice faking relying on the assumption that the industrial countries report accurately. This assumption seems for the most part realistic, given the results for interindustrial country trade reported in Gulati (1985). These estimates for trade-invoice faking with the industrial countries can then be blown up to generate estimates of world trade discrepancies by using weights based on the proportion of total trade that takes place with the industrial countries, assuming that the extent of invoice faking is the same for trade with the developing countries as for trade with the industrial countries. The results are given in table 3.11.

---

5. Rather than use a standard 10 percent adjustment for an f.o.b.-c.i.f. conversion, the precise figures for individual countries as reported in IMF, *International Financial Statistics*, are utilized. These range for the sample countries from 5 percent to 18 percent for the relevant time period.

Table 3.11 highlights the main conclusion of this note: while many countries[6] show up as underinvoicers of exports, they also show up as underinvoicers of imports. Given these counteracting effects, the usual presumption that capital flight is increased by such trade-invoice faking does not necessarily hold for these sample countries. That underinvoicing of exports is often utilized in generating an illegal outflow of foreign exchange is clear. It appears, however, that in most cases the increased supply of foreign exchange is more than made up for by the increased demand caused by those traders' underinvoicing imports to escape high tariffs or quantitative restrictions.

In our analysis of these eight debtor countries, we use trade data for a 16-year period. Table 3.12 presents frequency distributions for over- and underinvoicing which summarize the quantitative results in table 3.11. The important column is the last one which reflects the *net effects* of over- and underinvoicing. As it shows, in none of the eight countries analyzed is capital flight effected through trade-invoice faking in more than 7 of the 16 years. In fact, in each of the eight countries, for most of the period, we observe capital *inflows* due to the phenomenon of over- and underinvoicing. In the case of Chile, in every year of the 16 analyzed, capital inflows occurred, while in the case of Korea this was true in 15 of the 16 years.[7] Of special note is Mexico, which shows up as an underinvoicer of both exports and imports in each year of the sample period.

Since the underinvoicing of imports outweighs the underinvoicing of exports in most of the sample, current account deficits are in general being underestimated. This is because the figures used to generate balance of payments statistics are export and import figures as reported by the "home country" (rather than any group of partners). Thus, all three techniques to measure capital flight discussed above—as they use the current account balance either explicitly or implicitly through use of the "errors and omissions" figure—overestimate the level of capital flight, contrary to the usual presumption. Therefore, we can conclude that on average adjustment for over- and underinvoicing of both exports and imports reduces the estimate of the total amount of capital flight.

Table 3.13 compares the *magnitude* of capital flight which is detected through partner-country analysis for the eight countries with the results in

---

6. While this sample covers only 8 countries, the 101-country sample in Gulati (1985) verifies that in many cases underinvoicing of exports exists alongside underinvoicing of imports.

7. Korea is an outlier in the pattern of invoicing of exports as it shows up as a major overinvoicer of exports for all 16 of the years analyzed. One might hypothesize that explicit or implicit export subsidies would lead to such a result, or that it might reflect an attempt to insure against future imposition of "voluntary" export restraints, given the fact that restriction levels are quite often based on past exports.

Table 3.11 Capital flight through over- and underinvoicing, 1970–85
(million dollars)

	Argentina			Brazil		
	Under-invoicing of exports	Over-invoicing of imports	Net impact of mis-invoicing	Under-invoicing of exports	Over-invoicing of imports	Net impact of mis-invoicing
1970	148	−368	−221	47	−129	−82
1971	−949	−1,450	−2,400	81	−158	−76
1972	47	−210	−163	8	−283	−275
1973	374	−103	271	−274	−607	−880
1974	336	−541	−204	−82	−436	−518
1975	457	−40	417	712	628	1,340
1976	296	−202	94	−590	76	−515
1977	590	−317	272	119	−662	−544
1978	669	−1,082	−414	−130	−583	−713
1979	591	−2,958	−2,367	1,108	−252	856
1980	376	−2,266	−1,890	1,098	220	1,319
1981	616	−965	−349	551	−227	324
1982	785	−659	126	1,432	−1,559	−127
1983	898	−1,557	−658	204	−865	−661
1984	967	−1,170	−202	621	−2,623	−2,002
1985	206	−20	187	3,011	−1,018	1,993

	Chile			Korea		
	Under-invoicing of exports	Over-invoicing of imports	Net impact of mis-invoicing	Under-invoicing of exports	Over-invoicing of imports	Net impact of mis-invoicing
1970	−167	−56	−223	−87	−195	−282
1971	−31	−133	−163	−145	−53	−197
1972	−65	−262	−327	−174	−228	−403
1973	−137	−277	−414	−396	−454	−849
1974	−620	−306	−926	−93	−375	−467
1975	−231	−446	−677	−206	−56	−262
1976	−114	−282	−397	−123	−37	−160
1977	−69	−425	−494	−403	−679	−1,083
1978	161	−287	−126	−921	−1,052	−1,973
1979	−107	−364	−470	−1,172	621	−551
1980	−174	−775	−949	−1,128	356	−772
1981	−310	−520	−830	−2,073	2,703	630
1982	−202	−613	−815	−2,764	1,071	−1,694
1983	−452	−577	−1,029	−3,650	640	−3,010
1984	−189	−888	−1,077	−4,354	2,122	−2,232
1985	−310	−497	−807	−2,597	1,227	−1,370

	Mexico			Peru		
	Under-invoicing of exports	Over-invoicing of imports	Net impact of mis-invoicing	Under-invoicing of exports	Over-invoicing of imports	Net impact of mis-invoicing
1970	770	− 485	285	− 119	− 176	− 295
1971	770	− 539	231	17	− 220	− 203
1972	831	− 672	159	58	− 275	− 217
1973	1,451	− 1,415	36	83	− 466	− 383
1974	2,382	− 1,759	623	251	− 580	− 329
1975	1,971	− 1,804	166	306	− 565	− 260
1976	2,001	− 2,059	− 58	112	− 56	54
1977	2,788	− 2,168	620	115	− 48	67
1978	2,645	− 3,230	− 585	− 59	− 41	− 100
1979	3,171	− 4,023	− 853	− 126	− 896	− 1,022
1980	3,297	− 6,322	− 3,025	58	− 1,177	− 1,119
1981	4,067	− 6,474	− 2,407	155	− 1,257	− 1,102
1982	4,477	− 5,116	− 639	− 93	0	− 93
1983	2,304	− 7,134	− 4,830	− 85	0	− 86
1984	1,709	− 8,387	− 6,678	− 82	0	− 82
1985	2,462	− 5,058	− 2,595	− 75	6	− 69

	Uruguay			Venezuela		
	Under-invoicing of exports	Over-invoicing of imports	Net impact of mis-invoicing	Under-invoicing of exports	Over-invoicing of imports	Net impact of mis-invoicing
1970	− 59	− 77	− 135	− 425	153	− 272
1971	− 8	− 58	− 66	− 130	− 3	− 133
1972	− 29	− 72	− 101	− 128	− 60	− 188
1973	8	− 43	− 51	− 155	− 189	− 173
1974	− 4	− 94	− 98	− 242	− 110	− 352
1975	8	− 7	2	145	458	603
1976	32	− 75	− 43	− 205	82	− 123
1977	36	− 78	− 42	− 276	68	− 208
1978	19	− 248	− 229	− 53	1,186	1,133
1979	33	− 297	− 265	− 1,355	324	− 1,031
1980	47	− 386	− 339	− 1,090	1,069	− 20
1981	110	− 141	− 31	− 62	739	677
1982	414	− 214	200	− 163	1	− 162
1983	573	− 263	309	− 148	− 1	− 149
1984	821	− 177	644	− 154	0	− 154
1985	8	5	12	− 149	− 2	− 150

Table 3.12   Summary of trade misinvoicing, 1970–85 (months)

	Export underinvoicing	Import overinvoicing	Net capital flight
Argentina	15	0	6
Brazil	12	3	5
Chile	1	0	0
Korea	0	7	1
Mexico	16	0	7
Peru	9	1	2
Uruguay	11	1	5
Venezuela	1	10	3

Note: Number of months out of 16 that the phenomenon was observed.
Source: Table 3.11.

Table 3.13   Capital flight estimates and adjustments for over- and underinvoicing
(million dollars)

	1974	1975	1976	1977	1978
Argentina.					
D-H-T-U	800	0	− 200	900	3,000
Cuddington	36	− 163	266	− 618	1,497
Misinvoicing	− 204	417	94	272	− 414
Brazil					
D-H-T-U	300	3,000	− 1,600	2,400	4,400
Cuddington	64	427	− 496	618	− 299
Misinvoicing	− 518	1,340	− 514	− 543	− 713
Chile					
D-H-T-U	200	800	− 400	− 700	− 800
Cuddington	47	− 25	− 252	− 503	− 250
Misinvoicing	− 926	− 677	− 397	− 494	− 126
Korea					
D-H-T-U	− 300	300	300	1,100	2,600
Cuddington	− 69	− 453	− 112	12	1,524
Misinvoicing	− 467	− 262	− 160	− 1,083	− 1,973
Mexico					
D-H-T-U	1,600	1,100	3,500	4,300	800
Cuddington	1,272	1,285	3,331	917	517
Misinvoicing	623	166	− 58	619	− 585

D-H-T-U (1986) and Cuddington (1986). It should be noted that the over- or underinvoicing figures are not alternatives to these estimates, but should be treated as "adjustments" to them. As is evident from table 3.13, the magnitude of capital inflows (relative to levels of outflows estimated in D-H-T-U and Cuddington) effected through the trade mechanism as outlined above is quite large for Argentina, Chile, Korea, Mexico, Peru, and Uruguay; in some of these cases the over- or underinvoicing adjustment reverses the sign of capital inflows and would indicate that these debtor countries on balance might well have been the recipient of unrecorded capital movements.

Finally, tables 3.14 and 3.15 compare, for a slightly different and more recent time period, the results presented in Dooley (1986) and in the highly publicized Morgan Guaranty study. Again, in most cases, allowing for trade misinvoicing moderates the capital-flight estimates generated in these studies, in some cases greatly.

1979	1980	1981	1982	Total 1974–82	Total adjusted for misinvoicing 1974–82
1,700	6,700	7,700	−400	20,200	15,585
−1,693	2,301	8,680	4,978	15,285	10,970
−2,367	−1,890	−349	126	−4,315	—
1,100	1,800	−200	200	11,400	12,824
−1,227	351	390	379	206	1,630
856	1,319	324	−127	1,424	—
600	−200	−500	500	−500	−6,184
−416	−482	−899	792	−1,988	−7,672
−470	−949	−830	−815	−5,684	—
300	−600	−3,100	6,400	7,000	668
−516	−1,607	494	1,285	558	−5,774
−551	−772	630	−1,694	−6,332	—
2,800	7,300	8,200	6,700	36,300	29,968
1,147	4,826	11,510	7,558	32,662	26,504
−852	−3,025	−2,407	−639	−6,158	—

Table 3.13   Capital flight estimates and adjustments for over- and underinvoicing (continued)
(million dollars)

	1974	1975	1976	1977	1978
Peru					
D-H-T-U	− 100	1,400	300	− 100	500
Cuddington	72	826	328	112	− 51
Misinvoicing	− 329	− 260	54	67	− 100
Philippines					
D-H-T-U	200	300	500	1,000	700
Cuddington	n.a.	n.a.	n.a.	n.a.	n.a.
Misinvoicing	n.a.	n.a.	n.a.	n.a.	n.a.
Uruguay					
D-H-T-U	n.a.	n.a.	n.a.	n.a.	n.a.
Cuddington	82	38	13	− 42	− 159
Misinvoicing	− 98	2	− 43	− 42	− 229
Venezuela					
D-H-T-U	− 100	700	− 300	− 900	900
Cuddington	522	− 155	− 401	− 1,736	− 943
Misinvoicing	− 352	603	− 123	− 208	1133

n.a. not available.
— not applicable.
Note: Minus sign indicates a net inflow of capital. Estimates in table may not total to those above because of rounding.
Source: D-H-T-U and Cuddington figures are from Dooley, Helkie, Tryon and Underwood (1983) and Cuddington (1986).

Table 3.14   Dooley's estimates of capital flight and adjustments for trade misinvoicing, 1978–84 (billion dollars)

	Dooley	Misinvoicing	Adjusted total
Argentina	21.4	− 5.8	15.6
Brazil	5.0	− 1.0	− 4.0
Chile	− 1.5	− 5.3	− 6.8
Korea	3.6	− 9.6	− 6.0
Mexico	31.6	− 19.0	12.6
Peru	− 1.0	− 3.6	− 4.6
Venezuela	25.1	0.3	25.4

Note: Minus sign indicates a net inflow of capital.
Source: Dooley (1986) and table 3.11.

1979	1980	1981	1982	Total 1974–82	Total adjusted for misinvoicing 1974–82
300	200	200	100	2,800	− 1,104
13	187	− 468	148	1,167	− 2,707
− 1,022	− 1,119	− 1,102	− 93	− 3,904	—
300	− 300	700	500	3,900	n.a.
n.a.	n.a.	n.a.	n.a.	n.a.	n.a.
n.a.	n.a.	n.a.	n.a.	n.a.	n.a.
n.a.	n.a.	n.a.	n.a.	n.a.	n.a.
5	− 90	184	1,161	1,193	− 348
− 265	− 339	− 31	200	− 845	—
4,800	4,700	7,400	8,300	25,500	25,557
− 2,354	3,366	5,013	7,464	10,776	11,293
− 1,031	− 20	677	− 162	517	—

Table 3.15 Morgan Guaranty estimates of capital flight and adjustments for trade misinvoicing, 1983–85 (billion dollars)

	Morgan Guaranty	Misinvoicing	Adjusted total
Argentina	− 1	− 1	− 2
Brazil	7	− 1	6
Chile	− 1	− 3	− 4
Korea	6	− 7	− 1
Mexico	17	− 14	3
Peru	1	0	1
Uruguay	0	1	1
Venezuela	6	0	6

Note: Minus sign indicates a net inflow of capital.
Source: Morgan Guaranty Trust Company (1986).

References

Bhagwati, Jagdish N. 1964. "On the Underinvoicing of Imports." *Bulletin of the Oxford University Institute of Statistics,* November.

Bhagwati, Jagdish N., Anne Krueger, and Chaiyawat Wibulswasdi. 1974. "Capital Flight from LDCs: A Statistical Analysis." In *Illegal Transactions in International Trade,* edited by Jagdish Bhagwati. Amsterdam: North-Holland.

Cuddington, John T. 1986. *Capital Flight: Estimates, Issues, and Explanations.* Studies in International Finance, no. 58. Princeton, NJ: Economics Department, Princeton University.

Diaz-Alejandro, Carlos F. 1984. "Latin American Debt: I Don't Think We're in Kansas Anymore." *Brookings Papers on Economic Activity,* 2.

Dooley, Michael. 1986. "Country-Specific Risk Premiums, Capital Flight and Net Investment Income Payments in Selected Developing Countries," DM 86/17. Washington: International Monetary Fund.

Dooley, Michael; W. Helkie; R. Tryon; and J. Underwood. 1986. "An Analysis of External Debt Positions of Eight Developing Countries Through 1990." *Journal of Development Economics* (May).

Dornbusch, Rudiger. 1985. "External Debt, Budget Deficits and Disequilibrium Exchange Rates." In *International Debt and the Developing Countries,* edited by G.W. Smith and J.T. Cuddington. Washington: World Bank.

Gulati, Sunil K. 1985. "Capital Flight Through Faked Trade Invoices: 1977–83, A Statistical Note." Columbia University, New York, NY, May. Processed.

Morgan Guaranty Trust Company. 1986. "LDC Capital Flight." *World Financial Markets* (March).

Morgenstern, Oskar. 1950. *On the Accuracy of Economic Observations.* Princeton, NJ: Princeton University Press.

World Bank. 1984. *World Development Report,* Washington.

Comment

Michael Dooley

The paper by Cumby and Levich provides an excellent review and comparison of alternative empirical measures of capital flight. The authors show that there are important differences among the measures presented. More important is their argument that without some theory that relates these data to the rest of the balance of payments at a minimum and preferably to other important economic variables, we cannot hope to identify a preferred measure of capital flight or to evaluate the behavior of that measure. This is a particularly useful point because the implicit theory behind many discussions of capital flight may have little relevance for the historical data sets reviewed by Cumby and Levich. For example, it is often suggested that when residents acquire financial claims outside their home country, domestic real investment is constrained. This hardly seems relevant to the countries studied before 1983 since those countries received historically large net inflows of real foreign savings.

The importance of a theoretical framework can be illustrated by attempting to explain an empirical regularity that stands out for many of the countries studied. That regularity is that capital flight, measured in various ways, was greatly reduced either in 1983 or 1984 and, in some cases, both years. A framework that might help explain this pattern is suggested by considering a country not covered in the capital flight literature reviewed by Cumby and Levich. In the 1980–82 time period, private residents of the United States accumulated about $250 billion in claims on nonresidents. By the various measures of capital flight reviewed, somewhere between none and all of that would be classified as capital flight. It may be instructive to consider what the US experience would suggest in attempting to model capital flight.

In the years in which US residents acquired this substantial stock of claims on nonresidents, interest rates in the United States were high by historical standards, with the Federal funds rate averaging about 16 percent in 1981 and declining to 12 percent and 9 percent, respectively, in 1981 and 1982. The US dollar appreciated on balance relative to other major currencies and there was a small current account surplus—about $5 billion over those three years. Inflation was high by historical standards but it was reduced in 1982. Thus, it would appear that many of the factors often assumed to motivate capital flight from the developing countries included in many studies of capital flight seem not to apply in this case.

What was true in those years in the United States was that there were a variety of small "taxes" on domestic financial positions (taxes include a range of regulations which reduced the value of domestic financial assets).

There were interest-rate ceilings as well as small reserve requirements and insurance charges on some domestic deposits. These taxes made foreign financial assets relatively attractive for US residents. The small advantage offered by offshore assets, however, could hardly account for a $250 billion capital outflow from the United States unless nonresidents had been able to accept these funds and put them back into US financial markets on *relatively* better terms. It is usually the case that investors, other things equal, prefer claims on other residents of the same political jurisdiction because this minimizes political risk. But in unusual circumstances, investors prefer to have claims on nonresidents, and nonresidents prefer claims on residents. The result can be massive two-way capital flows in cases where the capital flow does not, itself, alter the incentives. In effect, residents and nonresidents can be thought of as arbitraging a tax differential through matching transactions. Such transactions do not require collusion among various parties. US residents only had to notice that instruments such as Eurodollar money market mutual funds were paying a higher yield than similar domestic instruments. The US resident, therefore, might liquidate a US bank deposit and bid for a Eurodollar deposit. The US bank that lost the deposit might in turn bid for offshore funds. Finally, the offshore funds could come back to the United States through an interbank transaction that enjoyed a slightly different tax status. The resulting two-way flow of capital had nothing to do with macroeconomic variables in the United States and in turn had no measurable effect on economic conditions in the United States.

Now how much of this analysis might be relevant to developing countries? Many developing countries have had a long history of direct taxes of financial positions in the form of interest-rate ceilings, outright taxes and, in rare cases, confiscation. The initial shock to the system may be some deterioration in the fiscal status of the government. To avoid additional taxes on financial assets, residents might bid for foreign assets. Before a capital flow is observed, however, some other transaction must also appear desirable to another party. If the only possible counterpart is a net export of goods and services, then the standard classical story of a depreciation of the exchange rate followed by a real transfer is relevant. Capital flight of this sort, however, could take years and would be of limited magnitude. The data set considered in the Cumby and Levich paper involves flows of billions of dollars over quarters. Under what circumstances might such flows be observed? If nonresidents see that yields on domestic assets in the *potential* capital-flight countries are rising (because its residents are offering to sell domestic assets), and if nonresidents feel relatively safe, that is, relative to residents, nonresidents will recycle the funds back to the capital-flight country's financial markets. So on the one hand, residents move money out to avoid an expected tax burden, and on the other hand, nonresidents return the money because they have, or believe they have, a preferred "tax" status. In fact, nonresident investors in developing countries have been offered foreign exchange and other government guarantees and in some cases may be in a relatively advantageous position.

This analysis of capital flight has a couple of appealing features. One is that it explains very large movements in financial capital over short time periods with very little macroeconomic effect in either country. The other is that it is capable of explaining why capital flight may have slowed dramatically in countries where overall economic conditions faced by residents remain very difficult. The process described above would come to an end when nonresidents become as fearful as residents that their financial claims would be taxed. In particular, nonresident investors might be a more attractive target for taxation as their investments grow larger.

A theory of capital flight can be stated quite simply. In any situation where residents of different countries can arbitrage an actual or an expected tax differential at little cost, they will do so. That can lead to a "grossing up" of financial positions across national borders—a process that will generate recorded and unrecorded capital flows of enormous magnitude. At the limit, if all investors mistrusted their own governments more than did nonresidents, all financial intermediation would be done offshore and "capital flight" would be a universal problem.

How should we evaluate the welfare implications of this type of financial transaction? If the capital tax on domestic financial capital is regarded as distortionary, and if these financial transactions allow investors to avoid the tax, there may be no welfare loss involved. In fact, an implication of this analysis is that to the extent that all residents can avoid the taxation, domestic real investment in the capital-flight country is unaffected by the expected tax burden. When nonresidents become equally fearful, it is no longer possible for residents to protect their financial wealth through financial transactions. At that point the world that Kindleberger (ch. 3) describes, in which residents must make a real resource transfer in order to avoid taxation, is relevant. Transfers of this type have very important macroeconomic and welfare implications, but such an analysis may have little to do with the data sets reviewed by Cumby and Levich.

Another interesting implication of this line of argument is that countries that attempt or are expected to attempt to tax financial positions relatively heavily will experience capital flight. But the fact that residents have acquired foreign claims does not, in itself, mean that the government's ability to generate revenue has declined. In this case, capital flight could be avoided only by forgoing the attempt to impose relatively high taxes on financial positions. In *either* case, the government would not collect the desired revenue.

Discussion

The attention paid to the definition of capital flight in many of the papers was mirrored in discussion scattered throughout the conference, here briefly summarized.

In the background paper for the conference, Lessard and Williamson had suggested that the choice was between a definition that selected out certain capital flows on account of their *causes* or their *effects*. Contrary to the position adopted in chapter 9, it seemed that the more common view was that it should be defined by its effects, with a number of participants taking the view that the term inevitably carries pejorative connotations.

Jagdish Bhagwati urged a definition based on the illegality of capital export, with wider concepts such as that advocated by Cumby and Levich or by the editors (ch. 9) being described as "capital outflow" rather than capital flight. He argued that it was such illegal outflows that were caught by the technique of partner-country trade comparisons that he had pioneered and that are exploited by Gulati in this chapter.

William R. Cline offered a taxonomy of different forms of capital flight, which he suggested might be defined as "accumulation by the private sector of net foreign assets during a period in which the public sector finds it necessary to accumulate net foreign liabilities or reduce its net foreign assets." He observed that this avoided including normal portfolio diversification (which is offset by inward investment) or private Japanese accumulation of US assets as capital flight, since in neither instance is there a net foreign-exchange flow that requires compensatory changes in the public sector balance sheet. But Donald Lessard suggested that this might more appropriately be termed "sovereign intermediation," and observed that Cline's definition would preclude considering as capital flight those instances in which the public sector was unable to finance an outflow of capital but instead had to resort to real adjustment. Cline argued that his definition could be extended to include this instance, the central point being the presence of private-sector foreign asset accumulation that forces the government to adjust on either the public capital account or the private current account.

Cline defined primary capital flight as flight financed by the provision of foreign exchange from the central bank to the private sector, out of the central bank's receipts of foreign exchange from its controlled access to export earnings, borrowings from abroad (private or public), or from its foreign-exchange reserves. In dual exchange rate regimes, primary capital flight includes that which is financed indirectly by government sales of foreign exchange to the free exchange market in an attempt to moderate the depreciation of the free exchange rate. He observed that from mid-1982 until mid-1985, the Mexican government did not directly provide foreign exchange for primary capital flight. It did, however, do so indirectly, by its sales of foreign exchange into the free exchange market in its attempt to ensure a smooth depreciation in that rate in nominal terms.

He defined secondary capital flight as that which is financed through a surplus on current account items permitted to trade in the free exchange market, when such surplus is not fully purchased by the government by intervention in that market. In Mexico, the surplus on tourism and border trade has largely gone into secondary capital flight, although in 1986 the government purchased some of this surplus for its reserves.

Tertiary capital flight was defined by Cline as that which is carried out through overinvoicing imports and underinvoicing exports. He noted that comparisons of Mexican and foreign trade data indicated that tertiary capital flight has been small because imports are underinvoiced, probably for smuggling reasons, by amounts equal to or exceeding the underinvoicing of exports.

Cline argued that the distinction between primary and secondary capital flight carried important policy implications. Foreign creditors have a right to insist that a debtor-country government curtail primary capital flight, because this is an area directly under its control. On the other hand, an increase in secondary capital flight might simply lead to a depreciation of the free rate in a dual exchange rate regime and in that way be self-financing, in which case he felt that foreign creditors should be expected to view it with greater equanimity.

It was Osvaldo Agatiello who first reminded the conference of Kindleberger's 1937 definition of capital flight as "abnormal [flows] propelled *from* a country. . . by. . . any one or more of a complex list of fears and suspicions," the definition the editors adopt in chapter 9.

With regard to the size of capital flight, Erhard Furst estimated that the total size of foreign deposits in Swiss banks amounted to some $600 billion. He noted that most foreign depositors received negative interest returns, implying that they were willing to pay a substantial premium for security (and also, incidentally, that withholding tax on interest income would have zero impact).

The main controversy on the magnitude of capital flight centered on recent Mexican experience. Cumby and Levich's estimates that, on certain concepts, capital flight might have amounted to over $25 billion in 1983–84 were strongly attacked by Cline, who estimated primary capital flight as at most $6 billion (even without allowing for smuggled imports). Ernesto Zedillo's analysis (ch. 7) shows a sharp curtailment after 1982, implying that the estimates of Morgan Guaranty and others for that period are seriously exaggerated. But Norman Klath replied that Morgan had used Mexican data in constructing its estimate, and that the main reason given for thinking that flight was overestimated in 1983–84—the increase in the registration of private-sector debt—implied that flight must have been even bigger in earlier periods.

Macroeconomic Determinants of Capital Flight: An Econometric Investigation

John T. Cuddington

Introduction

The very nature of capital flight makes it difficult to measure accurately. Nevertheless, the potential importance of stemming capital flight in order to reduce the burden of developing-country (LDC) debt makes the task of measurement essential. Once rough estimates of capital flight have been obtained, one must ask a further question before policy measures to deal with it can be evaluated: what are the determinants of capital flight?

The present paper updates and extends through 1984 (as data availability now permits) the earlier estimates of capital flight in Cuddington (1986) for eight heavily indebted developing countries. The potential impact of interest compounding of previous years' capital flight is briefly considered in order to get an alternative estimate of domestic asset holdings abroad resulting from capital flight.

The remainder of the paper considers the empirical importance of three macroeconomic (as opposed to political) determinants of capital flight:

☐ exchange rate overvaluation, and hence the expectation of major exchange rate realignment

☐ high interest rates in the US acting as a "magnet" for foreign capital

☐ the disbursement of new loans to LDCs. The latter factor has been of particular interest in recent policy discussions.

There is growing concern that it is futile to pour more funds into liquidity-constrained developing countries if a large portion of the increased lending merely flows right back out in the form of capital flight. Some observers

The author is Professor of Economics at Georgetown University.

Table 4.1   Capital flight estimates
(million dollars)

	1974	1975	1976	1977	1978
Argentina	36	− 163	266	− 618	1,498
Brazil	64	427	− 496	618	− 299
Chile	47	− 26	− 252	− 503	− 250
Mexico	1,272	1,285	3,331	917	572
Peru	72	826	328	112	− 51
Uruguay	82	38	13	− 42	− 159
Venezuela	522	− 155	− 401	− 1,736	− 1,072
Total	2,095	2,232	2,788	− 1,253	238

Source: IMF, *Balance of Payments Yearbook.*

Notes: 1. A positive figure denotes capital outflow. Figures do not necessarily add up due to rounding errors.

2. The definitions for estimating capital flight figures are those used in Cuddington (1985). The figures are obtained from the *Balance of Payments Yearbook*. The precise definitions are as follows—
Argentina: Net errors and omissions plus "short-term, other sectors."
Brazil: Net errors and omissions.
Chile: Net errors and omissions plus "short-term, other sectors."
Mexico: Net errors and omissions plus "short-term, other sectors, other assets."
Peru: Net errors and omissions plus "short-term, other sectors, other assets."
Uruguay: Net errors and omissions.
Venezuela: Net errors and omissions plus "short-term, other sectors, other assets."

3. The figures for 1978–82 have been updated by the IMF since Cuddington (1985) was written, and hence may differ somewhat from those reported there.

claim that capital flight is an important cause—although certainly not the only cause—of the debt problem. Others describe the causality as running in the other direction: capital inflows are a major "cause" or, at least, a prerequisite for capital flight because they increase the availability of foreign exchange needed to effect capital outflows. In the case of public-sector borrowing, the resulting increase in the potential for graft and corruption may also lead to higher capital flight.

Revised Estimates and the Effect of Compounding

Table 4.1 reports capital flight estimates from 1974 through 1984 using data from the IMF *Balance of Payments Yearbook* and the approach discussed in

1979	1980	1981	1982	1983	1984	Total 1974–84
−1,692	2,301	8,679	5,209	1,955	−1,635	15,837
−1,227	352	390	379	617	−406	419
−416	−482	−911	801	344	−439	−2,087
1,107	4,668	10,910	7,856	4,314	2,585	38,815
−112	187	−595	−462	417	557	1,277
11	−90	161	1,264	295	−149	1,425
143	2,574	4,748	7,112	715	1,210	13,660
−2,186	9,511	23,381	22,159	8,656	1,723	69,345

Cuddington (1986).[1] There, capital flight was defined to include short-term capital outflows by the private, nonbank sector. The precise line items from the balance of payments accounts used for each country are noted at the bottom of the table. The figures for 1983 and 1984 (the most recent ones available using the data from the *Yearbook*) show that the amount of capital flight shrank considerably in those years relative to its peak in 1981–82. In fact, two of the major capital-flight countries, Argentina and Uruguay, apparently experienced some repatriation of flight capital in 1984. In Mexico, the country with the largest cumulative capital flight, the outflow was reduced somewhat in 1983–84, although it still registered roughly $7 billion over those two years. Comparing the cumulative amount of capital flight to the increase in external debt over the period suggests that the residents of some LDCs have foreign asset holdings that are roughly half as large as their country's external liabilities. Of course, the bulk of the assets may be owned by the private sector, whereas the liabilities were largely incurred by the public sector.

The cumulation of capital-flight estimates, such as those in table 4.1, over successive years may understate domestic holdings of assets abroad because it ignores the growth in the value of these holdings from the investment income they generate. By merely adding the capital-flight estimates for individual years together to arrive at an estimate of foreign asset holdings, previous estimates implicitly assume that the owners of foreign assets consume 100 percent of the income earned each year on flight capital—but none of the principal. Although this is the type of behavior that a simple

---

1. The Cumby and Levich paper in this volume compares various estimates of capital flight (including mine).

Table 4.2 Capital flight with compounding, and gross external debt
(million dollars)

	(1) Cumulative capital flight without compounding 1974–84	(2) Cumulative capital flight with compounding 1974–84	(3) Gross external debt end-1984	(4) Capital flight to debt (2)/(3) (percentage)
Argentina	15,837	20,774	45,839	45
Brazil	419	425	104,384	0
Chile	− 2,087	− 3,708	19,959	− 19
Mexico	38,815	55,994	97,307	58
Peru	1,277	2,583	13,164	20
Uruguay	1,425	1,708	3,288	52
Venezuela	13,660	15,545	34,247	45
Total	69,345	93,320	318,188	29

Source: Table 4.1 for capital flight; IMF, *International Financial Statistics* for US Treasury bill rate (bond equivalent); and *World Debt Tables* for gross external debt.

permanent income theory of consumption would predict, one might expect flight capitalists to have a higher saving propensity for two reasons. First, to the extent that the wealth was obtained through illegal means (for example, smuggling, tax evasion, or violating foreign-exchange controls), conspicuous consumption would be ill-advised. Second, the fact that these assets may be far-removed geographically from the investors' "home base" may tend to discourage their liquidation for consumption purposes; repatriating the interest income may be infeasible due to exchange controls, or punitive at prevailing (disequilibrium) exchange rates.

It seems useful, therefore, to consider an alternative assumption about income on flight capital from previous periods. A simple assumption is that this wealth earns interest at a rate equal to the one-year US Treasury bill rate and that the entire proceeds are saved, thereby augmenting domestic assets abroad. How significant is this compounding effect? Making the conservative assumption that each year's capital flight does not occur until the last day of the year (so that there is no compounding in that year, only subsequent years), column (2) of table 4.2 shows the cumulative amount of domestic assets held abroad as a result of capital flight. For some countries, such as Argentina, Mexico, and Peru, the estimates are considerably larger than the previous estimates. On the other hand, for countries such as Brazil, which experienced modest capital flight in some years and reverse capital flight in others, the difference between the estimates with and without compounding is small.

Regardless of whether one prefers the estimates with or without compounding (or other estimates such as those of Dooley et al. [1986] or Morgan Guaranty [1986]), it is clear that capital flight is quantitatively very large in a number of high-debt countries. Whether any policy action can or should be undertaken to deal with this phenomenon depends critically on what motivates capital flight—and whether it reflects any discrepancies between private and social risks and returns.[2]

The Econometric Analysis

The rest of the paper attempts to isolate empirically the importance of the three economic determinants of capital flight mentioned in the introduction for the four countries in table 4.1 where capital flight was significant: Mexico, Argentina, Uruguay, and Venezuela.

A useful starting point for modeling capital flight is a standard portfolio balance or portfolio adjustment model in which LDC investors hold an array of domestic and foreign assets, and add to these asset holdings as saving grows over time.[3] If one assumes that the risk attached to various assets remains constant over time, which is surely a heroic assumption in situations where investors' reassessments of risk may be an important cause of capital flight, the asset demands in this framework depend on relative rates of return inclusive of expected devaluation.[4,5]

Thus, the capital flight equation takes the form:

(1) $\quad KF = b_o + b_1(x + r^*) + b_2 r + b_3 INF$

where KF is the change in domestic holdings of foreign assets in the

---

2. Various reasons why capital flight might be considered "bad," so that policy intervention is (potentially) welfare-improving, are suggested in Cuddington (1986). See also chapters 6 and 9 of this volume.

3. Dooley provides an extremely useful reinterpretation of regression results of the sort reported below, claiming that the rate-of-return variables proxy for different perceptions of financial and expropriation risk by domestic and foreign investors.

4. Admittedly, this approach leaves unanswered the fundamental question of what distinguishes capital flight from any other capital outflow, such as those motivated by portfolio diversification objectives. This issue is discussed by Cumby and Levich (this volume) and by Dooley (1986).

5. Regarding changes in risk: for Mexico, I experimented with the month-over-month variance in the domestic interest rate as a proxy for domestic financial and political risks in each year. This variable was typically highly correlated with the level of the domestic interest rate, however, so it added little explanatory power to the regression equations. Further experimentation with various risk measures would obviously be worthwhile in order to assess the effect of changes in risk perceptions on capital flight.

current period, r and r^* are domestic and foreign (for example US) interest rates respectively, x is the expected rate of depreciation of the domestic currency, and *INF* is the domestic inflation rate.[6]

Exchange Rate Expectations

The expectation that the domestic currency is soon to be devalued is undoubtedly an important determinant of the allocation of domestic wealth across domestic and foreign-currency assets. In modeling exchange rate expectations, expected devaluation was assumed to be a linear function of the gap between the current real effective exchange rate (REER) and its level in an appropriately chosen equilibrium year. (The exchange rate is defined so that appreciation of the domestic currency is indicated by a higher value.) That is, the expected rate of devaluation in the upcoming period equals:

(2) $x = a(REER - k)$

where k is the long-run equilibrium exchange rate and a indicates the speed with which exchange-market disequilibrium is expected to be corrected.[7]

The Regression Methodology

The approach taken here to estimate the importance of the foregoing determinants of capital flight was to start by estimating equation (1), after substituting for x using (2). Thus the regression equation includes the rate

---

6. In a recent paper, Eduardo Conesa (1986) has argued very convincingly for the inclusion of real income as a determinant of capital flight. Empirically, this variable turns out to be highly significant. His results differ in some respects from those presented here. This may be the consequence of: (1) his efforts to increase the data sample by going back to 1970 (although the possible structural shifts due to the collapse of the Bretton Woods fixed exchange rate commitment by the major industrial nations may make the inclusion of these extra data points dubious), (2) his inclusion of real income in capital flight regressions (which he finds to be highly significant— clearly, an interesting result) or (3) my greater care in specifying the error processes in the regressions, which was important in a number of the regressions reported below.

7. An alternative approach would be to use the rational expectations assumption that the anticipated depreciation in each period is equal to the actual rate plus a random factor, ideally with mean zero. An instrumental variable estimation approach would be desirable in order to deal with the errors-in-variables problem that the proxy for expectations undoubtedly entails. As the literature on the "peso problem" tells us, the gap between the conditional expectation of the change in the exchange rate and the actual realized change need not have mean zero in the case where speculation against the central bank is important.

of return variables (*REER, r*, r, INF*). A variable capturing disbursements of public and publicly guaranteed long-term debt, *DISBUR,* was also included in order to assess the hypothesis that capital inflows facilitate capital flight. Finally, serial correlation was dealt with (to the extent possible, given the small data sample) by including a lagged dependent variable or using simple AR or MA error specifications, as dictated by the data.

With 11 observations, the estimation is based on very few degrees of freedom. Thus every effort was made to eliminate insignificant regressors. All variables with coefficients whose *t*-statistics were less than unity were omitted from the regression, and it was rerun. This process was repeated a second time, if necessary, until only statistically significant variables remained. At each stage, the autocorrelation and partial autocorrelation functions for the residuals (with 0-to-5 lags) were examined to ensure that high serial correlation was not a problem.

It is well known that the foregoing "sequential approach" to model selection may overlook alternative, superior specifications due to the order in which individual regressors are deleted from the regression (or added, if the inverse procedure is used)—unless, by chance, the regressors are uncorrelated with each other.[8] Recognizing this, we calculated a correlation matrix including all the regressors and the regressand to see which variables were highly correlated. Where high simple correlations were found, we experimented with regression equations that replaced one of the colinear variables with the other, as well as equations that included them both.

The motivation for the foregoing approach is to ensure that the reported results were robust to minor changes in specification. This seemed especially important because of the small data sample.

Regression Results for Mexico

The general model for Mexico collapsed to the following once insignificant variables were omitted from the regression (only one pass was needed):

$$KF = -26{,}104 + 244\ REER + 0.31\ DISBUR + 1.02\ KF(t-1).$$

(3)   (5.31)   (4.97)   (2.24)   (6.01)

$\overline{R}^2 = 0.88$ DW = 2.20

Although the familiar DW statistic is reported, it is invalid in the presence of a lagged dependent variable. To check that the residuals were serially

---

8. As Kennedy (1985, p. 68) points out, "a specification search is best undertaken by beginning with a general, unrestricted model and then systematically simplifying it in light of the sample evidence. This approach (deliberate "overfitting") is preferred to or has more power than a search beginning with a very simple model and expanding as the data permit" (see Harvey, 1981, pp. 183–7).

uncorrelated, the autocorrelation (AC) and partial autocorrelation (PAC) functions with five lags were also estimated. Once the lagged dependent variable is included in the regression, the AC and PAC functions were very flat, indicating that the residuals were well behaved and resulted in a higher R^2. This specification was better than simple AR and MA error processes in that it left residuals that were better behaved.

The regression results are striking. They strongly support the finding in Cuddington (1986) that overvaluation of the exchange rate, and presumably fear of imminent devaluation, is an important cause of capital flight. Unlike in my earlier findings, however, the Mexican interest rate no longer enters with a *positive* sign once loan disbursements, *DISBUR,* is included as an explanatory variable. *DISBUR* is highly significant, lending support to the hypothesis that the inflow of foreign exchange from additional foreign lending did facilitate capital flight from Mexico. The regression coefficient suggests that roughly 31 cents out of each additional dollar of new long-term loans to Mexico over the 1974–84 period flowed back out in the form of capital flight. This obviously reduces the net benefit of external borrowing considerably. Furthermore, capital flight presumably reduces the Mexican tax base, making it more difficult to service external debt.

There is an alternative "Ricardian" explanation for the finding: when private residents see their government borrowing abroad to finance higher expenditure, they expect higher future taxes or inflation to service the additional external debt. By increasing their holdings of foreign assets, domestic residents secure a good hedge against the foreign-exchange risk being incurred by their government, as well as a good vehicle for saving to meet expected future tax obligations. This explanation assumes, perhaps implausibly, that the holders of foreign assets are, in fact, planning to pay their share of future taxes rather than using capital flight as a way of avoiding or evading them.

In the Mexican case, loan disbursements were highly correlated with the US Treasury bill rate during the 1970s and early 1980s. This, coupled with the fact that the US interest rate had the highest simple correlation with *KF* among all of the regressors, suggested that regressions with r^* be reconsidered. Minor experimentation with regressions including r^* yielded a slightly better fit than that in (3), but the residuals were not as well behaved:

$$KF = -24561 + 221 \, REER + 402 \, r^* + 0.94 \, KF(t-1)$$

(4)   (5.70)   (4.95)   (3.00)   (6.12)

$$\overline{R}^2 = 0.91 \qquad DW = 2.79.$$

The AC and PAC functions indicated that the residuals in this regression exhibited high first- and second-order serial correlation, which proved to be impossible to eliminate without ending up with a model that was obviously overfit.[9]

In short, equation (3), above, appears to have residuals that are considerably better behaved. From a strictly statistical standpoint, I prefer the results in (3) to those in (4).

Regression (4), like (3), points to exchange rate overvaluation as a determinant of capital flight, but now instead of disbursements the US interest rate enters. Unfortunately, the high correlation between r^* and *DISBUR* renders both of them (individually and jointly) insignificant when they are included in the regression equation at the same time. Nevertheless, the statistical significance of the US interest rate in (4) raises an important question: to what extent did tight US monetary policy and loose fiscal policy in the late 1970s and early 1980s contribute to Mexican capital flight, by raising real interest rates in the United States to artificially high levels, to the point where investment in Mexico appeared uneconomic?

Regression Results for Argentina

The best fitting capital flight regression for Argentina was the following:

$$(5) \quad \begin{array}{l} KF = -9{,}060 + 128\,REER(t-1) + e(t) - 0.75\,e(t-2) \\ (3.18) \quad\ \ (3.85) (1.95) \end{array}$$

$$\bar{R}^2 = 0.72 \quad DW = 1.86.$$

The above specification, which has a lagged value of *REER* and an MA(2) error process, yielded a better fit and flatter AC and PAC functions than did models with AR error processes or those including a lagged dependent variable. Admittedly, it is surprising that the lagged real effective exchange rate rather than the current value should be relevant in an environment where domestic residents are acutely aware of, and presumably respond quickly to, exchange rate developments.[10] In the Argentine case, there was no evidence that increases in loan disbursements were associated with higher capital flight. Furthermore, high US interest rates played no significant role once the real exchange rate was included in the regression.

---

9. The specification with the lagged dependent variable in (4) was better than any low-order AR or MA error specification.

10. The regressions using *quarterly* data in Cuddington (1986), on the other hand, did find the current exchange rate works better than the lagged value.

Regression Results for Uruguay

The best capital-flight regression for Uruguay is very similar to that for Argentina, except that the AR error process dominates the MA error specification (which did not converge):

(6) $KF = -2139 + 28\ REER(t-1) + e(t)$,
           (7.28)   (7.83)

where $e(t) = -0.68\ e(t-1) + u(t)$
           (2.54)
           $\bar{R}^2 = 0.78$ $DW = 2.84$.

Although this regression had the best fit, the PAC function indicated partial correlations of -0.45 and -0.58 at lags 1 and 2 respectively, suggesting that the model was not entirely satisfactory. An alternative model, which produced residuals that were better behaved, but had a considerably lower $\bar{R}^2$, was the following:

(7) $KF = -1709 + 15.06\ REER + 0.002\ DISBUR + e(t)$
                  (2.50)   (1.97)   (2.12)
           $\bar{R}^2 = 0.40$ $DW = 2.53$.

From a statistical standpoint, I prefer (7) to (6).
    Noteworthy in regression (7) is the small but significant (positive) effect of increased loan disbursements on capital flight. The US interest rate, on the other hand, did not enter significantly (or even with a t-statistic greater than unity) in any of the capital flight equations for Uruguay.

Regression Results for Venezuela

In Venezuela, the role of high US interest rates in drawing capital out of the country seems to have been particularly important, as was overvaluation of the real exchange rate, as the regression results confirm:

(8) $KF = -18203 + 142\ REER + 655\ r^* + e(t)$,
           (3.17)   (2.24)   (4.50)

where $e(t) = -0.53\ e(t-1) + u(t)$
           (1.17)
           $\bar{R}^2 = 0.64$ $DW = 1.96$.

Although the AR(1) coefficient in the error process in (8) is not statistically significant at conventional levels, this specification produced residuals that were most satisfactory. The regression results produce no evidence that capital inflows in the form of higher loan disbursements played a significant role in Venezuela's capital-flight problem in the late 1970s and early 1980s.

In addition to regressions with contemporaneous values of the explanatory variables (the best of which is reported above), we ran some with lagged regressors. In the case of Venezuela lagged regressors produced a regression with much better fit, although, admittedly, it is hard to explain why Venezuelan investors would respond to economic incentives with a one-year lag, rather than responding to current information. Also surprising is the finding that the inclusion of lagged inflation causes the real exchange rate to become statistically insignificant as a determinant of capital flight (although it still has a positive sign, as one would expect):

$$(9) \qquad KF = -12,170 + 41\ REER(t-1) + 185\ INF(t-1)$$
$$ (3.06) \qquad (1.10) \qquad\qquad (2.15)$$
$$+\ 933\ r^*(t-1) - 0.42\ KF(t-1)$$
$$(5.76) \qquad\quad (2.77)$$
$$\overline{R}^2 = 0.94 \qquad DW = 2.49.$$

The US interest rate remains highly significant. Thus, whether one chooses regression (8) or (9), there is evidence that high US interest rates exacerbated capital flight from Venezuela.

Concluding Remarks

The econometric analysis in this paper must be viewed with caution because of the small number of observations that were available, not to mention the lack of a convincing, generally accepted analytical framework on which the regression equations can be based. Nevertheless, several findings seem to be robust and have important policy implications. First, exchange rate overvaluation was an important determinant of capital flight in all four countries studied. Sound macroeconomic policy in LDCs is essential for preventing massive overvaluation of the domestic currency. If exchange rate overvaluation is allowed to develop, it will provide a strong incentive for domestic as well as foreign residents to reduce their asset holdings in the domestic currency in anticipation of the exchange rate depreciation that must ultimately follow. The incipient outflow is effected either through speculation against the central bank as it attempts to prevent the resulting exchange rate realignment, or via transactions with individuals who feel that they can avoid exchange risk—either by superior hedging techniques or because they have implicit or explicit government guarantees not available to other investors.

Second, for Mexico and Venezuela high interest rates in the United States seem to have exacerbated capital flight. The implication is that sound macroeconomic policy in the industrial countries, especially the United States, is also important in preventing capital flight from developing countries. If an inappropriate fiscal-monetary policy mix drives world interest rates to historical highs—and at the same time interest controls in many LDCs prevent their rates from climbing in step—then it is small wonder that smart money will begin to flow out of capital-scarce LDCs toward capital-abundant industrial countries where interest rates are artificially high.

Third, at least in some countries, notably Mexico, but perhaps Uruguay as well, capital inflows in the form of foreign borrowing seem to have facilitated or induced capital flight. Although this was not the case in all capital flight countries that borrowed heavily, it indicates a possible need for tighter administrative control over loan disbursements in countries where the leakage into foreign assets has been large.

References

Conesa, Eduardo. 1986. "The Causes of Capital Flight from Latin America." Washington: Inter-American Development Bank. Working paper.

Cuddington, J. T. 1986. *Capital Flight: Estimates, Issues, and Explanations*, Princeton Studies in International Finance, no. 58 (December). Princeton, NJ: International Finance Section Department of Economics, Princeton University.

Dooley, M., W. Helkie, R. Tryon, and J. Underwood. 1986. "An Analysis of External Debt Positions of Eight Developing Countries Through 1990." *Journal of Development Economics* (May).

Dooley, M. 1986. "Country-Specific Risk Premiums, Capital Flight, and Net Investment Income Payments in Selected Developing Countries." International Monetary Fund, DM 86/17 Washington. Unpublished manuscript.

Harvey, A.C. 1981. *The Econometric Analysis of Time Series*, Oxford: Philip Allan.

Kennedy, P. 1985. *A Guide to Econometrics*, Oxford: Basil Blackwell.

Morgan Guaranty Trust Co. 1986. "LDC Capital Flight," *World Financial Markets* (March), pp. 13–15.

Comment

Donald R. Lessard

The three papers of Cumby and Levich, Cuddington, and Walter provide important insights regarding the nature, mechanisms, and causes of capital flight. They also underscore the complexity of the phenomenon and how little we really know about it. I will focus primarily on John Cuddington's analysis of the causes of capital flight, but I will begin with a few general observations that apply to all three papers.

My first comment is on the limits of aggregate data in assessing the nature, magnitude, or causes (or cures for that matter) of capital flight. While Walter provides a general model of flight behavior at the individual level and a fascinating account of the mechanisms involved, he does not examine specific source-country situations. Cumby-Levich and Cuddington do, but their inquiry is restricted to aggregate measures, leaving many questions unanswered and unanswerable.

For example, while there clearly have been major episodes of flight from particular countries, is there chronic (continuing) flight as well? I doubt that this is discernible from aggregate data, since the data are so gross that only major fluctuations are likely to be captured. What is the position in the income (and wealth) distribution of residents who acquire foreign assets? Does this vary significantly across countries and episodes? What types of assets have residents liquidated in order to acquire foreign assets? Local bank deposits? Equity in owner-managed firms? Has the acquisition of foreign assets coincided with a "flight to real goods," with increased local borrowing by local firms, with government bailouts of failing firms? What types of foreign assets have residents acquired? Anonymous assets in Switzerland or Panama? Insured deposits in the United States?

Answers to these questions would provide a much clearer picture of the phenomenon and what can and should be done about it. In fact, most policy recommendations are based on implicit assumptions about a number of these issues. My point is not to criticize the papers presented today, which represent substantial contributions to the state of the art. Rather it is to appeal for more probing microeconomic analyses to go along with the macro-level inquiries. We need to know the composition of the asset portfolios of various groups of developing-country residents. At the moment, we really do not know what phenomenon we are studying.

My second general comment refers to the definition of "normal" capital flows versus capital flight. What is normal should be interpreted in terms of portfolio diversification: what we should expect residents to hold. Everyone acknowledges that residents can be expected to acquire some foreign assets for diversification, but little is said about how large these holdings should be. Recognizing that assets in less developed countries are very risky in their own right and yet virtually uncorrelated with the bulk of assets in the world economy, one might expect residents to hold as much as 50 percent to 60 percent of their assets abroad.[1] Therefore, what may be surprising is not the extent of capital flight, but the extent to which residents of less developed countries hold local assets.

My third general comment refers to the link between the nature of capital flight and its social costs. If the acquisition of foreign assets by residents is not offset by foreign inflows, there clearly are real effects in terms of capital formation, growth, and so on. The more interesting case is when capital flight involves "offshore intermediation" and outflows that are largely offset by inflows. In this case, residents effectively rent another country's jurisdiction for financial contracting. If the motive for doing so is tax arbitrage, then there is clearly an erosion of the local tax base. To the extent that financial markets are not informationally perfect, then the offshore shift of intermediation may raise the costs of, or reduce the access to, finance for local activities. Finally, and probably most important, such two-way flows typically involve sovereign intermediation in at least one direction.

In most developing countries, private funds flow out while the offsetting inflows involve sovereign promises. The sovereign, in one way or another, promises to make good on the resulting foreign obligations. Unfortunately, there are states of nature when it cannot meet all its obligations, and the typical response appears to be for the sovereign to discriminate among different classes of claims holders. In serious financial crises, resident claims come out fairly low in the pecking order. Therefore, capital flight involving the substitution of foreign funds backed by international leverage for resident savings may increase the likelihood of crises and the relative exposure of (the remaining) resident holdings of domestic assets.

Turning to Cuddington's empirical estimates, I would like to congratulate John for a very complete yet concise analysis of the causes of capital flight. His paper, like most work on capital flight, focuses on the phenomenon at an aggregate level. As such, it does not distinguish between private capital outflows that are offset by official borrowing and those that are not, and thus it does not address the "offshore intermediation" or "round-tripping" views of capital flight advanced by Dooley (1986) and others.

Cuddington views capital flight as a portfolio problem, with residents choosing between local and foreign assets based on their relative expected returns (interest rates) and associated risks. However, the models he

---

1. For an example of such calculations for residents of industrial countries, see Cooper and Kaplanis (1986).

estimates do not include any direct measure of the riskiness of source-country assets, nor are proxy measures carefully articulated. For example, although exchange rate overvaluation is the one common explanatory factor across the countries studied, the fear of devaluation should depend on the government's reserves and fiscal situation. The omission of such variables is disappointing, since I would expect variations in such risks to be key explanatory factors. This limits Cuddington's ability to distinguish between alternative hypotheses.

Consider his interpretation of the association between disbursements and capital flight. He views it as a liquidity effect, where the availability of foreign exchange enables the capital flight to take place. An alternative interpretation is that domestic assets held by residents are effectively subordinated to sovereign external obligations in the case of a fiscal crisis. To the extent that disbursements signal an increase in the probability of a fiscal crisis, therefore, they will trigger capital flight.

The difference in interpretation has major policy implications. Cuddington's interpretation supports the view of many that there should be no further lending to countries such as Mexico "since it is just going to flow out anyway." The alternative interpretation emphasizes the need to somehow reduce the debt burden in order to reestablish domestic capital formation.

It seems to me that it should be possible to make some headway in distinguishing between these two effects. One possibility would be to replace disbursements with a variable proxying for the probability of a fiscal or foreign payments crisis, drawing on the work of Cline (1984) or McFadden et al. (1985). One suspects, for example, that the relationship between disbursements and the crisis-probability variable would be very different in Mexico's 1976 and 1981 borrowing binges.

Similar comments apply to the findings on US interest rates. One suspects that this variable plays very different roles in different countries. My conjecture is that in the case of Mexico, for example, the major effect of high US interest rates is an increased probability of financial crisis. In the case of Venezuela, in contrast, with sticky local interest rates and an open capital market (during most of the period analyzed), one might expect that high US rates proxy for financial repression leading to "disintermediation" from Venezuela to the world financial markets. One could say, of course, that the US rates acted as a magnet in this case, but only because local rates were not allowed to adjust.

Obviously, the number of hypotheses that can be pursued with 11 degrees of freedom is extremely limited! But this calls for either a more complete theoretical model or more disaggregated data. It is reassuring that Cuddington (1986) obtains similar results for several countries using quarterly data. This could be done for other countries using data on nonresident bank deposits in the United States. While they represent only part of the stock of flight capital, there is no reason to believe that they do not move in tandem with the total stock.

References

Cline, William R. 1984. *International Debt: Systemic Risk and Policy Response.* Washington: Institute for International Economics.

Cooper, Ian, and Evi Kaplanis. 1986. "Estimation of Barriers to International Investment." London Business School Working Paper IFA-91-86.

Dooley, Michael P. 1986. "Country-Specific Risk Premiums, Capital Flight and Net Investment Income Payments in Selected Developing Countries," DM 86/17. Washington: International Monetary Fund.

McFadden, Daniel; Richard Eckaus; Gershon Feder; V. Hajivassilou, and Stephen O'Connell. 1985. "Is There Life After Debt: An Econometric Analysis of Creditworthiness of Developing Countries." In *International Debt and the Developing Countries,* edited by Gordon W. Smith and John T. Cuddington, Washington: The World Bank.

Discussion

Cuddington's finding of a significant "marginal propensity to flee" in several countries (0.31 in Mexico) provoked substantial discussion. Bhagwati suggested that, instead of showing that 31 cents of every dollar the commercial banks lent was wasted through an induced relaxation in debtor-country policies, the finding might be interpreted as showing that Mexican citizens were sufficiently alarmed to see their national debt mount as to take evasive action. He concluded that the banks might be able to help stem capital outflow by a greater willingness to deal with the debt overhang.

Vittorio Corbo argued that Cuddington's specification seemed to presuppose credit rationing, in which case the available funds should include the country's reserves as well as the flow of lending disbursements. Eduardo Conesa revealed that his own econometric estimates had indeed included the level of reserves and that these had proved to have explanatory power, a result that might be explained by the tendency of central banks to maintain an overvalued currency when reserves accumulated. Finally, Cline queried whether any estimate of the marginal propensity to flee that did not recognize a possible discontinuity in behavior in 1982 could be taken seriously.

Conesa sketched some of the results of his own econometric analysis into the causes of capital flight. He stressed particularly the finding that economic recession was an important cause of outflow, emphasizing that this had a ready economic explanation (low actual and expected profit rates in the domestic economy) and important policy implications. Specifically, it suggested that the excessively contractionary policies that had sometimes been involved in Fund programs could be counterproductive since the induced capital outflow might outweigh the improvement in the current account: indeed, a Fund program that injected substantial liquidity while insisting on domestic recession might be the worst combination of all from the standpoint of inducing capital flight. Despite some qualms about Conesa's econometric specification, many participants seemed convinced of his basic thesis that a restoration of growth was a necessary step toward the reversal of capital flight.

Hyman Minsky drew attention to asymmetries in the financial structure that he felt were crucial to the generation of a large volume of net capital flight. He argued that there was no reason to expect the residents of developing countries to be content with a portfolio dominated by local assets in a world where portfolio diversification had been cheapened by technological advance. But this need not be harmful if their financial infrastructure were as good as that of the developed countries, since then there would be an equivalent inward flow as the rich sought to buy high-risk, high-return assets in developing countries. Instead of being considered an irrational response to a rational world, capital flight should therefore be regarded as a rational response to an unpredictable world without the financial structure to allow those on one side of the market to take up the risks that those on the other side were rationally avoiding.

Barbara Stallings was critical of the tendency of most of the economists (Rudolf Hommes excepted) to overlook the political determinants of capital flight. However, Joseph Ramos noted that, although such a connection might seem plausible, it did not show in the statistics: the premium of the black market rate in Chile peaked before the political protests. Likewise, Zedillo replied that capital flight from Mexico had peaked at a time of political stability but poor economic management, and had declined and then reversed when economic management improved, despite an increase in political tension.

Several participants also suggested using pooled time series/cross-section techniques to get better estimates of the causes of capital flight, although it was replied that the gains would be at best small and the results could be misleading, because both theoretical considerations and empirical results suggested that parameters differ across countries. Cuddington argued that a better way to increase the data sample was to exploit the quarterly data available for Argentina and Mexico.

Conesa was highly critical of some of Cuddington's results, questioning especially whether they provided any convincing evidence for treating overvaluation as a cause of capital flight in Argentina and Uruguay, in view of the finding that the exchange rate variable enters with a one-year lag. Cuddington replied that his quarterly results did not have a lag, which did not entirely allay concerns, although most participants did not question the role of overvaluation even though they may have felt the evidence was less decisive than they would have liked.

Vittorio Corbo suggested that another way of compensating for the limited number of data observations would be to structure Cuddington's model more carefully, specifically by including the interest differential rather than the US interest rate as an independent variable. Cuddington replied that he had indeed experimented with the inclusion of interest differentials, but found no significant results, a finding that he attributed to the endogeneity of the domestic interest rate.

5

The Mechanisms of Capital Flight

Ingo Walter

This paper deals with flight capital from two perspectives—the conduits used and the deployment of assets. The first is a "flow" dimension that addresses the various techniques that individuals and business entities may use to redeploy financial and other assets under conditions of capital flight. The second is a "stock" dimension concerned with the investment vehicles that are available to achieve asset-holders' objectives with respect to return, risk, and confidentiality in the context of highly specific portfolio requirements.

We begin with some important definitional issues, and proceed to discuss in conceptual terms the core motives that drive those who engage in capital flight. We then proceed to consider, in turn, the conduits of capital flight and the vehicles that form the networks of asset deployment and ownership structures. We conclude with an assessment of prospects for inhibiting flight capital through governmental and intergovernmental action to impair the vehicles that make it possible.

Webster defines "flight" as "an act or instance of running away." To apply this definition to the phenomenon of capital flight requires both the attribution of certain motives to the asset-holder concerned and a frame of reference of the act of flight itself.

Asset holders in the ordinary course of events engage in constant redeployment in their search for an efficient portfolio—one that maximizes total returns under a given risk constraint. They continuously compare alternative portfolios domestically and internationally, and routinely engage in asset restructuring as risk-return perceptions of individual investment vehicles, currencies, and locations change. In any specific instance, the underlying investor motivation may be either return driven or risk driven, depending

The author is Professor of Economics and Finance, Graduate School of Business Administration, New York University, and John H. Loudon Professor of International Management, INSEAD, Fontainebleau, France.

on which parameter is perceived to have changed. Either one can trigger movement toward or away from a particular asset. Yet use of the term "flight" is rare indeed in discussions of ordinary portfolio adjustments of this sort. Investors may "flee" from IBM or General Motors stock, but the word is not often used in this context.

Rather, from the standpoint of the asset holder, common usage of the term "capital flight" appears to refer to an unfavorable change in the risk-return profile associated with a portfolio of assets held in a particular country, as compared with a portfolio held in other national jurisdictions. This altered profile, in turn, is deemed to be sufficiently inferior to warrant an active redeployment of assets—overcoming normal investor inertia as well as information costs and transaction costs that can themselves be substantial. In many cases the potential costs include running afoul of the law and risking punishment or violating an implied social contract. This has a bearing both on the conduits used in achieving asset redeployment and on the process of asset selection. In each case, confidentiality may play a significant role.

Governments normally follow multiple macroeconomic objectives that may include growth, employment, inflation, and balance of payments or exchange rate targets as well as more specific objectives related to prices of goods and services, income and wealth distribution, economic structure, public-sector financing, and ownership of the means of production. International flows of direct and portfolio investments under ordinary circumstances are rarely associated with the capital flight phenomenon. Rather, it is when capital transfers by residents conflict with political objectives that the term "flight" comes into general usage.

Asset redeployment by individuals or institutions in this context threatens attainment of one or more national objectives. It threatens to impose an economic cost on the nation and a political cost on those who hold office. As residents of the country concerned, asset holders who engage in such behavior are held by the authorities to be in violation of a social contract. This violation may involve illegal conduct, as in the evasion of exchange control regulations. Or it may involve conduct that is deemed immoral or irresponsible, and which could be made illegal in the future (Ramirez-Rojas 1985). Asset redeployment on the part of an individual or institution under such conditions is usually captured under the rubric of capital flight.

Beyond this, flight capital may also involve assets that have themselves been illegally obtained domestically (Blum 1981). Assets accumulated through criminal activities such as smuggling, financial fraud, bribery, racketeering, and corruption are obvious candidates for capital flight if shifting them abroad yields perceived reductions in the probability of disclosure, asset recapture, and possibly serious legal sanctions applied to the institutions or individuals involved. So are assets that have otherwise been accumulated legally but are involved in tax evasion. Criminal and tax-motivated capital flight obviously depend on the size and character of a nation's underground economy and will occur even in the absence of ordinary asset redeployment incentives based on comparative risks and returns. At a minimum it violates fiscal statutes and may violate a broad range of criminal statutes as well.

Correctly defined, capital flight therefore appears to consist of a subset of international asset redeployments or portfolio adjustments—undertaken in response to a significant perceived deterioration in risk-return profiles associated with assets located in a particular country—that occur in the presence of conflict between the objectives of asset holders and governments. It may or may not violate the law. It is always considered by the authorities to violate an implied social contract.

Motivations

Capital flight invariably involves trade-offs among four sets of factors: expected returns, information and transactions costs, risks, and confidentiality (Walter 1985).

Holders of financial assets, broadly defined, are generally thought to be driven by considerations related primarily to the nature of risks and returns. The behavioral characteristics of asset holders are thoroughly addressed in modern portfolio theory and can easily be adapted to include the international dimension. In the context of capital flight, their behavior may be conditioned as well by confidentiality regarding the size, location, and composition of financial or other assets that comprise a portfolio. Confidentiality clearly has value to the asset holder whenever disclosure would impose damage, or disutility, upon him or those with whom he identifies. This will be the case for flight capital if it is—or might in the future be—considered illegal or irresponsible, and the asset holder or his family continues to reside within the country.

If confidentiality has value, then asset holders engaging in capital flight should be willing to pay for it. They may pay by accepting a portfolio of assets that has lower expected real net returns than one assembled without regard to confidentiality considerations. Or they may pay by assembling a portfolio with higher covariances in expected net real returns among the constituent assets—a more risky portfolio—than if confidentiality were not a consideration. Or some combination of effects of confidentiality on returns and risks may be involved. It is possible to map out the trade-offs between confidentiality, risk, and expected returns using a standard analytical framework.

Confidentiality Versus Risk and Expected Returns

If confidentiality is not a free good, it must be "purchased" by putting together a portfolio of assets (or a single asset) that yields the desired level of nondisclosure. One "cost" of confidentiality to the asset holder involved in capital flight may thus be the difference between the expected yield on his confidentiality-oriented portfolio and the yield on a "benchmark portfolio" that would be put together by the same individual if confidentiality were not a consideration.

Besides the cost of confidentiality that may be imbedded in the differential expected real returns on assets, there is also the matter of differential risk. It seems likely that portfolios of assets containing greater degrees of financial confidentiality may also be more risky. For example, assets may have to be held directly or indirectly in certain countries, resulting in increased foreign exchange risk or country risk, or both. Or the portfolio may be forced into a configuration that is susceptible to increased interest-rate risk. Various ways of hedging risk—including the ability to diversify or to shift risk by means of futures and options markets—may not be available to portfolios subject to a high degree of confidentiality. One could argue that the degree of risk, defined as the covariance of expected future returns on the assets contained in the portfolio, will tend to increase with the confidentiality content of the portfolio.

Conventional views on the creation of "efficient" portfolios can easily be adapted to take confidentiality considerations into account. An efficient portfolio is one that maximizes investor returns, subject to a risk constraint, or minimizes risk given a particular return target. The individual's attitude toward risk, or risk-preference, together with the risks and returns available in asset markets, are the basic elements in the design of efficient portfolios. What happens when one incorporates an individual's desire for confidentiality motivated, for example, by capital-flight considerations? From the earlier discussion, the asset holder should be willing to accept a reduced rate of return or be willing to expose himself to a higher level of risk. That is, the individual will have to accept a reduced expected return or increased risk, or both. From a risk-return perspective he will be worse off. But the welfare gains from the enhanced degree of confidentiality may well outweigh the welfare losses incurred in the risk-return dimension. An optimum combination can be defined once the individual's preferences and the availability and cost of alternatives in the market are known (see Lessard, 1976 and 1983, on limits to diversification).

The basic model can be depicted quite neatly in figure 5.1. For convenience, we invert the horizontal "risk" axis to represent "safety," with a minimum-risk portfolio represented by point A on the axis, and asset covariance rising (safety declining) as one moves toward the origin. We know that asset

Figure 5.1 Confidentiality-risk-returns trade-offs and capital flight

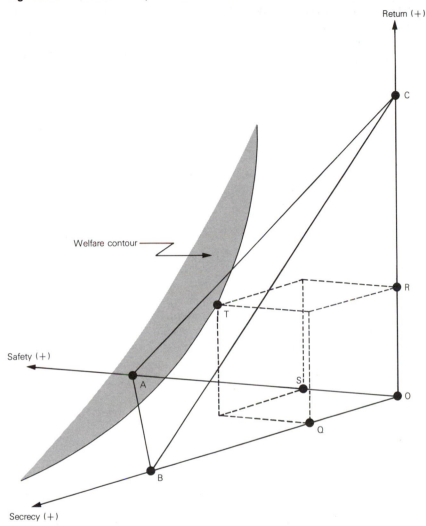

markets present the individual with a risk-return trade-off, here line AC, showing returns rising with increasing risk or decreasing safety. We also believe that these markets present a return-confidentiality trade-off, here shown as line CB, with C being the maximum attainable real portfolio returns when confidentiality plays no role whatsoever, and returns declining with increased confidentiality, perhaps eventually resulting in negative net returns to the left of B. Finally, we posit a confidentiality-risk trade-off, under the assumption that the acquisition of greater confidentiality forces the individual into a more risky selection of assets or closes off options for portfolio diversification or risk-shifting. This trade-off is shown by line AB in figure 5.1—increased confidentiality may have to be "purchased" by asset portfolios that embody a reduced degree of safety.

If we assume that all three market-determined trade-offs are linear, we can thus define the plane ABC in the three-dimensional space in figure 5.1. The individual involved in capital flight can choose any asset mix yielding a combination of safety, returns, and confidentiality that lies on the ABC plane. For example, if confidentiality plays no role whatsoever in the individual's objectives, he will want to operate along line AC at the "back edge" of the plane. Similarly, if returns are an immaterial consideration compared with safety and confidentiality, he will want to operate along the AB "edge" of the plane. If all three considerations are to be taken into account, he will want to position himself somewhere on the inside of the ABC plane.

The precise "mix" of the three attributes will be determined by the individual's preferences. We can depict the preference for safety versus returns by the shape of a contour (the shaded area in figure 5.1), which in the risk-return plane shows that the individual is willing to accept reduced safety for increased returns, but at a decreasing rate—that is, the individual is normally risk-averse. Similarly, the individual is willing to trade lower returns for increased confidentiality along the shaded contour in the secrecy-return plane, again at a decreasing rate. And he is likewise willing to trade lower levels of safety for higher levels of confidentiality along the shaded contour in the safety-secrecy plane. The shape of the three-dimensional contour itself depends on the marginal rates of substitution within the individual's preference set between each pair of objectives. The better any two objectives substitute for one another, the "flatter" the contour. The less they are regarded by the individual as substitutes, the more "convex" the contour will be to the origin at point 0.

We thus have in the shaded area in figure 5.1 a convex "preference surface" among the three objectives that defines the nature of an individual's relative preferences at a given level of welfare. If the surface lies "higher"—farther away from the origin—he will obviously be better off by being able to avail himself of more confidentiality *and* safety *and* returns. Conversely, a "lower" preference surface represents a lower level of personal welfare.

We can now complete the picture by combining the individual's confidentiality-safety-returns preference contour and the market's "supply" pattern defined by the ABC plane. Given the trade-offs dictated by the market, the individual in this example will want to obtain a level Q of confidentiality, which requires a portfolio of assets yielding S of safety and earns R of net real returns—at point T in figure 5.1, where the demand surface is just tangent to the plane representing the opportunity set. At this point the individual will maximize his welfare, given the alternatives available in the market. Of course, he could also operate with any other mix of confidentiality-safety-returns defined by the ABC plane. But any such mix would leave him worse off—i.e., on a *lower* preference contour—and consequently would make no sense. Nor could he reach a higher preference contour under existing market conditions. Point T thus represents the optimum attainable level of welfare.

How can the individual become better off and move to a higher preference contour? One way is for the market to throw off higher returns, as when global credit conditions tighten—point C is moved upward. Another is for the cost of confidentiality to decline, as when there is increased competition among vendors of assets embodying confidentiality—point B moves to the South-West. If new, less risky types of assets become available, or greater opportunities for diversification or risk-shifting present themselves, point A moves to the left. Any of these developments will raise the ABC plane and permit an increase in the individual's level of welfare—a move to a higher preference contour. Unless all three increase proportionately, however, the *shape* of the ABC plane will change as well, and hence the *mix* of safety, returns, and confidentiality will likewise be altered (the relative location of point T). Conversely, factors affecting reduced yields, confidentiality, and portfolio safety will leave the individual worse off, on a lower welfare contour.

Now suppose the ABC plane remains unchanged, but the individual's preferences shift. For example, if the asset holder's government lifts capital controls or grants an amnesty, he may no longer need the same degree of confidentiality. He would therefore operate at the tangency of AC and the preference contour, with point T moving onto line AC—he would end up better off in the risk-return dimension. If, on the other hand, the perceived benefits from confidentiality increase, point T would move to reflect a preference contour that is more "biased" in that direction than before. Similar changes in the mix would reflect an alteration in the relative preference for safety versus returns.

The acquisition of external assets in a context where confidentiality matters, on the part of individuals engaging in capital flight, can thus be thought of as a rational process—one that balances a number of perceived costs against benefits and in which perceived changes are likely to change behavior in rather predictable ways. If we assume that these asset holders are normally risk-averse, they will tend to prefer portfolios incorporating greater confidentiality together with lower covariances in expected future total returns, all else equal. That is, they will prefer rather conservative portfolios, both because of the reduced probability of disclosure and because they may be heavily and differentially exposed to risk at home.

Getting the Money Out

Having discussed the underlying motivations of those engaged in capital flight, we can now turn our attention to the specific conduits and vehicles involved. As noted earlier, the mechanisms of capital flight have two dimensions: transfer of assets, and deployment of assets. The matter of asset transfer is reasonably straightforward. In each case, the focus is on the nature of the vehicles involved and the associated costs.

Transfers via the International Payments Mechanism

Capital flight can occur via the normal channels of international payments, for example, via bank transfer from a local institution or the local affiliate of a foreign institution to a designated recipient abroad. The rate of exchange involved in such transactions may be market-determined. Alternatively, a disequilibrium rate sustained by central bank intervention may make such transfers especially attractive. Even in the presence of exchange controls, bank transfers may still be possible—though often at a less favorable exchange rate than those applicable to commercial transactions, or requiring bribes to those in charge of administering the controls.

Ordinary bank-transfer channels may not be suitable for financial assets generated from criminal activities, or those involving tax evasion, if the government has put in place a monitoring system of some sort which could lead to exposure. But for noncriminal funds, routine financial transfers as a vehicle for capital flight can be accessed easily and at low cost. Even in this case, however, an information trail may be created that could prove troublesome in the event of future changes in government policy.

Transfers via Cash Movements

If the channels of conventional interbank funds transfer are closed due to exchange controls, or appear unattractive due to cost or the possibility of disclosure, an alternative involves transfers of cash or monetary instruments payable to the bearer—most commonly domestic or foreign currency, travelers checks or cashiers checks.

Domestic currency may be taken out of the country and exchanged legally abroad for other currencies at market rates. In the absence of exchange controls (so that confidentiality is the only motive for cash as opposed to bank transfers) the rate of exchange obtained in this way may not be highly unfavorable and—even taking the chance of loss or theft into account—the transactions and information costs may be quite acceptable. Alternatively, foreign currency or other monetary instruments arising predominantly from tourist transactions may be purchased locally at prevailing exchange rates and physically transported abroad for deposit. Money laundering associated with domestic criminal activities and tax evasion from cash businesses are perhaps the most important forms of capital flight involving physical transport of currency in the absence of exchange controls, with disclosure the primary issue of concern to launderers in both cases (Bawley 1982; Tanzi 1982).

Currency movements are significant vehicles in noncriminal and nontax-related types of capital flight largely in the presence of exchange controls. Local residents purchase foreign currencies, travelers checks, and other bearer-type monetary instruments in the domestic parallel market, usually at a substantial premium over the official rate. The supply comes mainly from tourists and business travelers engaged in cash transactions seeking local goods and services at a discount in terms of foreign-currency cost. The all-in premium or discount—incorporating the chance of getting caught, the punishment involved, as well as the risk of loss or theft facing both the buyer and the seller—depends on the severity and efficiency with which the foreign exchange regulations are applied, as well as the underlying currency demand-supply relationship.

By definition, illegal currency movements involve smuggling (Koveos and Seifert 1986). Imports and exports of domestic currency are usually prohibited or severely limited for residents and nonresidents alike. Incoming nonresidents are often required to complete lengthy forms detailing possession of foreign currencies or monetary instruments. Outgoing nonresidents may be required to repeat this procedure, and any differences must be documented by receipts evidencing officially sanctioned transactions. Milder controls involve refusal to reconvert more local into foreign currency than was officially converted into local currency. A number of procedures are used. Depending on the difference between the official and parallel rates of exchange, nonresidents have an incentive to underreport foreign currencies on arrival and overreport on departure. Residents are normally limited in the amount of foreign currencies they can take out. In all cases, travelers are potentially subject to physical search, seizure, criminal sanctions, and loss through accident and theft (Bhandari and Decaluwe 1986).

Currency, travelers checks, cashiers checks, and other monetary instruments can be supplemented as capital-flight vehicles by bearer bonds and even registered securities that can be endorsed over to the buyer. These, however, generally involve greater information and transaction costs and therefore tend to be less useful in this context.

Currency movements at times seem to take on very significant proportions indeed. The US dollar appears to be the predominant vehicle currency, and Federal Reserve data and the size of reported interbank international currency transactions indicate that a significant proportion of US currency in circulation is actually held outside the United States. The media are replete with anecdotes of planeloads of cash crossing the Caribbean, suitcase-loads crossing European borders, and even hang gliders ferrying currency from French mountaintops to Swiss plains (Hector 1985).

Transfers via Precious Metals and Collectibles

As a substitute for currency movements, it may be possible to convert local currency to gold, silver or other precious metals, precious stones, jewelry, objets d'art, and similar assets that are potentially moveable abroad and which tend to hold their value in the face of domestic policies that erode the worth of monetary assets. All have for centuries served as traditional stores of value, as a "sink" for domestic savings—hidden in walls, worn as adornments and otherwise kept under the watchful eye of asset holders. They often lend themselves well to transport abroad and resale for foreign currency. The premiums involved, in relation to official exchange rates, tend to be similar to those associated with parallel-market purchases of foreign currency. Governments tend to restrict or prohibit imports and exports of any such items regarded as close substitutes for currency. Once again, international transfers usually involve smuggling. The associated costs and risks are similar to currency smuggling, and depend largely on the specific items involved.

Transfers via False Invoicing of Trade Transactions

Another standard technique of capital flight under exchange controls involves the issuance of invoices covering international trade transactions that deviate from agreed prices (Bhagwati 1964, and Gulati, ch. 3, this volume).

On the import side, the foreign supplier issues an invoice in excess of the agreed price of a product for which the buyer holds a valid import license. The buyer applies to the monetary authority for foreign-exchange authorization in the amount of the invoice and the buyer remits that amount in foreign currency to the foreign supplier—who then places the overage in an account belonging to the buyer and keeps the agreed amount, perhaps including the addition of a commission.

On the export side, the domestic seller issues an invoice for an amount in foreign currency less than the agreed price. The foreign seller places the difference (less any commission) in an account belonging to the seller and remits the invoice amount—which the seller surrenders to the monetary authority via approved channels in return for local currency at the official rate.

In both cases, false invoicing can succeed in moving flight capital from one country to another at very favorable exchange rates. From the country's perspective, of course, it creates shadow prices of traded goods or services that alter the terms of trade just as surely as a depreciation in the exchange rate. It also shifts the use of foreign exchange under the established exchange control regime from high-priority to low-priority uses. Consequently, checks are usually applied to determine arms-length prices for goods and services moving in international trade. These can be compared with invoice prices to detect over- or underinvoicing practices, which is more easily said than done for goods that are not commodities and for which pricing benchmarks are difficult or impossible to determine. It is even more difficult for services such as advertising, legal work, commissions, royalties, and fees. Consequently, some of these payments may simply be prohibited altogether. Officials in charge of checking prices present obvious targets for bribery and corruption (Gladwin and Walter 1980).

Capital flight through false invoicing is generally directly accessible only to local owners of businesses engaged in international trade, local affiliates of multinational companies, and stockholders in joint ventures who share with their foreign partners the incentive to limit distributions of local-currency earnings or to decapitalize the enterprise by moving assets abroad. It may also be indirectly accessible to linked businesses or individuals (suppliers and customers) who can themselves do transactions at off-market prices in local currency (including an implicit fee) leading to a transfer of assets abroad through false invoicing by the intermediary firm.

In certain cases, capital flight using the technique of false invoicing can be multiplied through a practice called "round tripping." Foreign-currency assets are accumulated abroad at the official exchange rate (minus transaction costs) via over- or underinvoicing. Some of these assets are then repatriated in the form of cash or other monetary instruments, which are converted back to domestic currency in the local parallel market at a premium. The gain in local currency can then form the basis for further false-invoiced transactions—in effect arbitraging the official and parallel-market exchange rates. The same thing can be achieved by individuals able to bribe exchange control authorities to agree to otherwise unauthorized disbursements at the official rate.

It is important to note that capital flight is only one motivation for transfer pricing. Others include tax avoidance or evasion as well as the common practice of setting intercompany transfer prices as a normal accounting operation in multinational firms. In the latter case, pure arms-length pricing and attribution of costs and revenues to individual products or services entering the channels of international trade may not be feasible, so that transfer prices become a necessary part of doing international business. Distinguishing this motivation from the others may be difficult or impossible for the responsible authorities.

Parallel Loans

A fourth vehicle for capital flight involves parallel lending between counterparties inside and outside the country of capital flight. As a simple example, individuals or companies A and B know and trust each other, but perceive different risk-return profiles with respect to assets held in Developmania. A lends B dollars in the United States and B lends A pesos in Developmania, agreeing to reverse the swap after a stipulated time period. B invests the dollars abroad and A invests the pesos locally. This affords B the opportunity to achieve foreign-exchange earnings, which can be retained abroad. The exchange rates and interest rates imbedded in the transaction will reflect the discount structure involved. Information and transaction costs, as well as counterparty default risk, make parallel loans a relatively difficult vehicle to access for purposes of capital flight.

Facilitators and Vehicles

We have noted that information and transaction costs as well as associated risks can be a problem in gaining access to transfer methods, investment vehicles, and alternatives in asset deployment with respect to flight capital. Information costs can be quite high, particularly for the ordinary, relatively unsophisticated investor whose knowledge about the vehicles of capital flight may be confined to the parallel currency market, and who may well be limited to holding foreign currency locally in the absence of knowledge about getting it out and investing it abroad. Indeed, information and transaction costs may account for the fact that capital flight has not in many cases been even more dramatic, particularly under conditions of virtually universal loss of confidence in domestic monetary and perhaps real assets. Many simply do not know how to get out, are afraid of getting caught, or fear loss of principal in the process.

There are, of course, facilitators. Domestic and foreign financial institutions, lawyers, accountants, airline employees, investment advisers, even government officials will variously provide information and occasionally act as couriers to make capital flight easier by either bending the rules, looking the other way, or violating the law on behalf of a client in return for a payment. In the process, a trust relationship is established which may turn out to be misplaced and lead to losses for the asset-holder—such transactions via intermediaries are highly susceptible to "agency" problems, discussed below.

It also seems clear that wealthy and well-connected individuals, as well as firms engaged in international trade, have far easier access to capital flight vehicles than do most people in the lower and middle classes and smaller domestic firms. This may be one reason why the kinds of government economic policies that most commonly trigger capital flight can have regressive income and wealth effects, and why even confiscatory national policies often seem to leave the rich very well off indeed (Overseas Development Council 1986; Rodriguez, ch. 6, this volume).

The Role of Banks

Much has been made in recent years of the role of banks as facilitators (Ayittey 1986; Henry 1986). Indeed, banks as a group constitute the most important vendors of financial services to parties engaged in capital flight. Their services include allowing unidentified clients to make deposits; allowing clients whose funds are not of foreign origin to make investments limited to foreigners; acting without power of attorney to allow clients to manage investments, or to transmit funds, on behalf of foreign-registered companies or local companies acting as conduits; participating in sequential transactions that fall just under national financial reporting thresholds; allowing telephone transfers, without written authorization, or failing to keep a record of such transfers; and entering false foreign account number destinations in wire transfers.

Banks can obviously follow careful procedures in vetting new clients, and failure to exercise due diligence could result in serious costs to the institutions themselves. But given the diversity of bank policies and practices, and the small volume of truly questionable transactions as compared to total banking volume, it is unrealistic to expect banks to devote substantial resources to filtering procedures that could reduce capital flight except in cases of obvious criminal activity.

Despite charges to the contrary (Henry 1986), banks of international standing tend to avoid direct involvement in the capital flight process itself. They generally have multiple domestic and foreign relationships with governments, public- and private-sector entities, individuals and multinational firms, and exposure, especially of illegal capital flight activities, is likely to lead to business losses greater than the prospective gains. On the other hand, all such institutions will actively solicit fiduciary and other business from individuals and institutions engaged in capital flight once the assets are safely offshore. They will also assiduously cultivate the various clients involved. In that sense they may help reduce information and transaction costs. But they will tend to stay well clear of illegal acts of capital flight. At the same time, among foreign-based financial institutions there are plenty of second-tier players and shady operators who have far fewer long-term stakes in the game, and are more than willing to turn a fast profit at the edge of the law or ethical behavior.

Portfolio Composition

Flight capital may be held in a variety of forms, covering a broad spectrum of real and financial assets. This includes bank accounts, certificates of deposit, stocks, bonds and other financial instruments, real estate, precious metals, jewelry and other collectibles. Each has unique risk, return, and confidentiality attributes that are of interest to the asset holder. They have in common the fact that they are held outside the political jurisdiction of home authorities—either onshore abroad or offshore—and thus are deemed acceptably safe from the problems at home and from unwanted disclosure.

Foreign real estate, equities, and debt instruments may provide good yield and security, but may be subject to host-country withholding taxes (unless the host country is also a tax haven) or negotiated disclosure at the request of the home country. Bearer certificates, beneficial ownership, trusts, and shell companies may provide added protection (see below).

An alternative, if somewhat narrower range of options, is provided by offshore assets. These may be held in the form of bank deposits or certificates in Eurobanking or booking centers that provide substantial exemption from taxation, although confidentiality may be eroded if deposits in offshore branches of home-country banks are involved (or foreign banks that do business domestically). Eurobonds provide another type of offshore asset. These are available in bearer form and can be purchased by individuals at retail, either on issuance or in the secondary market.

Not all types of assets involved in capital flight are available to everyone, of course. This is particularly true of some of the more interesting and complex types. Lack of information and financial sophistication, inertia, fear of getting caught, and size of transactions are some of the factors that inhibit people's access to some of the available capital flight "products." This leads to considerable market segmentation, which in turn gives rise both to constraints and profit opportunities among those who supply the vehicles for capital flight. We will review here several of the important vehicles.

Confidential Accounts

To a degree, all bank and fiduciary accounts involve a significant level of confidentiality, and all are identified by numbers. The basic idea of the classic confidential ("numbered") account is to permit current transactions to be performed by bank employees who nevertheless remain ignorant of the identity of the account holder—identified by a code, a number, or a series of letters (Chambost 1983). There are various internal numbering and control procedures used by banks, but the goal is always the same—to protect customers' identity from the bank's own employees, and to confine knowledge of that identity to a minimum number of individuals. The name of the owner is usually known only to one or two people, normally a bank director and an account manager. They alone have access to files that contain his true identity, which in turn are kept in the bank's safe and are accessible only under very restrictive conditions.

Private Agreements

A variety of structures can be used to facilitate ownership and management of assets outside deposit or fiduciary accounts of financial institutions. They usually avoid exposure to tax liability or financial controls in the country where the assets are held. A trust agreement (for example, in the form of a normal, discretionary, alternative, or disguised trust) may be used to establish the true ownership of securities or other assets registered in the name of one or more parties with whom the deed or trust has been created. In addition, an investment company may be set up that is both nonresident and tax-exempt. The latter will tend to be free of exchange control and financial reporting requirements and possibly subject to only an annual flat tax regardless of the amount of assets or profit. Examples in this category include arrangements that can be made in Switzerland and Liechtenstein involving beneficial ownership that appears in a fiduciary agreement but nowhere in the records of an official body.

Death is an obvious problem with respect to private agreements used in capital flight, due to a trade-off between confidentiality and the assurance that assets will indeed reach beneficiaries. Heirs or executors may first have to prove their own standing and the death of the principal before establishing any right to information about the assets involved. In countries with tight secrecy laws, banks will normally give only the current situation of the account (usually defined as that existing at the time of the last statement approved by the asset holder), and will oppose any attempt by the inheritors to trace past transactions. In the case of Switzerland, courts tend to consider that the right to bank confidentiality passes to the heirs (Achleitner 1981).

Shell Entities

Owners of flight capital may be able to improve the mix of returns, risk, and confidentiality by means of shell companies or captive banks. Shares in such entities are normally issued in bearer form, and no guarantees are required from the administrators. The name of the ultimate asset holder does not appear anywhere in writing, and even local attorneys who formed the company—possibly under instructions from foreign lawyers—may not know his identity. Panamanian administrators, for example, will give executive powers over a shell company to an unnamed individual without having any idea of what use is being made of the authority they have conferred. The ultimate owner of a shell company is faced with a choice between entering his own name on the executive power, or using someone else's name—in the latter case he will ultimately have to put his name to a fiduciary agreement (Chambost 1983).

A "captive bank" is an institution that exists purely for the benefit of one physical or legal person or group of people and may also take the form of a shell entity. Captive banks allow the owners to take advantage of substantial leverage in financing their activities. They can be linked to capital flight in a number of ways, both as conduits and in the management of assets. They are normally formed in tax and banking havens with tight disclosure laws, low reserve ratios, withholding tax on interest, and an absence of exchange controls. The true owner of the bank will be able to remain anonymous, if necessary. Captive banks are often set up as offshore entities, sometimes located in countries with no meaningful banking regulations whatsoever, and where all kinds of financial activities are permitted.

Bearer Securities

Securities that are sold in registered form comprise acceptable vehicles for flight capital in portfolios for which confidentiality is not a consideration or where the home countries of the issuers do not provide insight by foreign authorities. An alternative is bearer securities, notably Eurobonds, which are not registered in the name of the bondholder. Bearer bonds have long been attractive in the context of capital flight.

One example is the 1984 repeal of the US withholding tax (previously 30 percent) on interest payable on domestic bonds purchased by foreigners— a move designed to put the US capital market on a par with other financial centers while at the same time giving US private- and public-sector borrowers better access to foreign capital. Withholding had made US securities less attractive than securities issued in jurisdictions that had no withholding provisions (such as the Netherlands Antilles) or in the Eurobond market, and in jurisdictions (such as Switzerland) that rebate most or all of the tax to foreigners.

Whereas bonds in the United States can only be issued in registered form (with interest payable only to the registered owner), the bearer bonds that are common abroad (interest payable to anyone presenting a valid coupon) are obviously more attractive to investors concerned with confidentiality. The Treasury was thus caught in a bind by withholding tax repeal. Issuing bearer bonds would clearly foster tax evasion by residents of the United

States and was deemed unacceptable by a unanimous, nonbinding Senate resolution. Yet issuing registered bonds would make them unappealing to foreign investors even without the 30 percent withholding tax. So "special registered securities" were structured that require buyers to certify that they are not US residents, and the investment house must provide recertification each time interest is paid—yet without revealing the identity of the bondholder to the Treasury. Resale of such securities is made more difficult, and resale in the US market automatically precludes subsequent resale abroad.

The Principal-Agent Problem

Capital flight can generate considerable problems between the asset holder (the principal) and those responsible for establishing and maintaining the vehicles used and managing the asset portfolios themselves (the agents). Agents take on a fiduciary responsibility to carry out the principal's mandate as faithfully as possible, in return for commissions and fees that presumably reflect the value of services rendered.

An agency relationship thus exists whenever an asset-holder delegates decision-making authority, and it will involve both monitoring and bonding costs that can be either monetary or nonmonetary in nature. Divergences can occur between the agent's actual decisions and those decisions that would maximize the welfare of the principal, who will thus incur a "residual loss"—yet another cost to him of the agency relationship. Ordinarily, contracts between principals and agents provide appropriate incentives and sanctions for the agent to make decisions that will maximize the principal's welfare.

The principal-agent relationship in the presence of capital flight raises some unusual issues. Even under ordinary circumstances, interpreting and executing the principal's wishes may not be easy, especially if they change over time or the agent is poorly advised, and can lead to serious disputes. Or the agent himself may abuse his mandate by "churning" the portfolio to boost commission income, or by "stuffing" the portfolio with substandard securities he wants to unload. With capital flight the agent's role can become even more complex.

Ordinarily, agency-related disputes can be taken into court in civil suits, which then supersede private forms of dispute-settlement that have proven unsuccessful. But individuals engaged in capital flight may have difficulty taking the agent to court when a foreign legal jurisdiction is involved, when jurisdiction is unclear, or when such an action would compromise confidentiality—that is, when the suit would itself expose the act of capital flight. So the agent can acquire a certain immunity from the sort of redress usually available to asset holders confronted by agent misconduct. This in turn may tempt him to abuse his agency function, and enrich himself at the expense of the principal.

The real question is whether the shelter attributable to confidentiality and capital flight influences the behavior of the agent. On the one hand, the incentive is strong for agents to maximize their own welfare, since they are at least partially protected from retribution. In addition, asset holders involved in capital flight are fully prepared to pay even high agency costs as long as there are no unacceptable losses. On the other hand, the competition an agent faces from others and the future of his business, as well as traditions of prudence and competence, tend to impose constraints on abusive behavior. Still, this problem puts a real premium on selection of the agent, who must be depended upon to carry out his fiduciary responsibility with sensitivity to the client's often delicate circumstances without succumbing to the temptations that derive from his potential agency leverage.

Havens

Flight implies havens, and havens take the form of national states that provide an attractive range of real and financial assets to foreign-based investors, political and economic stability, a favorable tax climate for nonresidents, and various other attributes that generally are the obverse of conditions triggering capital flight in the first place. Havens take two forms. The first are countries within which assets arising from capital flight are actually held, either in direct or in beneficial ownership—the "target" countries. The second are countries that primarily serve as intermediaries or "conduits" of capital flight and support the required ownership, asset management, and confidentiality structures.

Targets

From the discussion of the interests of those engaged in capital flight, it is clear that target countries will tend to provide a favorable combination of asset safety, liquidity, yield, and confidentiality. The latter is a less important target characteristic, however, since it can be provided indirectly via one or more of the vehicles discussed in the previous section.

Countries that have large-volume, public- and private-sector issuers of securities, whether sold on domestic or international markets, will prove to be among the major targets for flight capital. With the securitization of international financial markets, these today comprise mainly the industrial countries. Given the financing needs of US corporations and the federal deficit, there is little doubt that the United States is by far the largest target country in this respect (Bhagwati et al. 1974; Ashekov 1981).

In other asset categories, such as real estate and direct participations in business enterprises, the United States is also likely to be a major target, although in the real estate area attractive opportunities are also offered by various other industrial countries that do not restrict foreign investment in this sector. Developing countries such as Paraguay have from time to time tried to position themselves as offering real estate investments for political flight capital from Western Europe, Hong Kong, and elsewhere. Especially where eventual residence and citizenship are involved, portfolio motivations underlying capital flight often become secondary to personal freedom considerations.

Conduits

The principle of national sovereignty ensures that foreigners will have limited insight into asset holdings—insight that is strictly controlled by domestic law and policy. One such safeguard is domestic bank secrecy law, which bars insight by national and foreign authorities alike. The other is the blocking statute, which effectively prevents the disclosure, copying, inspection, or removal of documents located in the host country in compliance with orders by foreign authorities (el Hadj 1979; Newcomb and Kohler 1983).

National sovereignty on the part of conduit countries is basic to capital flight vehicles, especially with respect to disclosure of information. Whereas some countries are quite willing to accommodate inquiries by foreign governments, others fiercely resist them. The view in conduit countries is that their governments cannot be held responsible for the consequences of economic or political conditions prevailing in others. And if they stand to benefit economically in the process of simply safeguarding their own sovereignty, so be it.

Countries that serve as havens for capital flight involving "criminal" behavior have a more difficult time justifying their actions on grounds of national sovereignty. But a crime may not be considered a crime unless it is committed on the territory of the haven country, which makes financial disclosure or freezing of assets associated with criminal offenses committed abroad difficult under most circumstances. An alternative position is that disclosure is warranted only if a crime committed abroad is also defined as a crime in the haven country. Here a case has to be made that the appropriate domestic due process and the associated legal tests are satisfied, which may not be easy in many instances and may be impossible in cases of simple flight capital. Even here, however, arm-twisting can be exercised if the country where the "crime" has been committed has sufficient bargaining leverage, and haven countries have on occasion been known to bend their own rules. Still, such intergovernmental leverage is in most cases unavailable to countries subject to capital flight.

Table 5.1 contains a listing of countries that would appear to be among the principal conduits for capital flight. Some of these are "functional" centers where transactions are actually undertaken and value-added is created in the design and delivery of financial services, while others are "booking" centers, where transactions are recorded but the value-added involved is actually created elsewhere (Senate Committee on Governmental Affairs 1983). Switzerland and Panama are cited here as interesting examples of functional conduits.

Switzerland

Placement of flight capital with institutions in Switzerland is encouraged by the basic competence and integrity of Swiss bankers, the credit standing of their institutions, and their position in the international banking community; the wide range of financial services that Swiss institutions can provide for clients; the liquidity and stability characteristics of assets denominated in Swiss francs, the freedom from exchange controls, government regulations and interference in banking activities; virtually unparalleled political stability; and tight financial secrecy laws.

In 1985 Switzerland had one bank for each 1,250 inhabitants (compared with 6,000 in the United States), and a financial sector that employed over 100,000 people (3 percent of the labor force) and generated Sw F 6 billion in tax revenues and Sw F 15 billion in net current account earnings. Financial institutions had estimated foreign deposits of Sw F 230 billion in 1984, and up to Sw F 1.6 trillion in fiduciary accounts. Swiss capital exports in 1985 amounted to Sw F 46 billion (*Economist* 1986).

Since no information is available on the geographic distribution of Swiss international financial flows, the country's role as a conduit for flight capital is impossible to pinpoint. Swiss financial institutions certainly cannot be considered guilty of encouraging or advocating the underlying activities that give rise to capital flight, although the country's position as a conduit nevertheless leaves it open to charges of aiding and abetting such flows. Swiss "guidance" of political flight capital is alleged to be substantial, particularly through overseas branches. For their part, Swiss institutions point to excessive taxation and irresponsible macroeconomic policies in other countries as the primary causes of capital flight. They maintain that they do not actively solicit funds that arise from evading either taxes or

Table 5.1 Preliminary inventory of capital flight conduits

Caribbean and South Atlantic	Europe, Middle East, Africa
Antigua	Austria
Bahamas	Bahrain
Barbados	Channel Islands
Belize	Gibraltar
Bermuda	Isle of Man
British Virgin Islands	Liberia
Cayman Islands	Liechtenstein
Costa Rica	Luxembourg
Falkland Islands	Monaco
Grenada	Netherlands
Montserrat	Switzerland
Anguilla	
Netherlands Antilles	*Asia-Pacific*
Nevis	Cook Islands
Panama	Guam
St. Kitts	Hong Kong
St. Lucia	Maldives
St. Vincent	Nauru
Turks and Caicos Islands	Vanuatu
	Singapore

Source: Ingo Walter, *Secret Money* (London: George Allen & Unwin, 1986).

currency controls, that they have no obligation to collect other people's taxes, and that in any case financial nondisclosure is hardly airtight in investigations of offenses that are defined as being criminal in nature under Swiss law.

They also point to the Convention of Diligence, a private agreement between the Swiss National Bank and the Swiss Bankers' Association, which prohibits signatories from doing business without knowledge of the identity of the counterparty—whether such business involves accepting cash or securities deposits, fiduciary activities, or the use of safe-deposit boxes— as well as withdrawals by clients of amounts in excess of Sw F 500,000. Clients may still avoid registering their names with a bank by having a professional lawyer, trustee, or auditor do it for them, but this individual must declare that he knows the principal personally and is not aware of any abuse of financial secrecy for criminal purposes. Only banks, and not the bankers themselves, can be punished under the Convention (Swiss National Bank 1985).

A number of arrangements for cooperation in legal matters have been concluded between Switzerland and other countries since World War II, focusing mainly on the concept of "bilateral culpability," which means that the activity under scrutiny must be a crime in Switzerland itself to fall under the terms of applicable legal assistance conventions. More recently, cooperation has been extended to capital flows involved in insider trading cases and misappropriation of funds by foreign public officials where official requests are received from the foreign governments concerned. The latter was "stretched" somewhat by the preemptive freezing of the Marcos assets in 1986, undertaken in the light of the confused political situation at the time in Manila (Tagliabue 1986). But the role of Switzerland as a solid conduit for flight capital remains largely intact.

Panama

Over the years, the Caribbean has become an area abundantly supplied with conduits. The reasons include proximity to both the United States and the major sources of flight capital in Latin America, country-risk profiles supported by important US political and economic interests in the region, and the ease of communication with the rest of the world. Panama is probably the only "functional" conduit in the region and has become the most widely used financial haven in the Western Hemisphere. Its position is bolstered by a Latin business culture and a special treaty that establishes the US dollar as legal tender on a par with the Panamanian colon. The country's secrecy laws are so tight that the banking authorities themselves are denied the right to audit deposits (Lessard and Tschoegl 1985).

Panama has statutes that facilitate the formation of shell companies, which can be created within a few hours or are held already formed and "on the shelf" by local law firms. In this way, an existing company can be bought for a small transfer fee from attorneys who create and hold these "vintage" shells. The exact number of registered Panamanian companies appears to be unknown, even to the government. The cost of establishing and maintaining shell companies is trivial.

There is no mechanism for policing offshore activities by Panamanian-registered companies. Any inquiries or complaints about an offshore company can be brought to the attention of the Ministry of Commerce, but this will only reveal the name of the company's registered local agent. There can be no release of information if the alleged crimes are not committed in Panama itself. Thus, the secrecy statutes in Panama and the fundamental territorial thrust of its criminal law go a long way in protecting asset-holders from disclosure and prosecution.

Panama has embarked on a policy of national development wherein the financial services industry is a central element. The banking sector in 1984 accounted for about 9 percent of GNP, employing over 8,000 people, with an annual growth rate during the early 1980s of 22 percent—compared with an overall national economic growth rate of 3 percent to 4 percent. Assets of Panama's banking system in 1983 amounted to about $49 billion with 130 banks, mostly branches of established international institutions. About one-third of the Panamanian banks are affiliates of Latin American institutions.

Prior to the creation of an offshore banking center in 1970, 241 "banks" operated in Panama. Through a weeding-out process, this number was initially cut to only 20, followed by a dramatic resurgence. The authorities still prefer to license only major international banks already headquartered in responsible foreign countries. They tend to reject applications from banks headquartered elsewhere in the Caribbean—as well as those from major banks' subsidiaries if these in turn are located in the Caribbean. A requirement of $250,000 paid-in capital precludes brass-plate banks. Nevertheless, because of US concern with the safety and soundness of Panamanian banks—a concern that was heightened by the failure of the Banco de Ultramar in late 1983—regulators have been reluctant to allow US institutions to participate in new Panamanian banks (Guttentag and Herring 1984). Nor have the strict licensing requirements for new banks prevented some already licensed institutions from engaging in highly questionable activities, including in particular money laundering for the drug trade.

Criminal activities may frighten away ordinary flight capital, with asset holders concerned that a Panamanian connection will be taken as presumptive evidence of criminal involvement. They also place a greater burden on the Panamanian authorities to restrict the use of shell companies with phony financial statements to defraud investors abroad. Progress by Panama in cleaning up its financial institutions will not, however, compromise its role as a conduit for some types of flight capital.

If there are national economic gains for the conduits of capital flight, then there will also be competition among countries that provide these services. The competitive variables will again comprise some combination of returns (including performance in portfolio management), risk associated both with asset deployment and with the conduit and its institutions, and confidentiality. Particularly the latter tends to be vigorously protected by conduit countries, since its perceived erosion will quickly drive flight capital away. New and innovative confidentiality attributes are eagerly sought after, although in most cases they cannot be created overnight, and marketing them can pose a difficult problem. A competitive hierarchy clearly exists, with very significant gains going to the preeminent, established functional centers and rather limited benefits accruing at the more highly competitive "booking" end of the market.

Returns on flight capital in forms such as bank interest, bond yields, rents, royalties, and capital gains are set by broad market forces that extend well beyond those engaged in capital flight. As discussed earlier, these returns may well impose an opportunity cost on asset holders—particularly if confidentiality is a major consideration—yet still be higher than the returns they would have sacrificed in order to succeed in capital flight. They thus enjoy a form of consumer surplus. Vehicles and instruments specifically geared to the capital flight market (confidential bank or fiduciary accounts, for example) may involve substantially higher opportunity costs, and hence a smaller surplus. Yet even these are largely list-priced. This is not the case with custom-tailored financial services for those engaged in capital flight, whose prices are set largely by bargaining. The vendor tries to ascertain how much his product is worth, given the apparent motivations of the client, and adjusts his asking price accordingly, drawing off some of the consumer surplus in the process.

Supply and demand thus interact in the markets for financial and other services provided to those involved in capital flight, just as they do in any other market. A hierarchy of differentiated vehicles and conduits exists, each with its own characteristics. The greater the demand, the higher the price. The more intense the competition among vendors and the easier the substitutability of capital flight products, the lower the price.

A few vendors have products with no good substitutes, so that demand for them may well be quite inelastic and their sellers are able to command high prices. Some traditional capital flight vehicles are easily available in some places but less so elsewhere. Others have been built up over the generations as secure repositories and can command high premiums. But high premiums also attract competitors, whose entry may alter the structure of the market. It is safe to say that higher levels of confidentiality, competence in financial management, and safety involve successively greater degrees of monopoly power in the definition of competitive structure and market organization of services catering to international flight capital.

Summary and Conclusions

Given the motives underlying capital flight, the vehicles that have emerged to serve the needs of asset holders are rather predictable. They must supply some combination of yield, safety, and confidentiality that is consistent with these motives, which can vary significantly from one case to the next and through time. Investors are willing to pay for the services required to undertake capital flight, in the form of lower yields or increased transaction costs or suboptimal portfolio selections, and this provides profit opportunities for individuals and institutions that provide capital flight vehicles. Governments responsible for the vendors tend to be on much the same wavelength, depending on the importance of the capital-flight business in generating real economic gains in the form of employment, income, and fiscal revenues. Any form of discretionary disclosure, reduced safety, reduced yield, or asset mismanagement will damage the value of what they have to sell.

Much has been made of "irresponsible" behavior among vendors of financial services catering to flight capital. This implies that they generate serious negative externalities, a charge that may well be justified in activities that facilitate the drug trade, organized crime, and political subversion. But what we generally understand to be capital flight is for the most part a symptom rather than a cause—a symptom of costs and risks imposed by governments on their own people. Designing and selling capital flight vehicles is a business, like any other, and irresponsible national economic policies give value to that business.

A variety of programs have been proposed to deal with ordinary capital flight (other than criminal flows and tax evasion). These include amnesties, "whitener" securities to encourage a return of capital, tightened exchange controls, and negotiated disclosure of foreign-held assets. Many exhibit an underlying contempt for human ingenuity, and some would do great damage to the role of privacy as part of individual freedom. None attack the fundamentals of the problem, the lack of confidence among asset holders—foreign or domestic—of a competitive risk-adjusted rate of return. Policies that restore such confidence alone attack the causes of capital flight.

References

Achleitner, Paul M. 1981 *Das Bankgeheimnis in Oesterreich, Deutschland und der Schweiz.* Vienna: Oesterreichisches Forschungsinstitut fuer Sparkassenwesen.

Ashekov, Nicholas. 1981. "Will Hot Money Spoil Miami?" *Institutional Investor* (September).

Ayittey, George B.N. 1986. "The Real Foreign Debt Problem." *Wall Street Journal,* 8 April.

Bawley, Dan. 1982. *The Subterranean Economy.* New York, NY: McGraw-Hill.

Bhagwati, Jagdish. 1964. "The Underinvoicing of Imports." *Bulletin of the Oxford University Institute of Statistics,* no. 2.

Bhagwati, Jagdish; Anne Krueger, and Chaiyawat Wibulswasdi. 1974. "Capital Flight from LDCs: A Statistical Analysis." In *Illegal Transactions in International Trade,* edited by J.N. Bhagwati. Amsterdam: North Holland.

Bhandari, Jagdeep S. and Bernard Decaluwe. 1986. "A Framework for the Analysis of Legal and Fraudulent Trade Transactions in 'Parallel' Exchange Markets." *Weltwirtschaftliches Archiv,* Fasc. 3.

Blum, R.H. 1981. "Offshore Money Flows: A Large Dark Number." *Journal of International Affairs* (Spring/Summer).

Chambost, Eduard 1983. *Bank Accounts: A World Guide to Confidentiality.* London: John Wiley.

Economist. 1986. "The Swiss Economy: A Survey," 6 September.

Gladwin, Thomas and Ingo Walter. 1980. *Multinationals Under Fire.* New York, NY: John Wiley & Sons.

Guttentag, Jack and Richard Herring. 1984. "Disclosure Policy and International Banking." The Wharton School, University of Pennsylvania (summer).

el Hadj, Elie. 1979. "The Economics of an Offshore Banking Center." *Euromoney* (September).

Hector, Gary. 1985. "Nervous Money Keeps on Fleeing." *Fortune,* 23 December.

Henry, James S. 1986. "Third World Debt Hoax: Where the Money Went." *New Republic,* 14 April.

Koveos, Peter E. and Bruce Seifert. 1986. "Market Efficiency, Purchasing Power Parity, and Black Markets: Evidence from Latin American Countries." *Weltwirtschaftliches Archiv,* Fasc. 3.

Lessard, Donald R. 1976. "World, Country, and Industry Relationships in Equity Returns: Implications for Risk Reduction Through International Diversification." *Financial Analysts Journal* (Jan.–Feb.).

————. 1983. "Principles of International Portfolio Selection." In *International Finance Handbook* edited by Ian H. Giddy and Abraham George. New York, NY: John Wiley & Sons.

Lessard, Donald R. and Adrian E. Tschoegl. 1985. "Panama's International Banking Center: Where Does It Stand and What Can be Done to Insure Its Continued Viability and Its Contribution to the Panamanian Economy?" USAID, January. Processed.

Newcomb, D. and A. Kohler. 1983. *Coping with Secrecy and Blocking Laws.* New York, NY: Shearman & Sterling.

Overseas Development Council. 1986. "Third World Capital Flight: Who Gains and Who Loses?" *ODC Policy Focus,* no. 5.

Ramirez-Rojas, C.L. 1985. "Currency Substitution in Argentina, Mexico and Uruguay" IMF *Staff Papers,* March.

Swiss National Bank. *Das Schweizerische Bankwesen.* Zurich: Swiss National Bank, various years.

Tagliabue, John. 1986. "The Swiss Stop Keeping Secrets." *New York Times,* 1 June.

Tanzi, Vito. 1982. *The Underground Economy in the United States and Abroad.* Lexington, Mass.: D.C. Heath.

Walter, Ingo. 1985. *Secret Money.* London: George Allen & Unwin.

US Congress, Senate, Committee on Governmental Affairs, Permanent Subcommittee on Investigations. 1983. *Staff Study on Crime and Secrecy: The Use of Offshore Banks and Companies.* Washington.

6

Consequences of Capital Flight for Latin American Debtor Countries

Miguel A. Rodriguez F.

External shocks and expansionist policies resulting in excessive absorption are a very limited part of the story behind the huge increase in Latin American external debt since the mid-1970s. For three of the four largest Latin debtors, at least half the increase in gross external debt ended up financing private capital flight.

This paper summarily deals with the consequences for debtor countries of this massive exportation of savings. The general conclusion is that, unlike the countries that allocated the borrowed funds to productive investment, those that used them to finance capital flight promoted a mechanism of regressive income redistribution, a structural disequilibrium in the public sector, and a process of transnationalization of domestic capital that dangerously hinder their development prospects.

We begin by laying out some facts. Then, after briefly discussing the causes of capital flight, we turn to explore its consequences for the source countries.

Some Facts

The balance of payments accounts provide the evidence on the relationship between external debt accumulation and capital flight. Table 6.1 shows the increase in gross external debt and in foreign direct investment for the four

The author, a Visiting Fellow at the Institute, is Professor of Economics at the Instituto de Estudios Superiores de Administración, Venezuela.

He is grateful to Felipe Pazos for many useful discussions on the subject, and to Asdrúbal Baptista, Gustavo García, Ricardo Hausmann, Janet Kelly, Nelson Ortíz, and Jaime Sabal, who also provided helpful suggestions.

Table 6.1   Components of the increase in gross external debt, 1974–83
(billion dollars)

		Increase in gross external debt	Current account deficit	Direct investment	Increase in reserves and other public sector assets	Capital flight[a]
Argentina	1976–77	2.6	−1.9	n.a.	3.4	1.1
	1978–82	31.0	10.7	2.5	−0.8	23.6
Brazil	1974–77	19.6	23.8	5.6	0.5	0.9
	1978–82	51.2	57.5	10.4	−3.3	7.4
Mexico	1976–77	8.8	2.7	1.2	−0.3	7.6
	1978–82	64.0	31.0	8.3	−0.5	41.8
Venezuela	1974–78	13.2 (10.5)[b]	−0.2	−1.0	9.6	2.8
	1979–83	19.8 (15.0)[b]	−9.3	0.7	−0.1	29.9

n.a. not available.
Source: IMF (various years), Frenkel-Fanelli (1986), Barros de Castro (1985), Diaz-Carneiro (1985), Ros (1985), and Rodríguez (1985).
a. These figures of capital flight may underestimate or overestimate the phenomenon. First, they do not take into account the accumulation of interest and profits that foreign assets produce abroad, since balance of payments data usually do not include these items as part of national income. This unrecorded income would therefore reduce the current account deficit and so increase the residual, capital flight. Smuggling, other nonrecorded imports, overinvoicing, and underinvoicing may further distort the data. See the importance of this for Argentina and Mexico in the text.
b. The numbers in parentheses are increases in public sector external debt.

largest Latin American debtors,[1] the size of current account deficits, the accumulation of international reserves, and the acquisition of foreign assets by the private sector.[2] For Argentina, Mexico, and Venezuela, the bulk of the borrowed funds financed, in the aggregate, an outflow of private capital. In Brazil, to the contrary, the increase in indebtedness had as a counterpart the large current account deficits that were experienced after 1974.

In Argentina, the upsurge of external debt took place in the 1978–82 period. Although the current account deficit during those years was about $11 billion, gross debt rose by more than $30 billion. Given the level of direct foreign investment and the fact that there was no accumulation of

1. Although one could show the numbers for Latin America as a whole, the four largest debtors account for more than 80 percent of the regional debt, and probably a larger percentage of capital flight.

2. The calculation of capital flight involved subtracting the current account deficit, plus the accumulation of reserves and other public-sector dollar assets, from the increase in debt and direct investment.

international reserves, this would have allowed capital flight of more than $23 billion. However, Frenkel and Fanelli (1986) estimate the outflow of private capital for the same period to be in the range of $15 billion to $20 billion. They point out that the official current account deficits underestimate the import bill, among other reasons because of the large unrecorded armament purchases (for as much as $7 billion according to some estimates; see Dornbusch [1984a]). In any case, more than half of the Argentine debt accumulation from 1978 to 1982 had capital flight as a counterpart. This phenomenon was insignificant in Argentina until the financial liberalization after 1978.

In Mexico, the situation is similar: the increase in debt was well above the excess of absorption over output. Capital flight has been persistent in Mexico, although most of it took place during the heavy borrowing of 1978–82.[3]

In Venezuela, the entire debt ended up financing capital flight. As can be seen from the data, this country accumulated a current account surplus of close to $10 billion between 1974 and 1983. This makes Venezuela a net creditor with the rest of the world, so the accumulation of gross debt was exceeded by the increase in foreign asset holdings of nationals. In particular, public external liabilities allowed in the end the acquisition abroad of even larger private assets. There is a sharp difference, however, between what happened during the periods 1974–78 and 1979–83. In the first period, this "exportation of financial intermediation" took place within the same public sector, with the funds borrowed by the nonoil state enterprises financing the accumulation of international reserves by the central bank and dollar assets by the Venezuelan Investment Fund (FIV) and the oil industry (PDVSA). In fact, as shown in table 6.1, the increase in gross public external debt in 1974–78, of about $10.5 billion, had as a counterpart an increase in reserves and other public sector assets of $9.6 billion, while capital flight was relatively minor. The latter developed with extraordinary strength in 1979–83, when the total increase in external debt of some $20 billion, plus the large current account surplus of more than $9 billion, financed outflows of private capital close to $30 billion in the aggregate. As we shall discuss below, the consequences of these two types of exportation of financial intermediation are considerably different.

Brazil was the only one of the largest Latin debtors that used its borrowed funds essentially to finance current account deficits after 1974. The outflow of private capital was barely 10 percent of the total increase in gross debt.

---

3. As in Argentina, the official estimates seem to underestimate the current account deficit in Mexico, leading to an overestimation of private capital outflows. Estimates by Jaime Ros (1985) of private acquisition of dollar assets for 1978–82 are close to $30 billion, which would give a ratio between gross debt and the private dollar portfolio similar to that of Argentina.

This opens a potentially wide gap between the medium- and long-term growth possibilities of Brazil vis-à-vis Venezuela, Argentina, and Mexico.

Causes of Capital Flight

Capital flight is commonly attributed to a number of factors, among them: overvaluation of the exchange rate, financial repression translating into negative real interest rates, fiscal deficits, tax evasion, risk factors, and external incentives provided by foreign banks and governments (Khan and Ul Haque 1987; ch. 4, this volume).

The recent history of the three largest Latin American exporters of private capital suggests that open overvaluation in an environment of free convertibility, together with a downturn in economic activity, were at the root of the huge outflow of funds that took place from these countries after 1978. In Brazil, on the contrary, where capital flight was minor, exchange rate policy generally avoided open overvaluation, and tight exchange controls were always in place.[4]

Fiscal deficits, though common for Mexico and Argentina, were not a problem in Venezuela, where the public sector accumulated a financial surplus from 1974 to 1983. Brazil, on the other hand, despite a large fiscal deficit, experienced little flight.

Risk factors, tax havens, and financial investment incentives in the industrial countries, though powerful incentives for shifting funds abroad when poor exchange rate and macroeconomic policies are in place, do not seem to be very important when the macro fundamentals are respected, especially when complemented with the additional safety of exchange controls.

We next briefly survey the capital flight experience of Argentina, Mexico, and Venezuela. The contrast to the Brazilian case makes clear the procyclical character of the phenomenon. The importance of the motives listed above in stimulating the huge outflow of capital from those countries since the late 1970s is also apparent.

Argentina

The most notable characteristic of the indebtedness process in Argentina is that it took place in the midst of stagnation of real economic activity: the

---

4. In Korea, which shares with Brazil a record of high growth, proper use of debt, and little capital flight, the exchange rate policy was also characterized by maintenance of equilibrium and exchange controls.

excess of absorption over current income explained perhaps only half the total increase in debt. Most of the debt was accumulated after 1978, as a consequence of maintaining a policy of financial and commercial liberalization that based the control of inflation on a gross overvaluation of the peso. The period prior to the financial and commercial reforms, namely 1976–77, featured a relatively strong external sector in combination with an upsurge in economic growth, as well as the accumulation of $5 billion in foreign exchange reserves. Since inflation was intractable in an economy with widespread indexation, in 1978 the government implemented an anti-inflationary plan that, relying on the relatively easy external situation, was characterized by: the preannouncing of the rate of exchange devaluation and increases in public-sector prices well below inflation; the opening of the economy by liberalizing imports and lowering tariffs; and financial liberalization involving the elimination of credit restrictions and exchange controls (Frenkel and Fanelli 1986, p. 2).

The main objective of the Martinez de Hoz Plan—the reduction of the inflation rate to the preset "tablita" levels—was never achieved, and the consequence was a severe overvaluation that sharply raised expectations of devaluation. In these circumstances, in 1980, the private sector began briskly to shift funds abroad. This process stopped only with the onset of the Malvinas Conflict, the reestablishment of full exchange controls, and the closing of the international capital market to Argentina.[5]

Mexico

The Mexican case is very like the Argentine one, in that the exchange rate became so grossly overvalued following financial liberalization that massive capital flight was the only possible consequence. In contrast to events in Argentina, the upsurge in debt took place in a period of explosive economic growth (1978–80), following the extraordinary increase in oil income after 1978–79. The favorable oil shock was partially offset, however, by a sharp increase in the world interest rate, given that the country was already a very large debtor by 1978 (Ros 1985; Frieden 1986). This, matched by a substantial increase in public spending after 1978, produced a huge fiscal gap that had as a counterpart a significant current account deficit. The acceleration of inflation, accompanied by a passive exchange rate policy, led to an open overvaluation of the peso by 1980–81. Against this background, the Mexican private sector, with a long tradition as capital exporter to the United States,

---

5. Besides the extreme financial instability created by the overvaluation and liberalization, the consequences on the real side of the economy were staggering, with GNP collapsing more than 10 percent between 1980 and 1982. See Dornbusch (1984b) and Frenkel and Fanelli (1986).

started an unprecedented attack on the peso in early 1981 that sent more than $20 billion abroad in a year and a half.[6]

Faced with serious trouble in the external sector, in February 1982 the government tried an orthodox policy package that included deep cuts in public spending and a massive devaluation while maintaining free convertibility. The results were recession, the acceleration of inflation, and a stepping up of capital flight. Since the current account deficit was sharply reduced during the year, capital flight became the main source of external imbalance, culminating in August with the depletion of all foreign exchange reserves, a moratorium, and the onset of the international debt crisis. In September, the Mexican government nationalized the banks and adopted full exchange controls.

Venezuela

The background for capital flight in Venezuela was also one of blatant overvaluation and free convertibility. However, there are some interesting peculiarities.

In the first place, although more than 80 percent of the increase in external debt was public, more than half of the current account *surplus* of $9.3 billion accumulated from 1974 to 1983 was also public (Rodríguez 1985). Contrary to what happened in Mexico and Argentina, where the fiscal deficits partially explained the current account deficits and thus partially determined the increase in the public external debt, in Venezuela the existence of a public-sector surplus during the period of debt accumulation made the public sector a substantial net creditor of the private sector. In fact, while government was the largest supplier of financial funds for private investment, the state enterprises had to borrow abroad to finance their investment projects. The financial resources of the private sector liberated by this peculiar dynamic of intersectoral savings flows allowed the latter the huge acquisition of assets abroad during 1981–83, when the economic situation made this propitious.

The Venezuelan case also shows the procyclical character of capital flows. During the period of explosive growth in 1974–78, the increase in the public debt all went to finance the accumulation of foreign exchange reserves, capital flight was minor, and the private sector invested at record levels in a booming economy. Moreover, the external debt did not pose any burden, since its service was guaranteed by the external assets accumulated by the same public sector (in fact, up to 1979 the interest earned on the public-

---

6. For an excellent account of the Mexican crisis, see Ros (1985).

sector dollar assets was larger than the interest payments needed to service the public external debt: Rodríguez 1985).

In contrast, when, in 1979—despite the second boom in oil prices—the new government started to implement contractionary policies, private investment collapsed, and private domestic savers hurriedly started to shift their wealth abroad. To be sure, this tendency was fueled in 1981, when the central bank kept fixed nominal interest rates well below international levels with the explicit aim of promoting a loss of reserves and, thus, a decrease in inflationary pressure in the economy. The policy absurdity was staggering. When interest rates were freed in mid-1981, capital flight stopped until early 1982. Then, the worsening situation in the oil market and open real appreciation sharply raised expectations of devaluation. This ignited a massive speculative attack on the bolivar that stopped only in February 1983, after all liquid reserves had been depleted and the government had temporarily closed the exchange market. In the meantime, the real problem of the Venezuelan external debt evolved, since the public external liabilities were no longer offset by public dollar assets, but ended having as a counterpart private holdings of assets abroad.

Brazil

The historical experience of Brazil has been unique. Since 1974, this country has implemented highly heterodox policies aimed at eliminating the enormous structural disequilibrium suffered by its external sector after the first oil shock. The centerpiece of these policies was an increase in public and private investment in tradables, to create the capacity to expand the medium- and long-run production of exportables and importables (especially oil). This is precisely what has been happening since 1984, when Brazil began to generate huge trade surpluses, allowing both full service of its external debt and high growth.

To accomplish this structural change, Brazil required a significant investment effort in energy, petrochemicals, minerals, heavy industry, and infrastructure, which it financed through external borrowing until 1982. The continuity of a competitive exchange rate policy, avoiding real appreciation and maintaining tight exchange controls, was also a central element of this externally oriented growth policy that prevented any significant capital flight.[7] The implementation of an aggregate demand policy aimed at promoting high growth during most of the post-1974 period was fundamental

---

7. The effectiveness of exchange controls in dampening capital flight is illustrated by the Brazilian experience. When growth slackened and overvaluation became apparent after 1980, capital flight continued to be relatively minor. See Barros and Pires (1985).

in inducing the Brazilian private sector to remain closely tied to the country and to invest internally, as well as maintaining foreign investment.

Not surprisingly, despite the severe external shocks of two sharp hikes in oil prices and the big increase in world interest rates on its large stock of accumulated debt, Brazil can stand the challenge of economic growth because of its characteristics not shared by the other heavily indebted Latin American countries.

Consequences of Capital Flight for Developing Countries

The great effort of capital accumulation needed for economic development generally faces a savings constraint, especially in countries of relatively low per capita income. For this reason, developing countries (including those already industrialized) have usually been net capital importers, to provide themselves with the saving and foreign-exchange flows needed to have enough income to achieve a process of self-sustained growth.

Capital flight is a perverse exportation of domestic savings and foreign exchange that, given the insufficiency of both in low-income countries, has consequences that may severely hinder their potential for growth. The first consequence is, precisely, the intensification of the shortage of foreign exchange and savings to finance investment in development projects. This weakens the growth of potential GNP, national income, and employment, and creates an inflationary bias if the countries that suffer from this export of national savings fail to scale back their investment efforts accordingly.

When capital flight is financed by external borrowing, the negative consequences multiply. Had the massive capital flight from Argentina, Mexico, and Venezuela been avoided with appropriate macroeconomic policies and controls à la Korea or Brazil, the effective net burden of these countries' external debt would be significantly less. Argentina's and Mexico's net external debt would be around $20 billion and $50 billion, respectively; Venezuela's, close to nil. For Latin America as a whole, Dìaz-Alejandro (1985) estimated private external assets at half the external debt. This means that the continent's direct cost of capital flight has been a rough doubling of the debt burden. Had it been avoided, the prospects for Latin America's future growth would be extraordinarily greater, even under the hostile external environment that has surrounded the region since 1982.

Income Distribution Effects

The worsening of the foreign-exchange constraint is not the only or even the most distressing consequence of capital flight. The income and wealth distributional effects are especially pernicious. Think for a moment of the Venezuelan case, where the external debt was entirely used to finance the acquisition of foreign assets by the private sector. The balance between gainers and losers has a very strong distributional bias, since the private agents with access to subsidized foreign exchange who transferred part of their wealth abroad have made extraordinary capital gains. Ownership of an external asset portfolio is, indeed, a privilege reserved only for the wealthiest in a developing country. The increasing external wealth accumulation of the few has been made possible by the massive external indebtedness of the public sector, which, after substantial real devaluations, has become impoverished proportionally. But, who pays for these public-sector losses? The gargantuan debt has to be serviced. Hence, to the wealth transferred to dollar-asset holders, has to be added the cost of an enormous income distribution from the bolívar income earners to the few who earn interest in dollars. In fact, the bulk of Venezuela's interest bill to banks for debt service ends up as interest, rent, and profit income for Venezuelans who hold assets abroad. Foreign banks just act as financial intermediaries between domestic agents. The forced savings needed to achieve the real resource transfer required by the debt service are possible only by the depression of real economic activity and real wages.

Indeed, we are witnessing a regressive redistributional mechanism massively transferring resources from workers and firms with bolívar income to the few possessing assets abroad. The same process has been going on in Argentina, Mexico, and, for that matter, in any other country that has financed capital flight with debt.

The ultimate implications of this redistributive process are complex. But, besides ethical considerations, some macroeconomic consequences stand out clearly. In the first place, having a highly regressive character, this redistributive effect weakens the internal market. The real wage and income deterioration affecting most of the population surpasses by far the real requirements of competitiveness for the external sector. This translates into an excessive contraction of private consumption and aggregate demand as a whole, which has direct repercussions on real production and employment.

Although the impact on national income is obviously lower, since part of it comes to originate abroad as returns on private external assets, a net welfare loss results from the loss of macroeconomic efficiency. This is due to the generation and accumulation of part of that income abroad: it is to be expected that internal investment would have social returns considerably higher in the source than in the recipient country.

Fiscal Effects

An important characteristic of the process of debt accumulation in countries beset by capital flight was the generation of a structural fiscal deficit that is not a product of excess public spending, but rather of the role played by the public sector in the indebtedness process and in the de-dollarization of private debt.

The government facilitated the capital flight by selling foreign exchange at privileged prices, while simultaneously borrowing abroad to sustain the overvalued exchange rate. When the funds were borrowed by the private sector, the liabilities were eventually made public by various mechanisms: for example, servicing the debt at the old parity after devaluation, or the erosion of private liabilities that took place in Argentina via acceleration of inflation while simultaneously fixing interest rates.

To the subsidized selling of foreign exchange and the ex post socialization of the private debt,[8] one should add other financial and nonfinancial subsidies that the government provided to private agents. The Venezuelan case is again archetypical in this respect. The public external debt was not a product of excesses of public investment over saving, since as already mentioned, the public sector generated a surplus in the period of debt accumulation (1974–83). Nevertheless, the government was the great financier (at very low interest rates) of the private sector's vast investment plans which, given government generosity, used very little of its own resources to finance its investments. The funds thus liberated were placed in financial assets, largely dollar assets held abroad. Even when government did not supply the finance, the firms borrowed abroad with the expectation of cheap dollars for repayment, while their owners quietly sent their substantial profits abroad. A large private net debt to the state also resulted, but the whole affair represented a huge financial transfer to the private sector, exacerbated because clumsy bankruptcy provisions and company laws with lax equity requirements made private liabilities partially worthless for the public sector.

The cost of the external debt, its socialization, and the vast transfers directed to the private sector opened a wide fiscal gap that the government has tried to close in all countries through reductions in public investment and social spending. Despite the "success" obtained in this direction, the gap is too wide to be feasibly filled by such a contraction in spending. Thus, besides the reduction in the level of real economic activity, one has to add the generation of a structural public-sector deficit, which is the transmission mechanism of the regressive redistribution of income and wealth in favor of the most privileged sectors of society.

Part of the distributive injustice resulting from capital flight, and the subsequent fiscal disequilibrium created with it, could have been avoided by application of the "capitalist rules of the game." After the sharp

---

8. About which the private sector seems to have always had very rational expectations.

devaluations needed at the outset of the crisis, these rules would have indicated bankruptcy proceedings for firms unable to service their debts, with other entrepreneurs, foreign or local (including governments), putting back to work the physical assets under new and more efficient management.[9] In fact, however, the "perfect foresight" of local entrepreneurs led them to borrow heavily abroad via their firms, while transferring their own wealth to external assets, convinced that the capitalist solution would never have a chance.

Another way of reducing the intensity of the distributive conflict and the fiscal deficit would be by the implementation of tax reforms affecting the top level of the income and wealth distribution. However, one of the bases of the vicious circle involving debt, stagnation, and more debt appears firmly established in countries like Argentina, Mexico, and Venezuela: capital flight is an extraordinary channel for tax evasion. The increasingly important part of the national income of these countries that is generated abroad (up to 15 percent in the Venezuelan case) as rents of the wealthiest segments of society does not bear any tax burden, neither from the source countries nor from the recipient countries which have become "tax havens."

Almost all external debt is public, since most private debt has been assumed by the public sector (often due to pressures from foreign banks and governments). In contrast, private external assets have remained private and are granted absolute protection and secrecy. Besides not reporting the interest income and profits earned by Latin American residents, foreign banks and governments have created various incentives to stimulate capital flight, and thus tax evasion from Latin American countries. A behavior considered criminal and subject to severe punishment in the advanced countries is actively promoted in the Latin American upper classes by the members of the Organization for Economic Cooperation and Development (OECD), especially the United States. This situation has a heavy foreign policy and economic cost for the United States. As Professor Dornbusch of MIT has pointed out, debts are being serviced to the detriment of US trade interests and by deep cuts in Latin America's investment programs. This is more so when we consider the debt originated by capital flight (Dornbusch 1986). One has to conclude with Carlos Díaz-Alejandro that this whole affair reduces the political legitimacy of continuing to service the external debt and creates a crisis of legitimacy for the private sector's role in Latin American development.[10]

---

9. In fact, the same owners would often have rescued their enterprises, using their huge holdings of dollars abroad.

10. On this, see the masterful analysis by Diaz-Alejandro (1984, p. 379).

The Exportation of Financial Intermediation

As noted, a main source of indebtedness for many countries in Latin America was the exportation of their financial intermediation, with a good deal of the funds borrowed by the public sector from the banks ending up financing private deposits in the same international financial system. Besides the macroeconomic, distributive, and fiscal consequences already discussed, this peculiar process had important additional effects reflected in destabilization of the domestic financial system.

The strengthening of the internal financial system is considered both a cause and a consequence of economic development. The healthy growth of domestic financial intermediation, besides being a factor stimulating the expansion of domestic savings, is a necessary condition to channel domestic financial resources efficiently through the savings-investment circuit. The huge capital flight suffered by Latin America in the recent past produced a significant weakening of national financial systems. This frailty and its contractionary effects on real income induced a reduction in domestic savings.

The financial instability evolved as a consequence of increasing overvaluation in an environment of free convertibility. The dynamics of the process were characterized by the increasing external borrowing of private and public firms and financial institutions, while wealthy private households (especially the firms' owners) simultaneously acquired assets abroad. After devaluations following the depletion of international reserves (and the drying up of external funds), the households with dollar assets reaped enormous capital gains, while symmetrical capital loss was suffered by agents with dollar liabilities. In the vast majority of cases, the financial system reached total insolvency. The natural course of events would have been a takeover of domestic banks by foreign ones, or the intervention of the central bank as lender of last resort to avoid such a takeover. This would have been tantamount to outright nationalization for some nonfinancial firms and most of the financial system, as happened in Mexico. Nationalization would seem to have been the appropriate counterpart in the public sector's balance sheet for assuming most of the nation's external debt. In the end the solution was a gigantic giveaway in the form of a massive capital transfer to the owners of financial and nonfinancial private firms, who kept intact their ownership of both domestic real and foreign financial assets, while escaping their dollar debt.

The exportation of financial intermediation also had further macro- and microeconomic consequences. To the structural weaknesses of the domestic financial system, financial liberalization added the burden of unfair competition with the international system. Once capital flight gained strength, it was thought that a tight domestic credit policy that raised interest rates could make it attractive to save locally. However, the high interest rates induced by policy were incompatible with an acceptable level of real economic activity, and induced a collapse in private investment. To be sure, this was also encouraged by increasing overvaluation, which shifted demand away from locally produced goods, and raised expectations of devaluation. Once these expectations were firmly established, no financial policy was restrictive enough to stop capital flight. In the meantime, skyrocketing interest rates, while ineffective in avoiding the export of savings, damaged the productive side of the economy.

The Transnationalization of Domestic Capital

Irrespective of the causes motivating it (overvaluation, risk, or even tax evasion), capital flight is considered a short- and medium-term transfer of domestic resources, directed to the acquisition of a private external portfolio thought to be usually composed largely of financial assets and some real estate. That the outflow of funds is not usually considered to be long-term is suggested by the general tendency of academic economists and others to propose policy measures intended to reverse that flow.

When the stock of wealth accumulated abroad is relatively small (perhaps up to 10 percent of the total private portfolio of a developing country), this perception about portfolio composition may be essentially correct. When the extraordinary capital flight from Argentina, Mexico, and Venezuela took place after 1978, besides the substantial quantitative increase of the external private portfolio, it would appear that a profound qualitative change in its composition may indeed have been taking place.

It is known that important groups of Latin American investors (especially Venezuelans and Mexicans) are progressively acquiring important stakes in corporations in the OECD countries. The continuation of this "transnationalization" of Latin American capital is bound to have significant consequences.

In the first place, the "takeover" of foreign firms and the acquisition of risk capital makes the return of the domestic funds to the source countries more unlikely. There is far more capital mobility when the exported funds take the form of a financial asset (such as a savings account or a CD in a bank), than when they involve ownership of a large brewery in Germany, the largest department store chain in Spain, or a very large stake in banking and productive enterprises in the United States.

If the reversal of the private capital outflows was thought to be difficult to start with, then the most important consequence of this portfolio shift has to do with its effects on private saving and investment behavior in the source countries, and hence on their level of real economic activity.

One of the inherent features of capitalist economic development is the growth in each country of a domestic capitalist class, which undertakes the bulk of the investment projects required to achieve ever higher levels of production, welfare, and per capita income. The consolidation of these native capitalists, intimately tied to the destiny of the domestic economy, is thought to have been a crucial factor making possible the progress of industrialization in the western developed countries. In recently industrializing economies, the flowering of this local bourgeoisie has also been one of the key factors spurring capitalist development and growth. When the latter is allowed to operate on a global basis, the returns to investment and economic growth of its own country cease to be crucial to its vital interests (because there are other more advanced economies, where economic, social and political stability make it more attractive to concentrate its investment and entrepreneurial efforts). One fears that the consequences for the source countries may be devastating.

The evidence is scattered, but with research effort in this direction it may indeed be possible to document how this progressive diversification of the Latin American private external portfolio, away from financial assets and toward equity, increases the severe negative effects of capital flight.

Concluding Remarks

Besides its destabilizing effects on the domestic economy and drain on foreign exchange and savings needed to finance productive investment, capital flight has had other severe consequences in countries where it has taken place. Since in the recent past almost all private capital outflows from Latin America have been financed, in the aggregate, by public external debt, this peculiar export of financial intermediation has initiated a vast process of regressive income and wealth redistribution. The counterpart of this has been depression, lower real wages, extreme financial instability, and generation of a structural fiscal disequilibrium that serves as the transmission mechanism of that process. The financial frailty brought about by the coexistence of increasing debt and capital flight has been "solved" almost everywhere by policy measures that deepened the vicious circle of regressive income and wealth distribution, fiscal disequilibrium, and protracted recession. Finally, the shift toward long-term direct investment that is occurring within the Latin American private external portfolio seems to have further consequences that worsen the already severe negative effects of capital flight.

From a policy point of view, some interesting options suggest themselves to prevent future outflows of private capital, and even to induce possible reflows.

From the examination of the recent economic history of the largest Latin American debtors, it seems clear that capital flight was most pronounced in countries having overvalued exchange rates and freely convertible currencies and experiencing an economic downturn usually exacerbated by contractionary economic policy. Contrary to conventional wisdom, inflation and budget deficits did not appear to be important factors stimulating capital flight.[11]

As a preventative to capital flight, there seems to be no substitute for sound expansionist macroeconomic policies featuring an equilibrium real exchange rate and increased public and private investment aimed at provoking structural changes in the productive side of the economy. These appear to be preferable to old-fashioned, orthodox budget cutting and anti-inflationary policies, since the induced recession creates an environment in which capital flight would ensue.

Although countries may usefully implement financial policies that make saving locally attractive, the historical evidence also seems to support the case for tight controls in the foreign exchange market. Debtor countries that experienced little capital flight (Brazil, Korea, Taiwan, and Colombia) always had exchange controls in place, whereas the larger exporters of private capital were under free convertibility. This suggests that domestic agents' propensity to save abroad can be substantially diminished when the transaction cost of shifting funds overseas is inflated by the imposition of controls.

A final word can be said on the policies of the industrial countries. Forcing full and timely debt service from Latin America is poor foreign policy, especially when the burden of capital flight is added to the transfer implied by interest payments. The dire effects of this removal of real resources from the region are well known. Thus, besides the search for approaches seeking a long-term solution to the debt problem, OECD countries' policies that stimulate capital flight should also be revised. In particular, changes in policies regarding taxes on interest income of nonresidents, deposit insurance, and sales of bearer bonds should be accompanied by a change in attitude with respect to the provision of information on asset holdings of Latin American residents to their respective governments. The resources that can be generated from this type of cooperation will provide room for expansionist policies in Latin America, which will create the best environment in which to consolidate the democratic awakening of the continent.

---

11. The contrast between Brazil and Venezuela helps to illustrate the point.

References

Barros de Castro, A., and F. Pires. 1985. *A Economia Brasileira em Marcha Forçada.* Rio de Janeiro: Paz e Terra.

Díaz-Alejandro, C. 1984. "Latin American Debt: I Don't Think We Are in Kansas Anymore." *Brookings Papers on Economic Activity* 2.

———. 1985. *El Universal,* 4 April.

Díaz-Carneiro, D. 1986. "Perspectivas do Endividamento Externo Brasileiro: 1986–90." Pontíficia Universidade Católica, Rio de Janeiro. Processed.

Dornbusch, R. 1984a. "External Debt, Budget Deficits, and Disequilibrium Exchange Rates." National Bureau of Economic Research Working Paper No. 1336.

———. 1984b. "Argentina Since Martinez de Hoz." Massachusetts Institute of Technology, Cambridge, Mass. Processed.

———. 1986. "The Bradley Plan: A Way Out of the Latin Debt Mess." *Washington Post,* 27 August.

Frenkel, R., and J. Fanelli. 1984. "Argentina: Un Caso de Endeudamiento Forzado." Centro de Estudios de Desarrollo y Sociedad, Buenos Aires. Processed.

———. 1986. "Del Ajuste Caótico al Plan Austral: Las Políticas de Estabilización Recientes en la Argentina." Centro de Estudios de Desarrollo y Sociedad, Buenos Aires. Processed.

Frieden, J. 1986. "Debt, Development, and Democracy: Five Latin American Borrowers from Boom to Bust and Back." University of California, Los Angeles. Processed.

International Monetary Fund. *International Financial Statistics,* various years.

Khan, M. and N. Ul Haque. 1987. "Capital Flight from Developing Countries." *Finance and Development,* March.

Rodríguez, M. 1985. "Auge Petrolero, Estancamiento y Políticas de Ajuste en Venezuela." *Coyuntura Económica,* Bogotá. December.

———. 1986. "Notas sobre el Ahorro, la Inversión y el Endeudamiento Externo Venezolano." Instituto de Estudios Superiores de Administración, Caracas. Processed.

Ros, J. 1985. "Mexico from the Oil Boom to the Debt Crisis. An Analysis of Policy Responses to External Shocks, 1978–85," Centro de Investigación y Docencia Económicas, Mexico. Processed.

Comment

Rudiger Dornbusch

Rodríguez's paper covers all the points that must be made in a thoughtful discussion of capital flight. There is little to add and nothing to disagree with. I particularly welcome the broad perspective, looking at capital flight not only as a reflection of the mismanagement that gives rise to it in the first place, but going far beyond to discuss the impact on public finance and on income distribution. This much broader perspective is certainly justified by the fact that, in a country like Argentina, public finance is wrecked by the pervasive habit of holding assets abroad and the associated systematic tax fraud. The extremity of the situation is signaled by the fact that real depreciation is good news for the middle class because their wealth is held primarily in dollars.

At the outset it is appropriate to indicate my prejudices. Surely, the lack of a hospitable investment climate is the basic reason for capital flight. But I do not believe that this is invariably the consequence of mismanagement. External shocks and bad politics (or fiscal systems that polarize income maldistribution) are as often a source. I quite emphatically agree with Rodriguez that 99 cents on the dollar of capital outflows from developing countries are socially unproductive. They involve speculation against burdens that must be borne by society in the aggregate and most of the time outright tax fraud. I find it difficult to agree with those who claim capital outflows as a basic human freedom in need of protection, enhancement, and codification.[1] I find myself outright baffled by the proposal for "amnesty international"—that those who committed tax fraud and exchange control violation should now be forgiven (once again) and allowed to repatriate their capital gains scot-free.

With prejudices thus set out, I would like to make some substantive points on three issues: the sources of capital flight, the effects, and the remedies, respectively.

Sources of Capital Flight

In my study of the link between budget deficits and external disequilibria in Latin America (Dornbusch 1985), I identified a combination of three effects as essential for a flight into foreign assets: massive overvaluation,

---

1. Ludwig von Mises, when asked about the high suicide rate in Sweden, is said to have answered: "Don't they have capital controls?"

transitory convertibility on either current or capital account, and government access to seemingly unlimited external finance.

I would emphasize here that there is not much difference between a flight into foreign financial assets in the form of CDs in New York, real estate in Miami, or into Swiss bank accounts, and two other, more parochial forms of holding foreign assets. One is the quite obvious shift into dollar currency, the other is a flight into imported durables which we might call quasi-dollars.

Argentina is the best case study of capital account liberalization combined with overvaluation in the Martinez de Hoz experience of the late 1970s. Estimates of the extent of capital flight differ, but my own reading is that in the 1978–82 period $25 billion went abroad, not counting accumulated earnings on existing stocks of external assets. Chile's case is the best example of an extraordinary flight into imported durables. With complete tariff liberalization and elimination of quotas the overvaluation of more than 40 percent brought about a record shift into importables. The private sector rightly perceived that importables were "on sale" and reacted by purchasing imported durables on an unprecedented scale.

In most other countries the reason for capital flight is some mix of the Chilean and Argentinian experience. The striking fact is that in 1979–82 every one of the newly industrializing countries reported in the Morgan Guaranty *World Financial Markets* showed a significant real appreciation. This is brought out in table 6.2 for a few countries, where an increase in the index signifies real appreciation. Note that compared to the annual averages the peak real exchange rates in Chile and Argentina, for example, show even larger overvaluation.

The table raises the interesting question why Brazil and Korea do not show stories of capital flight in the way other countries do. That fact itself has been questioned,[2] although nobody has suggested capital flight on the extravagant order of Mexico or Argentina. A good part of the explanation is that these countries have capital controls and enforce them quite vigorously. It is definitely not the case that they had consistently well-managed exchange rates or distinctly positive real interest rates.

Capital flight is not always and invariably the result of a sudden outburst of mismanagement. A good case in point is Mexico in 1986. The government had made significant adjustments in the budget and had been sustaining real interest rates at a level sufficient to draw in capital for more than a year. But when oil prices collapsed, capital moved out in anticipation of an inevitable currency depreciation and a deterioration of public finance.

An interesting question in the capital flight experience is why domestic *real* assets such as cattle, farms, real estate or productive capital in the traded

_____
2. See Morgan Guaranty, *World Financial Markets* (March 1986).

Table 6.2   Real exchange rates in manufacturing
(index 1980–82 = 100)

	Argentina	Brazil	Chile	Mexico	Venezuela	Korea
1976–78	73	116	75	98	95	92
1979	101	96	79	98	95	95
1980	116	85	95	104	93	96
1981	107	103	108	114	100	101
1982	76	112	97	82	110	103
Peak 1979–82	131	119	113	118	112	107
1983–85	74	85	86	86	98	96

Source: Morgan Guaranty.

goods sector should not behave like quasi-dollars. I am not familiar with any evidence that suggests that flight from domestic assets (money and bonds) also favors domestically located real assets. Of course, these assets are not exactly the same as actual dollar assets. They are subject to two kinds of special vagaries: domestic taxation and uncertainty about relative prices. In Argentina, for example, a compensated devaluation—i.e., devaluation with an export tax on agricultural products—means that a shift into dollars is preferred to a shift into agricultural assets which do not enjoy the same windfall because of the compensatory tax. One must assume that this disdain for domestic real assets on the part of asset holders is a reflection of systematic mistreatment of domestic real assets. If that is so, it is worthwhile documenting because it amounts to a more serious mistake than mistreating bondholders.

The Effects of Capital Flight

Capital flight has important macroeconomic and distributional consequences: it aggravates inflation and reduces the standard of living of those unable to participate in the evasion of the burden that populism or external shocks place on society at large.

For public finance, capital flight involves an extra burden for several reasons. First, when overvaluation induces capital flight, there is subsequently an extra burden of debt service. The government finances the capital flight by borrowing abroad. Once financing is no longer available, the budget has to adapt to the requirement of servicing the external debt. It is hard to raise taxes, which are already, for the major part, paid by wage earners. Other than investment, it is difficult to cut much in the budget. The remaining route is almost inevitably money creation to finance the budget deficit. The inflation tax, of course, creates a secondary round of capital flight and dollarization. If the government yields to financial liberalization, that cuts yet further into the scope for noninflationary deficit finance by reducing real balances and hence the base for the inflation tax.

Second, capital flight directly reduces taxable wealth or income. Once capital leaves it certainly is evading taxes in the home country and presumably also in the host country. That means, other things equal, a larger deficit and hence higher inflation.

Third, the real depreciation required to service external debts will raise the real value of external debt service and thus widen the budget deficit and the required inflation tax. All these channels point to inflation as the *consequence* of capital flight. Inflation may be the origin of capital flight, but once it takes place it has in itself a powerful inflationary impact. In the end it is hard to identify which is the chicken and which is the egg.

The income-distribution effects of capital flight are quite straightforward. Whoever succeeds in evading taxes and moving assets abroad does so at the implicit subsidy of an overvalued currency. Foreign assets are bought on sale while financing is plentiful and the exchange rate underprices external assets. In the second phase debts must be serviced. As is well known from the discussion of the transfer problem, service of the debt— incurred to finance capital flight—has a budget counterpart. The inflation tax that finances the debt service is paid predominantly by those holding domestic money, meaning workers.

To effect the transfer in terms of foreign exchange a real depreciation is required. Wages in dollars therefore must decline and the standard of living is cut as labor now is put on sale. It is apparent then that wealth holders are the beneficiaries of capital flight while workers pay the bill. There may be instances where costs and benefits are more diffuse, but I believe the simple distinction of workers and wealth holders captures the essentials of the distributional issue.

Remedies

Early to bed and early to rise makes man healthy, wealthy, and wise. What is the equivalent precept for avoiding capital flight? The simple answer is an undervalued exchange rate, ample reserves and good international credit standing, a budget surplus, a small domestic debt, and a low tax rate. In such an economy there is plenty of room to absorb shocks without the need to depreciate massively or to tax asset holders by inflation or levies. But of course that is not Latin America. There public finance is strained to the point where inflation taxes are an accepted part of tax collection, depreciation is the rule and external credit is overextended to the point of credit rationing. When external shocks happen they turn mediocre performance readily into chaos.

To get out of this vicious circle of capital flight and deterioration in public finance is nearly impossible. One obvious way is to write down (or off) all domestic debts and foreign debts as well. If such a move were accompanied by a dramatic increase in tax compliance, a reduction in tax rates, and a vigorous expansion in the tax base, the conditions for stability would be restored. But, unfortunately, advice commonly tendered runs in the direction of servicing debts at any price, even when it is quite clear that debts are already far beyond what ultimately can be paid.

Most of the burden of adjustment therefore must come from a more realistic exchange rate policy, shifting clearly to the region of undervaluation Korean style, and from a dramatic change in taxation. By comparison with industrial countries total tax collection (as a fraction of GNP) is very small in the developing countries. A widening of the tax base and a distinctly more vigorous enforcement of the tax laws (including frequent demonstration that tax evaders go to jail, US style) would help shift budgets toward balance in normal years. This should be combined with realistic real interest rates and real exchange rates. The combination removes the threat of always being on the verge of the abyss with collapse at the slightest disturbance.

Exchange rate policy and fiscal policy must be extra sensitive to exchange rate expectations. Real wage cuts in the face of external disturbances must be the assurance to asset holders that their wealth is not at peril. Of course, such a policy rule increases the variability of real wages as a means of stabilizing the real return on assets. That is a sad reflection of the fact that capital is mobile. But it certainly is not excluded that occasionally a wealth tax is also appropriate. This is particularly the case when public finance is so strained that it is the cause of capital flight. In those instances it is much better to do the unspeakable (but also the firmly expected).

A favorable setting in terms of the budget and the exchange rate is hard to achieve in periods of external shocks. Adjustments in exchange rates barely offset the impact of external shocks on the balance of payments rather than going farther so as to reinforce stability. Fiscal adjustments barely meet the extra burden external shocks place on the budget. In these conditions capital leaves in anticipation of increased vulnerability and almost certain deterioration of economic conditions.

What about stopgap measures to avoid and reverse capital flight while a basic consolidation of public finance is under way? Two means in particular are recommended: "amnesty international" and "positive real interest rates." In my judgment both are remedies that are deeply destructive of sound public finance.

It is commonly believed that tax amnesties and similar amnesties for people who engaged in illicit capital export are a valuable part of restoring a financial environment conducive to repatriation of assets, confidence, and financial stability. Of course, amnesty undermines credibility just as much as capital levies do. If either is expected as a rule of the game, it leads to anticipation and erosion of credibility. Anyone who argues in favor of amnesties must also support capital levies and occasional debt repudiation. No debtor is more credible than one who has no debts left. By contrast anyone honest but burdened with excessive debt is deeply suspect. After all, sound finance is to lend to people who do not need the money.

I also have difficulties with a policy of high real interest rates as a means of containing or reversing capital flight. High real interest rates, as they were used in Mexico to bring in capital with which to service the external debt, threaten bankruptcy for many firms and certainly put a stop to most investment. They deteriorate public finance by increasing domestic debt-service burdens. The perversity of the Mexican experience in 1985–86 is brought out by the fact that the government was borrowing expensive money (via a capital inflow) in order to service a comparatively low-cost external debt. Total debt in this event is growing more rapidly. If there is no expectation of ultimate default on the domestic debt, this is poor public finance. A better strategy would have been to increase external arrears pending a balanced budget position.

Debt-equity swaps are widely touted as an important means of returning capital. I find that implausible and rather agree with the point of view that they amount primarily to a substitution of debt reduction for direct investment inflows that would have taken place anyway. I also note that their domestic debt implications amount to substituting expensive for cheap debt. This is particularly true when most of the discount is passed on to the investor who is said to require a "hurdle" rate of return.[3]

I conclude in noting that an important aspect of capital flight is the existence of havens where capital can seek shelter from the turbulence visited upon developing countries. The exaggerated emphasis on financial liberalization, at the expense of good sense and productive activity, has found its most extreme expression in the US elimination of taxation of nonresident assets. A sounder policy would be, at a minimum, to tax foreign assets whatever we choose to do with the proceeds. The answer that there is always Switzerland is not a satisfactory reply.

---

3. I have discussed arguments against debt-equity swaps in greater detail in Dornbusch (1987).

References

Dornbusch, R. 1985. "Budget Deficits, External Debt and Disequilibrium Exchange Rates." In *External Debt Problems of Developing Countries,* edited by G. Smith and J. Cuddington. Washington: World Bank.

———. 1987. "Our LDC Debts." In *The U.S. in the World Economy,* edited by M. Feldstein. Cambridge, Mass.: National Bureau of Economic Research, forthcoming.

Discussion

Views were sharply divided about the welfare consequences of capital flight. In Dooley's analysis, as in Minsky's ideal world where financial intermediation in developing countries has improved to the point where portfolio diversification is symmetrical (see discussion, ch. 4), the effects are limited to erosion of the tax base and the exportation of financial intermediation. It became increasingly clear that it was necessary to distinguish sharply between that case, in which "capital flight" is one side of a two-way flow driven by the attempt to arbitrage tax differentials or the differential availability of guarantees, and the classic situations on which most of Kindleberger's historical survey focuses, in which a net flow dictated the achievement of a real transfer.

Kindleberger suggested that capital flight might actually be beneficial, in the absence of a net resource transfer, if it enabled residents to overcome distortionary tax systems. This suggestion was taken up enthusiastically, and without the qualification, by some other participants. Thus, Robert Heller argued that the crucial issue was whether investors succeeded in obtaining higher rates of return since this could be presumed to raise world economic growth. John Williamson contested this for the case where real transfer was needed, on the ground that the existence of a foreign-exchange constraint virtually guaranteed that the social value of foreign exchange to the domestic economy exceeded the private value to an individual investor.

Ingo Walter nevertheless subsequently argued that world welfare would increase if the flight were a response to distortions, while David Devlin found virtue in the existence of tax havens as a mechanism for integrating the world capital market and enabling investors to evade attempted theft on the part of their governments. However, Dornbusch questioned whether the tax systems in most Latin American countries could be characterized as attempted theft: he argued that what Argentina most needed could be described as a tax system designed by the Heritage Foundation, combining relatively low marginal tax rates with an assurance that everyone would actually pay tax on the whole of their income.

Case Studies

Chile

José Pablo Arellano and Joseph Ramos

Much as in the rest of Latin America, Chile's foreign debt has grown enormously in the past fifteen years, far more than its debt-servicing capacity. Debt has tripled in real terms, surpassing $20 billion in 1986, while gross national income (GNP) has grown but 10 percent. Thus, Chile's foreign debt today virtually equals GNP, up from 30 percent in 1973 (compared to 50 percent and 15 percent, respectively, for the whole region). To be sure, gross national income is not the only source for servicing debt. Foreign assets held by Chileans should be deducted, if in the public domain. Official foreign reserves ($2 billion) are in this category. Capital held by private Chileans might also help, if it could be taxed (which would require host-country cooperation).

Yet in practice this is not the case. Rather, the debt crisis has forced governments to "socialize" private debt, while capital flight has impeded their socializing the corresponding assets. Capital flight has thus exacerbated both the burden and the inequity of debt service. Hence, capital flight is important not just because of its impact on the economy, debt servicing, and income distribution, but for understanding how much of a role its repatriation might play in helping solve the debt problem.

In a nutshell, the results of this investigation suggest that capital flight in Chile was not severe, at least by regional standards—amounting in all likelihood to no more than $1 billion (or 5 percent of foreign debt). Understanding why it was not massive may help other countries reduce such flight in the future. Unfortunately, the modest size of capital flight means that its repatriation—even if it all returned—could reduce Chile's debt no more than 5 percent. In any case, one mechanism that Chile has designed to repurchase its foreign debt has proved useful in repatriating

The authors are economists at CIEPLAN and CEPAL, respectively. The views expressed here are exclusively those of the authors and in no way need reflect those of the institutions with which they are associated.

capital, and, despite its drawbacks, might be even more useful for countries that experienced greater capital flight.

The Magnitude of Capital Flight

Estimates of capital flight are beset with uncertainties, for much capital flight is designed to get around controls. Thus, it is unlikely to be registered, except incompletely in recipient countries. In much of the period examined, however, controls on capital exit were not strict—each Chilean could buy up to $10,000 a month in foreign exchange, and these controls were further relaxed for two critical months in mid-1982. Most capital flight from Chile through 1982 may have been registered under this provision (under which up to $1 billion a year gross in foreign exchange, 25 percent of the value of exports, was bought or sold in the height of the "boom" years).

In any case, we have made three estimates of capital flight based on: analysis of short-term capital outflows by the private, nonbank sector under the facility just described; a comparison of the growth of foreign debt (and so, of capital inflow) with the uses to which it was put according to the balance of payments—rises not otherwise accounted for being considered capital flight; and analysis of the growth of deposits held by Chileans abroad.

The first and third approaches are direct, one based on national data, the latter on recipient-country data. Yet both have their drawbacks: as regards the former, capital flight may have taken place under other forms (for example, under- and overinvoicing); as regards the latter, withdrawn capital may be held in bank deposits outside the major (reporting) financial centers, or it may not be listed under Chilean accounts, or it may be held in the form of securities rather than deposits. The second or indirect approach is thus a good check—all the more so if, as seems to have been the case in Chile, all foreign debt was duly registered.

The first method considers as capital flight all net short-term capital outflows by the private nonbank sector, unaccounted for by exogenous reductions in foreign lending, plus errors and omissions. On this definition, between 1975–84, there were net outflows in only two years, 1982 and 1983, amounting to $801 million and $343 million, respectively (table 7.1). However, since the bulk of the outflow in 1983 is explained by the unilateral reduction of short-term credit lines on the part of foreign banks (as a response to the intervention of the banking system[1] by the government in January 1983), capital outflow would appear to have been limited to 1982, and to $800 million.

---

1. The "intervention" of the banks refers to their temporary takeover by the state.

Table 7.1   Chile: estimates of capital flight
(million dollars)

	Method 1[a]	Method 2[b]	Method 3[c]
1976	n.a.	+275	n.a.
1977	n.a.	+195	n.a.
1978	n.a.	+154	n.a.
1979	n.a.	+213	n.a.
1980	n.a.	+580	n.a.
1981	n.a.	+149	n.a.
1982	−801	−734 (−680)[e]	−270 (−80)[f]
1983	−343[d]	+38 (−97)[e]	−620 (−440)[f]
1984	n.a.	+957	n.a.
1985	n.a.	n.a.	(2.230)[g]

n.a. not available.

Note: Throughout (−) signifies capital flight; (+) signifies capital inflows.

Sources: (1) United Nations Economic Commission for Latin America and the Caribbean (ECLAC), *America Latina y el Caribe; Balance de Pagos 1950–84*, (Cuadernos Estadisticos de la CEPAL, United Nations, Santiago, 1986). (2) Ibid, and Central Bank of Chile (October 1985, table 2). (3) IMF, *International Financial Statistics*, May 1986, and Bank for International Settlements, *International Banking Developments*, various numbers October 1983–January 1986, and IMF, *International Financial Statistics Yearbook*, 1985.

a. Method 1: Short-term capital outflows by the private nonbanking sector, plus errors and omissions.

b. Method 2: Increase in foreign debt, plus direct foreign investment, less the deficit on current account, less the increase in reserves.

c. Method 3: The increase in deposits of Chileans (not banks) in major international financial centers.

d. All or most of the $343 million are explained, not by an increase in short-term capital outflows, but by a decrease in short-term international bank lending to the nonbank private sector.

e. The first estimate includes changes in official reserves only; the estimate in parentheses includes changes in commercial banks' foreign assets as well.

f. The figure in parentheses is net of increases in overseas deposits because of interest earnings abroad.

g. Total deposits held abroad by nonbank Chilean depositors in 1985.

The second approach estimates capital flight from the relationship between the increase in foreign debt and the uses to which it was put. The net increase in foreign debt plus direct foreign investment (or net capital inflow) is equal to (spent on) the trade deficit plus interest payments (or deficit on current account) plus the increase in reserves[2] plus capital flight (a residual). On this definition, capital flight in the period 1975–84 was again limited to the two years 1982 and 1983 (table 7.1); on the first variant (including just the change in official reserves), $734 million, and nil in 1982; on the second variant (including changes in commercial banks' net foreign assets), a total of $777 million, $680 million of it in 1982 and $97 million in 1983.

Finally, the third approach directly estimates capital flight as the increase in deposits held abroad by Chileans (other than banks). Such data are available in this detailed form from the IMF only as of the end of 1981; but, happily, this coincides with the period of maximum capital flight according to our two previous estimates. On this definition, capital flight amounted to $530 million to $890 million, according to whether or not one deducts the increase in deposits due to interest payments received on assets already held abroad. Yet, at odds with our former estimates, the bulk of capital flight on this measure was recorded as taking place in 1983. As for the period before December 1981, no such detailed data are available. However, there are Bank for International Settlements (BIS) data on *total* deposits held abroad by Chileans. If one excludes the increase in official reserves in this earlier period (1978–81), once again the increase in overseas deposits would appear to be fully accounted for by the increase in official reserves. Thus, these data also suggest that .capital flight was limited to 1982–83.

In short, while there are differences in the three estimates, all point to a level of capital flight in Chile of under $1 billion, and to the years 1982–83 as the critical years for such flight. Thus, by regional standards, capital flight in Chile in the post-1979 crisis period was relatively low. Yet this was not so much because the yearly rate of capital flight was low, for it was not— indeed, capital flight in 1982 (probably some $700 million) amounted to over 40 percent of Chile's increased foreign debt, 70 percent of its fall in official reserves and 130 percent of gross national savings in that year. Rather, it was because capital flight was limited to a very brief period in Chile, unlike Argentina, Mexico, and Venezuela, where it was large for five or more consecutive years. And its impact was devastating, for it both contributed to, and resulted from, the 14 percent fall in GDP in 1982.

Causes and Mechanisms

Three questions naturally arise: why was there so little capital flight (relatively speaking) from Chile; what mechanisms were used to take out

2. There are two estimates: the change in official foreign reserves less gold and the same, plus the increase in the foreign assets of commercial banks (this latter because of the control, direct and indirect, that the central bank is thought to have over them).

capital; and why such flight as occurred was so heavily concentrated in 1982–83?

Beginning with the last point, two of the estimates suggest that capital flight was largely limited to 1982, a view supported by the following additional bits of information:

☐ The largest loss of official reserves by far took place in 1982, when over $1.10 billion were lost. In 1983 reserves fell only $650 million. Moreover, capital inflows of medium- and long-term maturities also declined sharply in 1983 (to $1.2 billion, down from $1.7 billion in 1982). Since the magnitude of capital flight is limited by the amount of foreign exchange to which it has access, this suggests the bulk of the flight is likely to have taken place in 1982.

☐ The fall in reserves was especially sharp in the second half of 1982, and particularly during the third quarter (table 7.2), when restrictions on capital outflows and inflows were fully lifted. As of late 1982, very tight capital restrictions were imposed.

☐ The data on Chilean deposits in the United States (table 7.3) show an increase of $900 million during 1982, just as official reserves were sharply falling.[3]

The fact that capital flight was so heavily concentrated in 1982, and especially in the third quarter of 1982, suggests both the causes of flight and the principal mechanism utilized. Like exchange rates elsewhere in the region, Chile's had lagged so that domestic prices and costs by late 1981 had risen 30 percent to 50 percent relative to the peso price of imported goods in the period 1978–81. Thus, a good case could be made that the currency was significantly overvalued, all the more so since in this same period the price of petroleum (which is a key import) had doubled. To be sure, gross capital outflows increased, but the attraction of the Chilean economy plus confidence were so high that capital inflows swamped outflows. Indeed *net* capital inflows reached nearly $5 billion in 1981 (100 percent of exports, raising Chile's gross foreign debt by over 40 percent that year), despite the lag in the exchange rate, the bankruptcy of one of Chile's oldest and most highly reputed firms (CRAV), and the intervention in November 1981 of eight banks and financial institutions (which accounted for 25 percent of total private bank credit).

To be sure, much could be explained by the attraction of Chilean interest rates (table 7.4) which rose to 3 percent per month in real peso terms and

---

3. To be sure, part of this could be a transfer of funds to US dollar accounts from European accounts in anticipation of the further appreciation the US dollar was then experiencing, and continued to experience through 1984.

Table 7.2 Chile: monthly loss of international reserves
(million dollars)

	Reserve loss	Reserve loss plus increase in short-term central bank liabilities
September–December 1981 (average)	82	n.a.
January–May 1982 (average)	60	n.a.
June 1982 (month of devaluation)	154	n.a.
July 1982	206	n.a.
August 1982	139	189
September 1982	299	349
October 1982	74	224
November 1982	231	281
December 1982	−206	−306
January 1983	625[a]	575
February 1983	213	263
March 1983	162	162
April–June 1983 (average)	11	77

n.a. not available.
Source: Central Bank of Chile, monthly bulletins.
a. Includes the use of an IMF credit of $450 million.

Table 7.3 Liabilities to Chileans reported by banks in the United States by month (million dollars)

	1981	1982	1983
January	501	771	1,347
February	431	815	1,280
March	549	951	1,068
April	539	992	1,204
May	526	1,224	1,345
June	508	1,224	1,385
July	566	1,442	1,385
August	538	1,170	1,472
September	491	1,293	1,612
October	538	1,447	1,697
November	505	1,444	1,783
December	664	1,626	1,842

Source: *Federal Reserve Bulletin,* various issues.

Table 7.4   Chile: real interest rates and index of real value of stock market shares (deflated by the consumer price index)

	Peso loans[a] (per year)	Dollar loans (per year)	Index of value of stock market shares (real) (1969 = 100)
1976	51.4	−21.6	165
1977	39.4	−0.8	269
1978	35.1	2.7	484
1979	16.6	0.2	562
1980	12.2	−9.8	1,037
1981	38.8	10.5	823
1982	35.1	81.9	623
1983	15.9	11.5	397
1984	11.4	33.7	396
1985	11.1	27.0	388

Source: Central Bank, *Monthly Bulletin*.
a. An annualized real interest rate on short-run (monthly) nonindexed peso loans.

closer to 5 percent per month in dollar terms, given the fixed exchange rate. Nevertheless, it must be noted that until mid-1982, unlike Argentina and Uruguay (which had far freer mobility), capital inflows had to remain in the country for a minimum of two years before they could be withdrawn (with increasing reserve requirements the shorter the loan). And such long-term capital inflows increased by 60 percent between 1980 and 1981, long-term capital accounting for over 75 percent of capital inflows to Chile in 1981. Thus, it was not only short-term interest rates that attracted capital but also the confidence inspired in both domestic and foreign investors by the liberalization process and increasingly lower inflation. Chileans increased their dollar indebtedness sharply in 1981 to avoid paying high rates on peso loans. It is now clear to everyone that this confidence was misplaced and that investors seriously erred in their assessment, but only a minority was clamoring for devaluation by mid-1981. Had confidence been lacking, long-term capital inflows would have fallen in 1981 (instead of shooting up), the proportion of short-term funds in overall capital inflows would have jumped (rather than falling from 30 percent in 1980 to 24 percent in 1981), and Chileans would have reduced, not increased, their dollar indebtedness.

Why Chile seemed so attractive is another question. Certainly the economy had recovered and expanded briskly since the recession of 1974–75. Yet the 6 percent per year GNP growth and the 11 percent growth in the volume of exports during the "boom" years (1976–81), while good, was hardly spectacular, not even by Latin American standards. There were also many signs of weakness: a very low national savings rate (12 percent); double the historic rates of unemployment; persistently high real interest rates (30 percent a year on average); the high and rising level of foreign debt; a lagging exchange rate; and a composition of growth strongly skewed in favor of nontradables. Nevertheless, the fact is that confidence there was. Not only had income flows grown smartly, but the value of capital assets had grown spectacularly (table 7.4)—stock prices sextupling in real terms between 1976 and 1980, after having already tripled since the Allende period. And certainly the insignificant differential between the value of the dollar on the parallel market and the official price (table 7.5) suggested no lack of confidence, but quite the contrary.

Thus, notwithstanding the relative ease with which capital could be taken out, confidence, however misplaced, buttressed by—but not simply based on—high domestic interest rates was such as to make capital flight an unattractive option right through the end of 1981.

By the end of 1981, however, and certainly in early 1982, a devaluation was being seriously discussed. Moreover, discussion no longer centered on whether Chilean and international prices were grossly out of line—this was obvious—but on whether it was less costly to achieve the needed real depreciation via a devaluation of the exchange rate or a reduction of wages with the exchange rate remaining fixed. Thus, only at the last moment, as a significant devaluation became extremely likely, did capital flight get under way.

The principal mechanism for capital flight was the general purpose purchase of foreign exchange from the central bank at the permitted rate of $10,000 a month per person. Since the central bank chose to defend the exchange rate (at 39 pesos per dollar), valuable reserves were drawn down to finance such flight (some 70 percent of the loss of reserves in 1982), while the minimum time restriction of two years on capital inflows was eliminated.

Since this did not work, in mid-June the peso was finally devalued after three years of fixity. The devaluation lessened confidence both because it broke with announced policy and because it was relatively slight (a mere 18 percent, moving the dollar to 46 pesos). Thus capital flight further intensified, inducing the authorities to float the peso as of August in an attempt to stem the loss in reserves and to permit a more active monetary policy to brake the sharp fall in output (GNP fell 14 percent in 1982). Immediately upon floating, however, the dollar shot up to between 65 pesos and 70 pesos. Since this was well above the central bank's views as to the appropriate long-run exchange rate, the government intervened to bring the dollar down to 60 pesos, but at the price of a further loss of $500 million

Table 7.5   Chile: evolution of the exchange rate
(period average)

		Official rate[a]	Parallel rate[a]	Index of real effective exchange rate (1982 Q:1 = 100)[b,c]	Ratio of parallel to official rate
1975		4.91		174.2	
1976		13.05		148.4	
1977		21.53		122.9	
1978		31.66		137.6	
1979		37.25		139.6	
1980		39.00		124.2	
1981		39.00		104.2	
1982		50.91	54	119.4	1.06
1983		78.84	92	143.5	1.17
1984		98.66	113	145.6	1.15
1985		161.08	180	181.7	1.12
1982:	1	39.00	41	100.0	1.05
	2	40.34	42	103.0	1.05
	3	55.01	58	129.4	1.06
	4	69.28	77	145.2	1.11
1983:	1	74.96	99	150.6	1.32
	2	75.34	91	140.5	1.21
	3	79.75	86	140.4	1.08
	4	85.31	93	142.6	1.09
1984:	1	88.05	97	143.5	1.10
	2	90.00	113	140.1	1.26
	3	95.62	116	141.0	1.21
	4	120.95	124	157.6	1.03
1985:	1	135.82	139	162.4	1.02
	2	152.14	172	171.7	1.13
	3	175.50	200	192.3	1.14
	4	180.87	210	200.7	1.16

Source: ECLAC on the basis of data supplied by the Central Bank of Chile and the International Monetary Fund.
a. Pesos per dollar.
b. See the technical appendix to ECLAC's *Economic Survey of Latin America 1981* for the methodology and sources used.
c. The nominal exchange rate was deflated by the consumer price index, as corrected by R. Cortazar and J. Marshall for the period 1975–78, and thereafter as calculated by the National Institute of Statistics (INE).

in the months of August and September. (During this dirty float, there was no restriction on the amount of dollars purchased, irrespective of purpose.) Finally, at the end of September, to stem the loss in reserves and the continuing capital flight, the authorities decided to limit the general purpose purchase of foreign exchange to $1,000 a person per month ($3,000 for overseas travel) and to set the exchange rate at 66 pesos, with future devaluations according to the inflation differential. This closing of the principal mechanism for capital flight, together with an exchange rate two-thirds higher (and over 50 percent higher in real terms) than in June, finally succeeded in sharply reducing, if not ending, capital flight.

The further shock came in 1983 with the state's intervention to stave off the financial collapse of most of the remaining private banks.[4] Given the restrictions on capital outflows, pressure was brought to bear on the parallel rate, whose differential peaked at 33 percent over the official rate in the first quarter of 1983. But by the end of 1983 the differential was down to 10 percent, as the crisis was weathered.

Hence, the avoidance of capital flight, which confidence alone had achieved up to 1981, in 1983 required both stiff capital controls and a high exchange rate.[5] But a high exchange rate alone is obviously a costly substitute for confidence.

How important then are capital controls in stemming capital flight? Chilean experience suggests that when confidence exists, as up to 1981, such controls are not binding. Moreover, we are inclined to surmise that controls alone could not long substitute for basic macroeconomic equilibria. Yet capital controls would seem to be especially useful policy *complements* when dealing with crises of confidence (as in 1982–83), over and beyond basic macroeconomic equilibria. For events like runs may, if not compensated, or controlled, lead to self-fulfilling, procyclical downspins. If allowed

---

4. This episode served as a pretext for the foreign banks to insist on the government's assumption of Chile's private-sector external debt. Thus, immediately upon the government's intervention in the domestic banking system, foreign banks demanded a government guarantee for their heretofore unguaranteed loans to the private financial sector as a precondition for rescheduling Chile's external debt and cut off all short-term loans to provide "bite" to their insistence. Because the government position was extraordinarily weak in early 1983, politically as well as economically, it caved in to the banks' pressure to guarantee and so socialize most of Chile's private-sector external debt. Thus, whereas in 1982 only 38 percent of Chile's foreign debt was public or publicly guaranteed—a point which might have positioned it well to ride out the debt crisis—because of this pressure, by 1986 this proportion had grown to 72 percent.

5. Additional factors are that capital inflows were low and cash flow in pesos was even lower in 1983, for the country was in a depression. Then, too, the intervention of the banks slowed the financing these banks gave to conglomerate-related firms, thus further reducing the possible demand of firms for dollars.

to run their course fully, they can entail gross discontinuities in all market values (over- and undershooting in exchange rates, real wages, asset values, and interest rates) and risk a major economic and financial collapse. Thus, full capital liberalization in August and September 1982 was precisely the opposite of what was required, and no doubt helps explain the particular severity of the depression of 1982. By the same token, the establishment of capital controls in late 1982 helps explain why the ensuing intervention of the banking system in early 1983 could be withstood with virtually no further loss in output or capital flight, and with an exchange rate no higher than that already prevailing before the financial collapse.

To be sure, what matters is not only the existence of formal controls but their efficient administration. In this regard, although capital controls were not very stiff in neoconservative Chile, those that did exist were well administered. Moreover, long experience with inflation and devaluation meant that creditors and debtors were eager to register debt fully so as to have ready access to foreign exchange when these debts had to be paid. When the crisis came, Chile thus had its debt well and fully registered. This made it easy, for example, to avoid the normal pressure for the prepayment of debt (a typical form of capital flight) as the crisis approached.

Finally, an indication of the role played by overoptimistic expectations in explaining the lack of capital flight prior to 1982 is the disproportionate increase in consumption (imports and otherwise) which took place in 1981. Asset holders probably felt they were wealthier (since the value of their domestic assets had increased far more than their income) and thus chose to bring their consumption in line with perceived permanent wealth. Wage earners probably took as permanent the almost 12 percent real increase in take-home wages[6] registered in 1981, and spent it on consumer goods. Per capita consumption rose about 9 percent that year, but per capita income remained unchanged. Hence the unprecedented increase in foreign savings (7.4 percent of GNP) was matched by an almost equal decline in national savings.

Chileans perceived their options as far wider than portfolio theory's mix of foreign and domestic financial assets. Rather they chose from among: consuming domestic goods, consuming foreign goods, investing in foreign equipment (investment), or investing in "private reserves" (capital flight). The lagged exchange rate lowered the relative price of the last three options. The overoptimistic expectations (greater perceived wealth) increased the

---

6. Much of this increase reflected the sharp decline in inflation beginning at the end of 1980, which gave rise to an unexpected, and in this sense possibly transitory, increase in real wages, along with a once-and-for-all increase in take-home pay arising from the decreed reduction in the payroll tax to be financed out of reductions in future social security benefits.

demand for the first two. In short, the income (wealth) effect dominated over the substitution effect, and given the possibility of purchasing foreign goods (imports) or foreign assets (capital goods or capital flight) more cheaply because of the lagged exchange rate, Chileans chose to import goods and raise their consumption to match their perceived increase in wealth. Capital flight was also low prior to 1982 because Chileans chose to use their increased indebtedness to finance consumer imports rather than build up their overseas assets.

Repatriating Capital Flight

How much capital can be repatriated and what can be done to bring it back, or bring back sooner hot money that fled?

The motives for capital flight are multiple: some transitory (speculative), some permanent (for example, portfolio diversification). Of the $2.2 billion held in bank deposits abroad by Chilean nonbank investors,[7] probably a bit less than half is transitory—the result of the depression and massive devaluation of 1982. It is this $1 billion that Chile can realistically hope to attract; the rest is of a more permanent character.

As to this capital which "fled" seeking transitory gains in 1982, the bulk should return naturally to realize these gains as confidence is restored and as asset values and the peso begin to appreciate. It is important to keep this point in mind before designing policies to accelerate the return. For it is not so much a question of attracting this capital back as of bringing it back *sooner*. A country should pay a high price to bring this capital back only if it would otherwise stay abroad. The merits of policies to speed up the return must be evaluated against this criterion.

Apart from restoring basic macroeconomic equilibria and reducing uncertainty, there seem to be five principal means of accelerating the repatriation of capital.

First, the possibility of further real depreciation of the currency must seem unlikely. It should be noted, however, that in the second semester of 1985 the real effective exchange rate was above its historic 1975 peak, and was almost 100 percent higher than in 1981.

Given the highly procyclical nature of capital flows, the exchange rate needed to encourage capital return might, for some time, be well above that

---

7. This, of course, is a minimum estimate of all Chilean nonbank assets abroad, for much capital may be in the form of assets or securities, some may be in accounts not attributed to Chilean residents, and still more may be in bank accounts outside the major financial centers. In any case, our earlier estimates suggest that "hot" money, which left during the exchange crisis, does not amount to more than $1 billion.

needed to achieve the desirable trade balance. A dual exchange rate might be considered during such an interim: a high or clearly overshot rate (for some time) for new capital flows (since these adjust rapidly to lagged exchange rates and interest rate differentials, and expectations are critical); and a lower one for trade and repayment of old capital. Had a special incentive been desired to attract capital back sooner, instead of devaluing across the board as strongly as in late 1982, a special rate could have been set for new capital. This might have been, say, 20 percent higher than the commercial exchange rate, but fixed so that it would appreciate in real terms over time (with inflation), coming to equal the regular exchange rate within a reasonable period of a year or so, since the regular rate would continue to be devalued in accordance with inflation.[8]

It would thus be attractive to bring back capital as early as possible, and to the extent that the differential was not too great (20 percent) and that it disappeared in a relatively brief time, the effect on the trade balance via over- and underinvoicing would not be great. In the long run, real exchange rates, the trade balance, and capital flows would be the same, but with a temporary dual exchange rate, capital would flow back sooner for any given (commercial) exchange rate.

Second, interest rates could be made more attractive. Yet this largely affects short-term capital. Moreover, higher interest rates would raise the financial cost of already overly debt-burdened firms.

Third, many would-be-repatriates are reluctant to bring in dollars through the central bank because they fear tax inquiries. A tax amnesty (partial or full) on capital returned within a specified period might be considered for this purpose. Although amnesties set poor precedents (and much capital flight may possibly return via the black market anyway), amnesty may significantly increase the amount repatriated since it makes investment much easier, and is especially helpful to large investments (for which it might otherwise not be possible to justify funds).

Fourth, many firms that would want to return capital will be reluctant to do so, to the extent that their financial situation borders on insolvency. It is thus fundamental to clarify the debt situation of most firms, either by speeding up bankruptcy proceedings or by forcing mergers and takeovers or designing feasible debt-repayment programs. This is no easy matter, but once it is achieved, capital may flow back to save firms (as may have been the case in Mexico in 1985), rather than holding back (as in Chile, at least up to 1985, while the threat of insolvency still hung over many firms).

---

8. If it were judged desirable to attract only medium- and long-term capital (presumably Chilean capital flight would be expected to return to stay), the special exchange rate could be limited only to capital brought in for more than one or two years.

Fifth, a more direct approach (the "stick" versus the previous "carrot" or inducement policies) is to seek cooperation with tax authorities of recipient countries to interchange information on overseas bank deposits of nationals. Such information might be used to bring overseas accounts under the control of the central bank (subjecting them to its authority) and could thus bolster the net reserve position of the country. Alternatively countries could attempt to confiscate (tax 100 percent) all undeclared accounts held overseas, embargo them and authorize their use as payment or collateral for its foreign debt.

The Chilean authorities have designed a special program which encompasses several of the above features in connection with the purchase of its foreign debt. The program is designed to take advantage of two facts: that part of Chile's foreign debt is presently being traded some 30 percent below its face value and that, because of capital flight, Chileans hold dollars abroad that can be used to buy back this discounted debt. Without dollars with which to buy back its discounted debt, the losses incurred by the banks were, until now, of no benefit to Chile.

The program is designed to remedy this latter problem by tapping Chilean funds abroad through the parallel (black) market to purchase discounted foreign debt and allow the exchange at par of that dollar-denominated debt for the reduction of domestic (peso) debt or certain types of investment. The program thus offers, in effect, a special exchange rate for such capital inflows along with a de facto tax amnesty on unreported earnings brought back.

There are two such programs for investors, one for Chileans, the other for foreigners. Since our interest is in repatriating capital from abroad, we will focus on that for Chilean investors (under chapter 18 of the regulations on foreign exchange).[9] All Chile's registered foreign debt of more than one year maturity can be purchased (abroad) and exchanged in Chile for pesos or peso-denominated debt of the issuing institution. The central bank sets a monthly limit on the total that can be so exchanged (to avoid significantly raising the price of the dollar on the parallel market) and auctions off to commercial banks the right to effect said transactions. As a result of the operations, the foreign debt is lowered by the amount auctioned off every month. Recent studies[10] show that the profits of the operation, derived from the 31 percent average discount on Chile's foreign debt, have been distributed

9. In fact, however, the incentives given foreigners to convert debt into equity have forced the authorities to provide similar possibilities for would-be Chilean investors (Chapter 18 modified), since otherwise Chileans tended to bring back capital as if it were foreign investment.

10. Aninat y Méndez, "Análisis de las Operaciones con Titulos de Deuda Externa: Algunas Consideraciones Financieras y Económicas," *Informe de Coyuntura Economica Nacional,* no. 22 (9 June 1986); and Gemines *Análisis de la Coyuntura Económica,* (September 1986).

roughly as follows: 5 percent, the differential between the value of the dollar at the official and parallel market rates, to suppliers of dollars on the parallel market; 2 percent as commissions to agents for matching would-be debt purchasers and investors; 9 percent in the form of the discount received by the Chilean commercial bank in order to be willing to prepay its own foreign debt or have a firm use this debt to prepay its own debt with the bank; 14 percent as the rent extracted by the central bank in auctioning the valuable privilege of effecting such a transaction; and 1 percent profit to the investor.

How effective have such programs been in repatriating Chilean capital from abroad? Three points are worth drawing attention to: the amounts, the costs, and the use of the funds so repatriated. First, the central bank auctioned off rights to effect transactions for about $20 million to $40 million per month under this program (Chapter 18), a total of $280 million, in the program's first year.[11]

How much of this is repatriated capital is another question. Ideally, all of it would be, in which case the program's natural limit would be on the order of $1 billion. However, as is true with any system of multiple exchange rates, it might also be diverting funds from the trade balance and into the parallel market to lower Chilean debt at the expense of greater imports and growth, with a lesser effect in repatriating Chilean capital abroad.

The second question concerns costs. The incentives provided by this capital repatriation program are three: the premium the parallel market pays over the official rate; the fact that now that the domestic debt reprogramming seems over, and the basic solvency of most firms and banks has been clarified, the repatriation of capital has been made more attractive; and that de facto amnesty is given to the entire operation, with anonymity of investors being assured through legislation protecting bank secrecy (for banks are the intermediators of these operations). What is truly surprising is how relatively slight the monetary incentive is: the parallel market differential is but 5 percent at present, down from 15 percent a year back. This suggests, on the one hand, that much capital is coming back not because of these programs but because the real effective exchange rate has never been higher in the last twenty years and uncertainty has been significantly reduced. On the other hand, it suggests that the implicit amnesty on capital flight was probably the most important of these three incentives.

---

11. Most recently (mid-1986) the central bank has modified Chapter 18 to allow Chilean banks and firms to exchange their own foreign debt (acquired with dollars from abroad) for equity in themselves, thus saving on the percentage paid out in auction, but subject to approval from the central bank and limitations on profit remittances. This second program has only recently been developed, with one major operation, to capitalize the Edwards Bank. In total, through 30 June 1986, in their first year of operation, Chapters 18, 18 modified, and 19 have permitted operations totaling $409 million.

Third, concerning use, this program allocates the repatriated funds entirely to debt amortization. The merits of such an extreme allocation are hardly obvious. Among other things, it seems to imply that the current discount on Chile's debt is so large that it is preferable to divert funds from imports of intermediate and capital goods, which would speed growth, to debt amortization. Hence, it bets heavily that the worst of the debt crisis—both the region's and Chile's—is over, and so implicitly plays down the foreign exchange constraint (and its especially high current multiplier) on growth.

In short, this program, instead of attracting capital back sooner, seems simply to channel it into the reduction of foreign debt. If this program did not exist, provided there were some form of amnesty, capital would probably continue to be repatriated at a similar rate (which would help explain why the parallel market differential has declined despite the increase in the demand for dollars generated by the program), but it could be channeled in any proportion the central bank wished between amortization of discounted debt and growth. Thus, it would seem preferable, in general, to segregate the capital repatriation component of the program from that of debt amortization, and attack each separately.

Colombia
Rudolf Hommes

The Colombian government adopted a very strict exchange control policy in 1967. Under this regime, it has been illegal for Colombians to hold foreign assets without authorization of the central bank Office of Exchange Control. The increase of unauthorized holdings of foreign assets, such as bank deposits abroad or real estate, would therefore be an indicator of capital flight. But for Colombia, and probably Bolivia and Peru as well, changes in the holdings of foreign assets would tend to overestimate the size of capital flight, since some nationals of these countries earn very large incomes abroad through illegal drug trade.

In fact, this trade produces capital flight from the United States toward these same countries, since detection of drug-related assets carries a risk of confiscation by the US authorities. This positive flow of funds counteracts the effects of funds fleeing Colombia as a result of such traditional causes as political risk or the disarray of macroeconomic variables. Despite the neutralizing effect of the drug-related positive flows, however, there was

The author is editor, Estratégia Económica y Financiera, Bogotá, Colombia.

significant capital flight out of Colombia, particularly in 1983–85 according to the Morgan Guaranty estimates, which show negligible capital flight in 1976–82, increasing to $0.7 billion in 1983–85. *International Financial Statistics* estimates that foreign bank deposits by residents of Colombia amounted to $2.6 billion at the end of 1985, of which $1.8 billion was deposited in US banks. These levels of asset holding are by no means inconsequential since $2.6 billion amounts to 19.8 percent of Colombia's total recorded foreign debt and 37.7 percent of the registered private foreign debt. This capital flight can usually be traced primarily to economic variables, but political variables are also very important.

Political Risk

Political risk is one reason for legal and illegal capital flows. It affects investors' perceptions of the probable outcome of investment decisions, and even the probability of survival of the investor, as a person or as an institution. In Colombia, the political climate deteriorated in the 1980s, compared with the previous decade. For example, the number of incidents involving political violence (kidnappings, terrorist acts, assassinations, invasions of towns or private property) increased very rapidly during the 1980s. There were 1,072 such incidents in 1976–80 and 2,736 in 1981–83. Of particular importance to investors is the practice of kidnapping for ransom that guerrillas and criminals use to raise money. This type of incident grew from a recorded total of 47 in 1974–80 to 268 in 1981–83, and to 476 between 1984 and September 1985. There were 498 recorded assassinations of civilians due to political violence in the first eight months of 1985, compared to a total of 407 political murders in all of 1974–80.

The figures reported here were taken from the official presidential report on the peace process.[1] Although it may underreport the level of political violence, there is no need for further gruesome detail to convey the picture of a rapidly growing political risk for investors. It can by itself explain capital flight in the 1980s, even in the absence of macroeconomic causes, which were also a likely reason for the flow of funds abroad.

Forecasting Exchange Rate Movements

Between December 1984 and December 1985, the Colombian peso was devalued 18.5 percent in real terms, and 50 percent in nominal terms. This

---

1. Ministerio de Gobierno, República de Colombia, *Paz* (a report on the Peace Policy of the Betancur Administration).

drastic devaluation could be foreseen since 1982, when the index of the real exchange rate showed a 32.3 percent real appreciation of the peso from the 1975 level, which is considered an adequate standard by the Colombian economic authorities and by the International Monetary Fund (IMF). In 1983, according to this index, the peso was overvalued by 35.9 percent. This overvaluation was not corrected until October 1985. Simultaneously, net international reserves dwindled from $5.6 billion in 1981 to $4.9 billion in 1982, $3.1 billion in 1983, and $1.8 billion in 1984 (in 1985 they climbed to almost $3.0 billion).

During this period, the international banks contributed to the crisis, cutting commercial credit to Colombia and pushing for an IMF intervention, which usually heralds devaluation and recession. The average investor, given this public information, could easily guess the direction of future exchange rate movements and thus had an incentive to take steps to protect his liquid assets. Because local foreign-exchange-denominated financial assets ("exchange certificates") were available only in limited amounts issued by the central bank, most investors had an incentive to place their assets abroad.

This is indeed what happened. During 1980 and 1981, the black market exchange rate was below the official exchange rate (i.e., the dollar was at a discount), probably reflecting an excess supply of illegal foreign exchange. This differential, which was 5 percent in December 1981, disappeared during the first quarter of 1982. Beginning in June 1982, a premium over the official exchange rate was paid for the dollar sold in the parallel market. This premium reached a peak of 35 percent in June 1983, which coincided with the 1975–86 maximum overvaluation of the real exchange rate, some 41.2 percent over the average 1975 level.

The Efficiency of the Parallel Market

In April 1985, a naive forecasting model to predict the peso exchange rate was published by *Estrategia*.[2] The dependent variable was the devaluation in a given quarter, and the independent variables were the internal and external nominal interest rates, and the black market premium at the beginning of the quarter. These three variables explained 95 percent of the variance of the nominal devaluation for the quarter ended in any month from January 1980 through April 1985. The variable with overriding explanatory power was the ratio of the official to the parallel exchange rate

---

2. Rudolf Hommes and Martha Bermudez, "El Papel de las Expectativas de Devaluación," *Estrategia*, no. 87, p. 18.

at the beginning of each quarter. This indicates that those prices successfully and correctly incorporated available information about the future of the exchange rate.

Although the model has a negative bias due to the long record of overvaluation of the peso and to the rapid adjustment during 1985, it indicates that the actors in the parallel market have access to correct information about the future, and that this is incorporated in the parallel exchange rate. This in turn suggests that the market is not thin, is likely to be efficient, and is therefore a suitable mechanism for capital flight.

The Speculative Nature of Colombian Capital Flight

At first glance, the relationship between the level of foreign interest rates and the parallel market premium over the official exchange rate would be expected to be positive and significant. The relationship between this premium and the domestic nominal interest rate would be expected to be negative and also significant. But while the latter relationship holds true, the former apparently does not. In fact, from January 1980 through June 1985, the black market dollar premium was negatively affected by increases of either the internal or the external nominal interest rates (adjusted for inflation and devaluation).[3] The size of the premium was also found to be a crucial element negatively affecting the net flow of funds in the personal services and tourism sections of the balance of payments, both well-known vehicles for repatriating capital to Colombia.

One possible explanation for the negative correlation between the premium and the international interest rate is that an increase of the international interest rate restricts the availability of legal foreign credit to firms operating in Colombia, forcing them to repatriate capital. This can be done by increasing the net flow of services and tourism, or the supply of parallel market dollars. This makes sense when internal interest rates are raised to counter changes in the external rate to prevent capital flight, as was done in Colombia during the period analyzed. No adjustment, of course, is necessary when external interest rates go down. This way, repatriation is encouraged both when international interest rates go up, and international liquidity contracts, and also when they come down. Appropriately, the model described shows that the internal nominal interest-rate elasticity of the black market premium is higher than the external interest-rate elasticity.

---

3. Rudolf Hommes and Martha Bermudez, "Determinantes del Precio del Dólar Negro," *Estrategia*, no. 89, p. 13.

The Riskiness of the Parallel Market

Trading in the Colombian parallel market is condoned, but it is still illegal and thus risky. A popular joke among stockbrokers illustrates the ambiguous status of such trading:

A well-known firm of stockbrokers was robbed by individuals who entered the building claiming to be investigators from the Exchange Control Superintendency. Although they walked away with 50 million pesos, the manager was relieved when he learned that they only wanted to steal the money in the safe and not to look at the company's transaction documents.

This ambiguous status creates opportunities for fraud, which generates uncertainty.

Detection by the authorities is punishable by fines as high as 200 percent of the value traded or transferred abroad. US authorities also ask questions when Colombians enter the United States carrying more than US$5,000 in cash or securities and investigate bank accounts with deposits over US$10,000. This may deter most Colombian investors from transferring funds abroad, particularly to the US market, and the Colombian authorities may regard the restrictions imposed on Colombian citizens' financial transactions as an additional positive by-product of the antidrug effort.

These difficulties suggest that the funds supplied so efficiently by the parallel market must be transferred through institutional channels. These may be found in the overvaluation of registered imports and the undervaluation of exports, or through the unrecorded prepayment of legally registered foreign currency debts, aided by banks fearing for the quality of their portfolios. This suggests that the opportunities for capital flight are greater for persons and institutions involved in international trade: exporters, importers, and banks, both Colombian and multinational.

Policies for Repatriation of Funds

The overvaluation of the peso was a major inducement for speculative capital flight. The 1985 devaluation corrected this imbalance, and the government's current policy is one of moderate real devaluation. These policies for repatriation of funds are already proving effective. The personal services account of the balance of payments showed revenue of US$233 million for the first eight months of 1986, compared to $60 million for the same period in 1985. In 1984, these revenues amounted to only $33 million. The devaluation policy is undoubtedly paying off on this front. This success is also reflected by the decline of the premium of the black market dollar over the official rate, which decreased from 1.6 percent in December 1985, to 0.7 percent at the end of July 1986. A drastic reduction of the inflation rate in the second quarter of 1986 also helped the trend toward a real devaluation, which positively affects expectations about future devaluation.

Unfortunately, the political causes of capital flight have remained unchanged. In the first eight months of 1986, there were 115 kidnappings, 247 fatalities among the armed forces and another 294 wounded, while 410 civilians were assassinated in armed confrontations between the army and guerrilla factions. The peace process has been severely criticized, and there have been attempts by right- and left-wing extremists to isolate the leading guerrilla group (FARC) from the peace process, by the systematic assassination of 16 members of the opposition party linked to FARC, including two congressmen. The government has announced radical reforms to appease the armed opposition, but the situation may get out of hand if such reforms are not approved quickly. Unemployment is running high, around 14 percent, and inflation started to climb in August 1986 after a quarter of relief.

Finally, some institutional mechanisms have been approved to induce the repatriation of funds. In June 1985, the Colombian Congress authorized the government to issue special "bonds for the repatriation of capital" to be traded in the international markets. Bond holders can redeem these in foreign exchange at maturity, or exchange them at any time for central bank paper denominated in dollars and traded freely in the Colombian stock market. The same law provides that when the holder of the repatriation bonds agrees to trade them for central bank paper or when they are redeemed at maturity by Colombian citizens living in the country, there will be no investigation or sanctions related to the implicit violation of the exchange-control regime that is derived from holding these bonds. The law also confers tax exemption or special tax treatment for the proceeds of conversion of these bonds to central bank paper.

At the present time, when Colombian public debt documents are being traded at approximately 87 percent of their face value in the secondary markets, these repatriation bonds offer Colombia a very attractive opportunity to reduce its external debt service and nationalize a fraction of its foreign debt. A leading US investment bank is studying a proposal by the Colombian government to issue the repatriation bonds with attractive yields that would make them marketable in international markets for bona fide investors. Additionally, they would offer the special inducements described for Colombians willing to repatriate their foreign holdings, and they would be tradable for outstanding Colombian public-debt documents at face value. Since these documents can be acquired at a discount in international markets, this could be a very profitable channel for multinationals to transfer funds needed by their Colombian subsidiaries or to make new capital investments.

At the same time, it would help Colombian public finances, since present interest rates are below the coupon interest rates of public debt and because the anticipated redemption of repatriation bonds would imply a net reduction of external debt. Given Colombia's improved credit situation, as a result of the coffee boom, it can be hoped that the international banking community will regard the repatriation bonds as legitimate and marketable financial instruments.

Regardless of the attractiveness of these instruments, the lessons of the Colombian case may be summarized as follows: currency overvaluation and political uncertainty encourage capital flight. One of these factors has been corrected; the other one remains unresolved.

Mexico
Ernesto Zedillo

My discussion of the Mexican case is made up of three parts: first, the issue of measurement of capital flight; next, some general observations on the causes of the phenomenon under study; and, lastly, some comments on possible actions to stop and reverse capital flight.

The Extent of Capital Flight

Other participants have pointed out the difficulties involved in measuring capital flight. One thing is for sure: international banking statistics such as those published by the International Monetary Fund (IMF) or the Bank for International Settlements (BIS), though useful indeed, tell only part of the story. This is chiefly due to the following facts:

☐ Investments other than bank deposits do exist. Real estate is a noticeable example that might well apply to the Mexican case; but other financial assets, such as bonds and equities, whose ownership by nationality is hard or even impossible to track, are surely used.

☐ The existence of offshore banking centers (such as Panama, Netherlands Antilles, Cayman Islands) makes possible the creation of deposits through "letter-box" or "brass-plate" companies. This implies that the true nationality of many depositors cannot be traced.

The author is General Manager of Fircorca at the Banco de Mexico. These observations are his sole responsibility and should not be attributed to his employer.

Despite these difficulties, estimates of capital flight have to be made by one means or another. A very old, but still very popular, method of estimating capital flight has been used extensively during the last year or so—particularly to assess the extent of capital flight from Latin American countries, including my own country. This method estimates capital flight as a residual, by assuming that capital inflows (increase in external indebtedness and direct foreign investment) finance capital flight unless they finance the current account deficit and the reported (official and commercial bank) external reserve accumulation. By pursuing this approach, it has been reported by *World Financial Markets* (WFM) of Morgan Guaranty that $53 billion fled Mexico during 1976–85.

Although I am ready to report on statistical evidence supporting the notion that the phenomenon of capital flight has been quite sizable in the Mexican case, I would also like to suggest that the estimates provided by WFM and others tend to exaggerate the dimension of the phenomenon. Like many other analysts, I have reservations about the "residual" approach as a methodology to estimate capital flight. Its main shortcoming is that all of the errors-and-omissions item of the balance of payments is taken as capital flight. This implies, for example, that smuggling of imports—certainly of some importance in a protected economy such as Mexico's—is included in the capital flight measure. In turn, export underinvoicing and import overinvoicing, if significant, would tend to underestimate capital outflows, when measured through errors and omissions. Putting aside these methodological caveats, the main problem in the WFM estimate stems from the data used in their calculations to determine the inflow of external savings, which they measure—apart from net direct investment inflows—through the change in the gross external stock of debt.[1]

This is not the proper occasion for a tediously long analysis of statistics. A couple of examples will illustrate my point. In recent issues of the *World Debt Tables* of the World Bank, substantial increases in the total size of Mexico's external debt are reported for years such as 1983 and 1984. These increases are far greater than the amounts raised by Mexico through the forced or concerted lending exercises of those years. The apparent increase in indebtedness—beyond the actual new lending—comes mostly from the increase in the private sector's external debt figures. These increases are not, however, the result of actual additional indebtedness. They come from a wider coverage of the debt-reporting systems. Before Mexico adopted

---

1. I should say, however that the WFM analysts are not to be blamed entirely; as shown later, the main blame falls on the institutions that report on stocks of external indebtedness—both national and international—for not warning users of statistics about their very serious problems of comparability over time. Yet, WFM analysts should have checked the consistency over time and across countries of the data they used in their calculations.

exchange controls in late 1982, it was not mandatory for firms to report their stocks of external liabilities to the financial authorities.[2] In fact, not until 1983 was the official and mandatory registry started in order to obtain statistics with a significant coverage. Clearly though, this peculiar situation—which, unfortunately, has not yet been granted a footnote in the relevant publications—provides a very distorted view of the availability of external resources to the Mexican economy during recent years.

Another problem arises from the evolution of supplier or trade-related direct credits. The reduction of Mexican imports, plus accelerated collections by trade creditors, have resulted in a significant outflow of resources to settle these obligations, which, under normal conditions, would have been rolled over. Although these payments are reported in the official Mexican balance of payments statistics, estimators of capital flight have decided to ignore them, and consequently take such payments as capital flight.

Considering all of the aforementioned, if the "residual" approach to estimation of capital flight is to be used at all, it is much more desirable to rely on the flow data of external indebtedness reported in the country's balance of payments. These flow figures are more consistent with the other items in the balance of payments, and also more consistent over a time period, than the figures obtained from ad hoc sources. Table 7.6 contains an estimate of the "residual" for a rather long period, 1970–85.

Notice that the current account figures have been adjusted by deducting the imputed interest on identified deposits of Mexicans abroad, an item that is consistently included in the Mexican official statistics. This adjustment—quite logical in the context of estimating capital flight—has not usually been made in other estimates of capital flight. Several conclusions can be drawn from table 7.6.

First, the residual suggests that persistent capital flight began to occur around 1973. Probably only in the three-year period 1978–80 did the phenomenon disappear for all practical purposes.

Second, however, the bulk of the "residual" is found in very specific years: 1976, 1981, and 1982 were years of massive capital flight. It is striking that the "residual" for 1981–82 was $18 billion, although not all of that should be attributed to capital flight since smuggling was probably sizable during those years.

Third, while capital flight has admittedly plagued the Mexican economy and taken on rather large proportions, especially in particular years, the "residual" of table 7.6 suggests that estimates provided by other analysts are exaggerated. Recall that WFM provided an estimate of capital flight

---

2. The Mexican balance of payments compilers relied on a questionnaire sent to a large sample of firms to calculate external indebtedness of the private sector. These data were never reported in the *World Debt Tables*.

Table 7.6 Mexico: balance of payments residual
(million dollars)

	Net flow of external savings[a]	Change in international reserves[b]	Change in other official and domestic banks' assets[c]	Current account balance[d]	Residual
1970	897.3	−102.1	−1.1	−1,318.0	−523.9
1971	845.9	−200.0	9.4	−1,035.0	−379.7
1972	760.1	−264.7	−4.5	−1,111.0	−620.1
1973	2,535.5	−122.3	−5.1	−1,740.1	668.0
1974	4,348.8	−36.9	−3.7	−3,552.9	755.3
1975	5,651.5	−165.1	16.7	−4,718.9	784.2
1976	5,924.1	1,004.0	−47.1	−3,937.0	2,944.0
1977	3,299.5	−657.1	−64.9	−1,890.8	686.7
1978	3,743.3	−434.1	−15.8	−3,226.6	66.8
1979	6,335.3	−418.9	17.6	−5,702.3	231.7
1980	12,686.8	−1,018.5	−559.0	−11,787.5	−678.2
1981	30,616.5	−1,012.2	−3,033.9	−16,837.3	9,733.1
1982	10,576.9	3,184.7	1,490.7	−7,027.1	8,225.2
1983	2,269.6	−3,100.8	−1,196.0	4,442.6	2,415.4
1984	1,941.3	−3,200.8	687.3	2,904.2	2,332.0
1985	−181.8	2,328.4	368.6	−597.5	1,917.7

Source: Banco de Mexico, Dirección de Investigación Económica.
a. Net increase of external indebtedness—public and private—plus net flow of direct foreign investment.
b. Change in gross reserves.
c. From 1980 onward includes external assets of domestic banks and of PEMEX.
d. Net of interest received on identified deposits of Mexicans abroad.

from Mexico of $53 billion for 1976–85, which is almost twice as much as the "residual" reported in table 7.6 for the same period. Particularly misleading is the WFM estimate of $17 billion for the 1983–85 period, which is $10 billion over the figure in table 7.6. Furthermore, I would submit that even the "residual" of $6.7 billion for 1983–85 in table 7.6 may be an overstatement of the size of capital flight during this period. From my day-to-day interaction with debtor firms and foreign banks, I am aware that significant repayments of external debt have been made through the free foreign exchange market—repayments that are not reported by firms and cannot be detected by the balance of payments compilers.

I am therefore reluctant to accept a figure as high as $6.7 billion as an estimate of capital flight for 1983–85. But this is, of course, simply my personal opinion, since I do not have—at least, not yet—firm statistical evidence to support this belief. I suspect that the foreign bank creditors of the Mexican private sector could, if they wished, help to quantify their quiet and unreported disengagement from Mexico, which is now wrongly identified as capital flight. Obviously enough, such disengagement has macroeconomic effects quite similar to those of capital flight.

Causes of Capital Flight

Needless to say, looking at length into the causes of capital flight would require a thorough review of Mexican economic policy and politics during the last fifteen years, a task that is impossible in this presentation. Instead, I intend to sketch certain macroeconomic facts that have characterized the capital flight period of recent Mexican economic history. I will not attempt to incorporate these facts into a formal theoretical or econometric framework. I simply want to suggest that very obvious violations of the basic rules of prudent internal economic management, which in turn had adverse social and political effects, might explain capital flight up to 1982. Since then, some external events—particularly the debt crisis—have come more prominently into play.

The following facts are surely associated with capital flight:

□ The first year in which some capital flight can be detected, 1973, is also a year in which the balance of payments disequilibrium enlarged significantly. The current account deficit grew almost 60 percent. Furthermore, the net flow of external savings increased more than threefold over the level of previous years. Since 1973 the total external debt has increased 10 times in nominal terms.

□ It is clear that, until 1982, capital flight was "financed" with external borrowing. Since 1983 capital flight has been "financed" mainly with trade and current account surpluses. It is peculiar that bankers' nervousness about lending money to finance capital flight is only of recent vintage. What was going on before the 1982 breakdown was not of concern at the time. Lending to developing countries (even if they were capital-flight-prone) was praised as the great achievement of international banks in recycling the oil surpluses. This point of view can be found in back issues of the same publication that is now so outspoken about capital flight.

□ Data in the first column of table 7.7 indicate that the beginning of capital flight coincided with exhaustion of the process of financial "deepening" that had characterized the Mexican economy during the previous two decades.

Table 7.7   Mexico: financial intermediation and real interest rates

	Total financial intermediation[a]	Real interest rate	
		Mexico[b]	Abroad[c]
1970	30.7	5.22	3.43
1971	32.3	4.44	1.34
1972	32.3	2.99	−0.23
1973	30.8	−10.11	−10.11
1974	27.1	−8.65	−8.30
1975	27.6	−0.51	−3.89
1976	26.5	−13.11	31.86
1977	23.8	−6.45	−1.55
1978	25.7	−1.68	−6.36
1979	26.9	−3.61	−6.53
1980	26.8	−4.65	−10.97
1981	28.5	5.30	2.78
1982	29.4	−22.61	235.41
1983	27.0	−3.11	−36.01
1984	27.0	0.68	−8.27
1985	26.7	6.16	30.20

Source: Banco de Mexico, Dirección de Investigación Económica.
a. Average stock of monetary instruments and banking and nonbanking savings instruments as a percentage of GDP.
b. Compounded weighted average return of most representative instruments discounted by the December–December rate of inflation.
c. Simple average return on instruments of up to one year maturity in the Eurodollar deposit market adjusted by the rate of peso depreciation and discounted by the December–December rate of inflation.

□ Table 7.7 also shows that the reversal and later stagnation of the process of financial deepening is associated with the behavior of real interest rates in Mexico. The first year of sizable capital flight was also the first year domestic real interest rates became highly negative, quite in contrast to the positive real levels registered in previous years. Negative real rates resulted from the combination of higher inflation and artificially repressed nominal interest rates. Note also the gap between domestic real rates and foreign real interest rates.

□ Not surprisingly, the years with the most acute capital flight were also years of exchange rate overvaluation, as shown by the real exchange rate index of table 7.8. Observe the degree of overvaluation registered in 1976 and in 1981. In this respect, 1982 was an exception. After the February

Table 7.8   Mexico: real exchange rate

	Index[a] (1970 = 100)
1970	100.2
1971	100.5
1972	104.4
1973	109.6
1974	98.9
1975	96.0
1976	87.1
1977	132.4
1978	126.0
1979	120.3
1980	110.2
1981	89.2
1982	116.9
1983	134.1
1984	112.8
1985	97.0

Source: Banco de Mexico, Dirección de Investigación Económica.
a. Mid-year value, 133 currency GDP-weighted basket.

devaluation, the real exchange rate was hardly overvalued during the year. Yet, other factors such as ill-founded economic policy actions and associated uncertainly fueled capital flight and further devaluation.

☐ The domestic side of the overall macroeconomic disequilibrium involved public finance. Table 7.9 presents a long series of the public-sector deficit. Rather than look at the overall or nominal deficit, observe the evolution of the "operational" deficit. Again, capital flight begins in 1972 after the abandonment of the policy of moderation in deficit financing. The worst years of capital flight occurred around the years of major operational deficits. After 1982, the operational deficit has dwindled—indeed, it has become a surplus if the inflationary component of interest on the external debt is also deducted from the figures in table 7.9. At the same time, however, the external debt burden—as measured by the well-known concept of net transfer—has become enormous, and inflation has proven to be uncontrollable so far.

☐ The internal disarray of the 1970s coincided with the enormous expansion of international financial markets. Until 1982, this expansion provided abundant external resources to finance the external disequilibrium. At

Table 7.9   Mexico: public sector deficit (percentage of GDP)

	Overall	Operational
1970	3.78	3.59
1971	2.47	2.21
1972	4.93	4.54
1973	6.86	4.94
1974	7.25	5.31
1975	10.01	8.75
1976	9.89	6.51
1977	6.73	4.33
1978	6.68	4.76
1979	7.61	5.28
1980	7.85	4.58
1981	14.75	11.60
1982	17.55	7.34
1983	8.99	− 1.30
1984	8.63	1.11
1985	9.95	1.74

Note: The operational deficit excludes interest payments that compensate for inflation ex post.
Source: Banco de Mexico, Dirección de Investigación Económica.

the same time, it also made it easier than ever for Mexicans and other Latin Americans to place their savings abroad. In particular, the emergence of offshore banking centers made it easier to save abroad without having the resulting income taxed.

Summing up, the causes of capital flight until 1982 do not call for extremely sophisticated analyses. A well-identified case of excessive fiscal expansion induced a deteriorating macroeconomic environment character- ized by double-digit inflation, sizable current account deficits (despite soaring oil revenues between 1978 and 1982) and an enormous growth of the external debt. In this context, a major policy mistake was the suppression of domestic interest rates and the overvaluation of the exchange rate. These two expedients permitted only temporarily lower inflation than otherwise, but at the cost of greater capital flight and higher external indebtednesses.

The effects of domestic policy mistakes were magnified by the way the international financial markets evolved during those years. The expansion of international financial markets meant not only easy access to external resources by borrowing governments, but also easy access by domestic savers to an attractive menu of—very often nontaxable—financial assets.

This taxation aspect is of paramount importance in explaining why the local availability of dollar-indexed instruments was not sufficient to stop massive capital flight when the risk of major devaluations became evident. The risk of internal debt repudiation, associated with episodes of fast growth in the fiscal deficit as in 1981 and 1982, was also important in explaining the failure of dollar-indexed financial assets to stop massive capital flight. Needless to say, the worst fears were confirmed in August 1982, when the Mex-dollars were declared dollar-inconvertible, and an exchange rate lower than the free rate was used to redeem them.

The story after 1983 is somewhat different. Real adjustment of the Mexican economy—as measured by the relevant fiscal and balance of payments variables—should be an undisputed fact. Yet, the dramatic reversal of external lending flows has implied an enormous transfer of resources, achieved through very fast devaluation and an almost unavoidable acceleration in inflation. The real adjustment that the economy needed, generation of a net transfer of resources abroad, worsening terms of trade, and an inflationary environment, have resulted, on average, in negative economic growth since 1982. All of this leads to a scenario hardly conducive to retaining internally 100 percent of the country's savings.

A Few Suggested Remedies

Let me start by suggesting that capital controls are not the answer. This judgement is not based on any ideological prejudice. It is derived from observing the experience of other countries, and from recognition that Mexico's peculiar geographic situation makes it even harder—I would say impossible—to establish effective restrictions on the export of capital. Successful controls require total control of current account transactions, together with efficient repression of parallel (or black) foreign exchange markets, both within and outside the territory of the country implementing the controls. Mexico's rather diversified current account transactions—comprising diversified imports and exports, tourism, and border trade—make it impossible to control all sources of inflow and outflow of foreign exchange. Moreover, our proximity to the United States makes it impossible to avoid the development of a parallel peso-dollar market abroad, even if such a market could be avoided within the national territory.

In addition, reflection on the experiences of several Southern Cone countries has made me quite skeptical about implementing successful controls on the capital account even where the geographical situation is different from Mexico's. Brazil is sometimes cited as an example of a country that used strict foreign exchange controls to curtail capital flight. My economic suspicion is that the pursuit of more consistent financial policies, particularly liberal interest-rate and flexible exchange rate policies, were more relevant to the Brazilian experience. I reject therefore the idea that capital controls could help to solve the Mexican problem. In fact, it would make it even worse and would nullify any chance of significant capital repatriation in the future.

Let me now refer to another idea: debt-equity swaps. This time it comes from the free-market-oriented camp that is very much in fashion. According to proponents of debt-equity swaps, debtor countries should take advantage of the fact that their international "IOUs" are marketed with significant discounts. It is said that as long as the debtor governments were willing to accept a smaller discount than the one prevailing in the market, the external debt could be swapped for internal debt and, in the process, would provoke larger inflows of direct foreign investment (DFI) and the return of domestic capital from abroad.

As an economist, I find the scheme rather naive and, possibly, counter-productive. When debt-equity swaps are used to attract DFI, as in the Mexican program already in operation, there is no true warranty that the swap will attract *additional* foreign investment. To the extent that it does not, debt-equity swaps may simply serve to pay off external debt at the expense of reducing other capital inflows, such as DFI. Giving up scarce capital inflows may prove very costly even in the face of substantial discounts on the foreign debt. The bottom line of my argument is, perhaps, that debt-equity swaps are a rather inefficient way of subsidizing foreign investment and may simply facilitate the disengagement of foreign creditors from debtor countries. One should also question, from the perspective of public-debt management policy, the wisdom of substituting internal debt for external debt, when the public sector has already crowded out the private sector from domestic credit markets and a rather tight monetary policy is still needed.

Equally fragile is the case for debt-equity swaps as a means of repatriating domestic capital. As long as effective foreign-exchange controls are impossible, "round-tripping" cannot be avoided. This practice—buy dollars in the free market, buy debt, sell debt; buy dollars, buy debt, and so on—is a real possibility as long as the fundamental causes of capital flight are not corrected. Therefore, the risks of using debt-equity swaps as a means of repatriating capital are considerable in terms of exchange rate instability and associated consequences.

Having disposed of capital controls and debt-equity swaps, what can then be done to solve the problem? Some observers would say that there is the Mexican approach of the past year: the application of a highly restrictive credit policy with its implicit marginal reserve requirements on commercial banks as high as 90 percent, currently around 75 percent. By drying up the domestic credit market, firms have been forced to repatriate a portion of financial assets abroad, consequently alleviating the acute shortage of foreign exchange caused by the drop in oil prices early this year. Given the natural lag of balance of payments figures, it is not yet possible to provide statistical evidence—through the "residual"—to support the belief that capital flight eased or, in fact, reversed during 1986. Yet, the fact that Mexico has continued to service its foreign debt, and that the liberalization of foreign trade has continued without exhausting foreign-exchange reserves (despite the oil price drop), does suggest that something is going right.

Needless to say, however, an overly restrictive monetary policy cannot be an effective, sustainable solution. Sooner or later its benefits are bound to be outweighed by its costs. Under 1986 conditions (a loss of about $8 billion in oil revenue, which translates into an enormous loss of fiscal revenue, as well as the absence of foreign credit during most of the year) there was no better alternative left for the country's monetary authorities than to apply a very tight credit policy together with rapid exchange rate depreciation. But, clearly, this cannot and should not be a permanent state of affairs, and its usefulness as an expedient to reverse capital flight has to come to an end soon.

This problem has to be addressed with policies sustainable in the medium and long run. I will list only what I see as broad, necessary conditions to cure the capital flight disease.

□ First of all, a return to an environment of economic growth in the context of inflation well below current levels is the main precondition for a permanent reversal of capital flight. One is hopeful that the new stage of stabilization policy now being launched by the Mexican government will achieve its chief objectives.

□ Second, the domestic banking system has to be liberalized with respect to the determination of deposit interest rates. It is important to accept the way international financial markets have evolved as a fact of life, and to allow domestic financial intermediaries to compete on a sounder footing to attract domestic savings. This criterion should also be applied in dealing with the placement of government paper. The introduction of dollar-indexed debt instruments—already under way—is also important in tackling the problem.

□ Third, a solution to the external debt problem that is perceived by the population to be sustainable in the long run will also be required. Having participated in the recent negotiations, it is best if I refrain from expressing my view on whether the deal just obtained will do the trick.

Last, but not least, a profound reform is needed to achieve tax neutrality between debt and equity financing. The present Mexican tax system, not unlike that of other countries, is significantly debt-biased. Furthermore, provision should be made in our tax laws to ease—at least temporarily—the taxation of capital gains derived from exchange rate devaluations, which is a prerequisite for any significant repatriation of capital. Fortunately, it seems that these ideas are now under serious consideration by the Mexican tax authorities.

8

Panel on Policy Issues

Rimmer de Vries

First let me say that you are doing a great public service by holding this conference on an important and relevant issue of public policy. The proceedings were fascinating, and I am sure you will get some valuable conclusions from the commissioned papers.

Some history may be of interest. The paper that attracted my interest in this subject was done by Sjaastad in 1983 for a conference in Geneva. Sjaastad pointed out the liquidity aspect of the debt crisis by emphasizing that the net asset position of Latin American countries had not deteriorated nearly as much as their gross debt positions, since their residents had built up large investment positions overseas. He did not talk about flight capital, as I recall. But his paper encouraged me to unravel his "net flows" into gross flows, and that exercise led to some large outflow numbers, which were dubbed "capital flight." When I mentioned the results to my management, they suggested that we bury the whole issue—and I believe a similar reaction occurred in some official institutions—because they were afraid that Congress, hearing about all the capital flight, would never approve the IMF quota increase.

I also asked my staff to reconstruct the past balance of payments of the large debtor countries assuming no capital flight. The results were astonishing. Argentina, for example, would have had an external debt of only $1 billion by the end of 1985 had there been no capital flight, and of course a much better current account as well. This is interesting because we are still debating how to measure capital flight—whether to use a narrow definition or a wider concept, which would include the earnings on overseas assets that are not repatriated. Bill Cline uses the narrow definition and we use the broad one because it is more consistent with standard balance of payments concepts. Also, if you want to know what would have happened

The author is Senior Vice President, Morgan Guaranty Trust Co.

to the external debt if there had been no capital flight, you have to use the broader definition, because the debt resulting from capital flight has to be serviced. If the earnings of the overseas assets are not repatriated to service this debt, new debt has to be acquired. So you are back again to the broader definition. These conceptual and computational difficulties drove home that it was a serious problem. Had there been no capital outflows or flight, the external debt position of almost all the heavily indebted countries such as Mexico, Argentina, and Venezuela would have been very manageable. The net external position of Mexico is probably better than that of Korea.

One other comment. When we finally published our estimates in a small technical article in *World Financial Markets*, many believed they were arrived at from in-house statistics. They are, of course, completely based on published balance of payments and external debt statistics. However, from what I know some American and Swiss banks are doing in this field, it is easy to err on the conservative side! Thus, if anything, the numbers we published are underestimates and the higher Bank of England numbers probably are closer to the mark.

Now, what is the purpose of having this conference? One concept that I have not heard discussed yet is "restoration of creditworthiness." The purpose of the entire debt strategy is to make troubled debtors get back into the credit markets, to get money to flow voluntarily again to them. If you do not have that objective, you do not treat capital flight as a serious issue. In fact, as Rudi Dornbusch does, you poke fun at it and at debt-equity swaps and tell cat and dog stories. But if you really want to restore creditworthiness, build and restore viable and competitive economies and equitable societies, so that those countries can go back to the free and voluntary credit markets, then you will look at all the suggestions made to stem capital flight and to turn it around.

In the September issue of *World Financial Markets*, where I review and discuss a paper that Rudi Dornbusch presented at a Federal Reserve conference, I mention that the issue of flight capital is part and parcel of solving the debt crisis. Rudi had stated that the return of flight capital is like the last car of the train. I would like to put the caboose up front. As pointed out, a great deal of the external debt buildup of recent years is directly the result of flight capital. The corresponding assets are abroad; how can we get them back? Yesterday, we heard many suggestions about what could be done: the need for the right policies, exchange rates, and so on. But before we get a return of flight capital, we have to find ways to repatriate the earnings of these overseas assets. Suppose the average rate of return on these assets is 6 percent, which is low. If returned to the home country, a country such as Mexico would be able to pay 40 percent of its debt service out of these earnings. Thus, after the first step, i.e., stopping capital flight, comes the task of securing a return of the earnings of these assets to help service the debt that was created by the capital flight in the first place. That was the whole point of Sjaastad. The net asset position of countries such as Mexico, Argentina, and Venezuela is very good.

It is also interesting to remember that the United States, in its balance of payments program in the 1960s, incorporated the repatriation of investment earnings in its schedule. US companies had to bring all or part of these earnings back. It was part of a formula that determined how much new investment capital they could take out. I would like Mexico and other countries to start tapping those huge earnings. In the Mexican loan package of $12 billion, about $4 billion of ex ante capital flight is included. This represents two years of earnings of overseas assets actually not repatriated, though recognized in the current account. Because they assume the earnings will not be brought home, the banks are asked to put up more cash, and more debt is created as a result.

Furthermore, a good part of the $12 billion will be used to build up reserves. For what purpose? In the past, reserves were used to defend the exchange rate. The more that is done, the more unrealistic the rate becomes, and the more capital flight occurs. In the final analysis, reserve buildup leads to capital flight. Thus I will be very surprised if much less than half of the $12 billion will de facto finance capital flight (using our broad definition). We will, of course, not know until the end of 1988.

To prevent it from happening, the Mexicans have to pursue the right policies, particularly in the interest and exchange rate areas. But, in addition, I am convinced everything has to be done to make extra inducements and encouragements. Last night, Jim Ammerman of the US Treasury mentioned tax treaties. Many of these capital movements are made to evade taxes. Since tax reasons are certainly very important in motivating flows, we should certainly work on tax treaties.

But, first of all, we have to agree it is a serious problem. I am not sure the authorities always did believe it is a serious problem! Until today, they have been trying to minimize the numbers. So first we have to recognize that a large part of the debt problem is related to capital flight. That is why this conference is important.

A second point I want to make deals with debt-equity swaps. We are going to hear a lot more about this type of instrument. At this time, it is still small and I would not want to portray it as the latest gimmick in the list of quick and easy solutions to the debt problem. Nevertheless, when I looked into the activity and size of the market for this type of instrument, I was very pleasantly surprised. This is an extremely active market; it is a new, emerging market; it is a profitable market. This is great because this will make it grow. It is an encouraging beginning, it is a good concept and with the proper stimulation and proper attitudes, I believe it could make an important contribution to solution of the debt problem. Why? Because it will contribute to the restoration of creditworthiness. It would, in fact, make both the borrower *and* the lender stronger. The latter is important. Banks are not going to add to their exposure voluntarily until they feel comfortable about their loan-to-capital-ratio for a country. In other words, even when a country is creditworthy, the bank also has to be in a position to add to its loans. The debt-equity swaps can make contributions to both lender and borrower. These swaps require a policy to encourage the private sector, a policy to stimulate equity investment (whether by foreigners or citizens), and a desire to reduce or slow down the growth of the country's external debt. All these elements are important in the restoration of creditworthiness. It would encourage foreign investment because the foreigner is able to obtain local currency at a very attractive rate through the swaps. Those banks that are unhappy with their claims have an opportunity to sell them, probably at an increasingly better rate as the market broadens and deepens. To me, these are all key elements in the process of solving and overcoming the debt problem.

Who gains and who loses? The big winner is the country. The holder of the claim takes a cut. It has to declare a loss. But it may feel better with the claim off its books. The country has less debt and more investment. Importantly, the buyer of the bank's claim can be a foreign investor, say Japanese or American, but more likely a citizen. That means a return of flight capital. I am therefore glad that Mexico is in the process of developing a debt-equity swap program, which has the potential of reaching $100 million a month. It would be the second largest in Latin America after Chile. With the proper encouragement this program could help stabilize the debt level for the next few years. In other words, while these countries still need an increase in loans of say 2 to 3 percent per annum, a good part of this increase could be offset by these swaps so that debt levels would nearly stabilize, while exports continue to grow. The key debt-to-export ratio would begin to fall, assuming some export growth. Thus, while not a solution, it could make a significant contribution to the debt problem and also help bring back privately held assets abroad.

One final comment. This type of program is far more effective, efficient, and equitable than debt relief. Both programs would reduce debt levels: one through the marketplace, voluntarily, the other through mandatory, congressional instructions. Why should the US Congress ask banks to give debt relief to countries that have tens of billions of dollars of assets? This is not the way to restore creditworthiness. This is a dead-end road. Furthermore, the market program is a going concern and can be accomplished over the next five years. It would take several years of haggling in the Congress to come up with anything. The market is a quick, effective, very democratic way. Of course, the politics are different. The market way means strengthening the private sector, creating equity, encouraging foreign investment. The Bradley way is exactly the opposite. It is socialization of debt, the pushing back of the private sector and getting governments more heavily involved. My guess is we will give the debt-equity swaps a try first!

Pedro-Pablo Kuczynski

The term "capital flight" conveys a moral judgment. Savings, it is argued, should stay where they are the most needed, namely in the debtor countries. Under this view, a Japanese who puts his money in New York is being "good" while a Latin American who does the same is "bad."

The fact is that the Latin American seeks the highest return in relation to risk, like any other investor; the problem is that in a number of countries, risk, both political and economic, has been too high. Among the indicators of economic risk are inflation that has exceeded the return on savings, unrealistic exchange rates, local deposits denominated in foreign currency forcibly converted into local currency (Mexico 1982, Peru 1985), nationalization of banks and other assets, and, most important, economic depression in the wake of the debt crisis and the subsequent commodity-price depression. Political violence and governmental incoherence have been additional important contributory factors. Hommes's paper on Colombia gives an excellent analysis of the interaction of economic and political factors. The supply of capital because of these motives faced the demand from a receptive international capital market in full bloom and, at least until 1984, with high real interest rates.

The largest single potential asset which most Latin American economies other than Brazil have today is the money that is kept abroad. Most of it fled from the mid-1970s to about 1983, especially during the crisis period 1981–83. In addition, however, private capital outflows have continued in several cases after 1983.

It is illusory to think of the return of this asset, or even the partial return of it via the reflow of earnings, until there is a continuous, determined and successful effort to reestablish the confidence of private investors. No schemes such as guarantees or amnesties can replace confidence. The main ingredient for confidence is sustained growth. It has begun to appear in Brazil in 1985–86 and also in Colombia. Elsewhere sustained growth is still elusive.

The author is Co-Chairman, First Boston International, and Managing Director, The First Boston Corporation. The opinions herein are personal.

A note of caution is needed on the amount and nature of capital flight. First, the popular picture in some circles in the United States, that a majority of upper-income Mexicans and other Latin Americans are engaged in capital flight, is wide of the mark. For example, the $100 billion sometimes mentioned for the period 1975–83 would represent close to half the disposable savings[1] of the whole of Latin America in that period, an improbable but not impossible number. Second, there is no precise measure of the sums involved. Only approximations are possible, as the variations in the numbers presented in this volume attest. While there is no question about the trend of outflows, which was most pronounced in 1981–83, it is simplistic to take, as some have done, the reported current account deficit and subtract known financing and uses of financing, such as the accumulation of reserves, and label the difference "capital flight." Unrecorded trade, both exports such as drugs in some countries and smuggled imports of prohibited or high-tariff consumer goods, a high probability in several countries, make it very difficult to be at all confident about "capital flight" numbers.

The most likely recipients of flight capital, US banks, recorded $37 billion of outstanding private Latin American deposits at the end of 1983, compared to $16 billion in 1981 and an average outstanding of $9 billion in 1977–79, but even these sums include working capital of Latin American banks and companies engaged in foreign trade and its financing. Without downplaying the importance of private capital outflows, it is important not to exaggerate the phenomenon, especially when the statistical sources are conjectural.

The commercial lenders to Latin America had available to them in the early 1980s, the peak years of lending and also of private capital outflows, the very same numbers which are today used to decry "capital flight." Yet they continued to lend, after some hesitation, in 1979–80. In 1981 the merry-go-round spun around one more time, providing the tonic for easy economic policies, especially exchange rate overvaluation in countries such as Argentina, Mexico, and Venezuela—the three major capital flight countries. It is, however, a gross distortion to claim, as some have done, that the "private banking" departments of some lending banks were deliberately seeking the money that their loan departments were putting out; rather, the point is that easy money contributed to lax policies, especially exchange overvaluation, which provided the incentive for private capital outflows.

For the future, the main thing that yesterday's lenders can do is lobby hard for more funds and lending by the multilateral development banks. Given the sharp decline in involuntary lending by the commercial banks, not much can be expected from that quarter for some time. A promising development is the growth of debt-equity swaps. But in the end more

---

1. In the sense of personal, noncontractual savings.

official capital inflows will be required, at least for a few years, to get growth going again. Countries that do not grow are not good magnets to retain their own savings, let alone attract new investment.

The borrowers have to reform, as they have indeed been doing in most cases since 1982. The recent book coauthored by Bela Balassa, Gerardo Bueno, Mario Henrique Simonsen, and myself contains a lengthy analysis of the needed reforms. Two points are worth emphasizing. First, in general it is continuity of sensible economic policies that counts, not just short-lived changes in policies. Second, exchange rate adjustments after the fact are always too late in relation to capital flight. By then, the horse is out of the barn. Realistic exchange rate policies must influence exchange rate expectations: continuity in policies is here again fundamental.

Much has been made of the potential benefits of capital controls. Maybe so, but I doubt their ultimate value unless they are preceded by realistic economic policies, especially continuously realistic exchange rates. Brazil and Colombia were reasonably successful in keeping private capital at home: capital controls may have helped but the main stimulus was a realistic exchange rate policy sustained over a long period. There is little that controls can do against the top-heavy income distribution in most Latin American countries or political volatility. These are features endemic to underdevelopment. The best way out is to reestablish the international and domestic setting that will favor investment and growth.

Miguel Urrutia

Capital outflow from Latin America is a permanent and normal phenomenon, which can be justified on the basis of rational portfolio-management criteria. The outflow can accelerate and become capital flight when political risk increases or when wrong economic policies lead economic agents to anticipate massive devaluations of the national currency or significant increases in the relative profitabilty of investments abroad.

The statistics show massive outflows of capital in Argentina between 1978 and 1982; in Mexico between 1981 and 1985; and in Venezuela between 1978 and 1985. The papers at this conference analyze the causes of these episodes of capital flight: overvaluation of exchange rates and expectations of future devaluations; rapid growth in public debt, which

The author is Manager of the Economic and Social Development Department of the Inter-American Development Bank.

allowed governments to maintain overvalued exchange rates despite massive capital flight; and economic stagnation, which made local investments unattractive.

Since there are clear social costs involved in this outflow of capital, it would seem justified to study mechanisms which will minimize capital flight. I will first discuss the measures that can be taken in source countries.

In yesterday's session, various participants expressed the fear that there had been excessive talk of using controls to stem capital flight. The point was repeatedly made that the controls generate inefficiencies and are seldom effective.

I do not sympathize with that point of view. Both Mr. Ramos and Mr. Hommes, in their presentations on the Chilean and Colombian cases, stressed that controls had been useful in stemming capital flight. In Chile, the dismantling of controls made possible a spectacularly rapid loss of international reserves.

Let me emphasize, however, that there are certain things that exchange controls should *not* attempt to do. In particular, they should not be used to maintain an overvalued exchange rate. Neither should they be used to maintain negative real interest rates.

While exchange controls should not be used as a substitute for sound macroeconomic policies, they may still be useful for avoiding extreme volatility in capital flows in economies whose exports are dominated by commodities whose prices fluctuate violently and which are trying to diversify exports. In such economies, external credit moves in a perverse way. It is available when commodity prices are increasing, and when external credit is inflationary, and it disappears like morning dew when commodity prices decrease. Intervention to limit this type of perverse behavior seems justified, for futures contracts and speculation unfortunately have not dampened the impact of commodity price fluctuations.

Exchange controls may not be very effective if underlying conditions create very strong incentives for capital flight. This has happened when war intensified in Central America, or internal violence escalated in Colombia (see the paper by Rudolf Hommes) or Peru, or when massive devaluation became a certainty in Venezuela. Nevertheless, exchange controls may mean that capital flees in months instead of days, and this is in itself a gain. In addition, exchange controls may be much more effective in stemming the flow of hot money into a country when commodity prices are increasing. This is because creditors have learned that honeymoons in Latin America are short, and that in order to get out one must have legally registered debts. The present debt crisis is due not primarily to capital flight but to excessive inflows when oil and commodity prices were on the upswing.

The Institute for International Economics has published, with some fanfare, a study on a new strategy for development in Latin America.[1] It recommends intervention to maintain a real exchange rate with few fluctuations as a strategy for export promotion. The recommendation, based on the analysis of the reasons for success of the export strategies of Japan, Korea, Taiwan, and Brazil, is correct. But how can a country keep fairly constant real exchange rates without exchange controls if commodity prices, and foreign credit, fluctuate widely and in the same direction? Japan and Korea certainly kept tight and effective exchange controls until export diversification was well under way.

It is important to repeat that exchange controls are only useful for avoiding short-run panics, runs, flights, and hot money inflows. To achieve this, the controls do not have to be extensive and expensive. They need only increase the cost of information and transactions, and decrease the speed with which the central bank's international reserves are depleted or increased during runs out or in. The controls keep banks and other financial intermediaries trusted by the public from providing respectable outlets for capital flight near every metro stop. In countries as diverse as Chile, Colombia, and Japan, exchange controls make capital outflow costly because the widespread branch network of banks and supervised financial institutions do not sell unauthorized foreign exchange to the public.

Rimmer de Vries emphasized that banks like Morgan Guaranty engage in personal banking in Latin America because it is legal, and that if they did not, others would simply replace them. Exchange controls would, however, increase transaction costs, if they persuaded the major international banks to abandon activities that facilitate capital flight.

Finally, in some Latin American countries, exchange controls may be a crucial aid in the fight against drugs. The drug racketeers in fact are only caught when they try laundering their money.

In summary, if one does not believe that floating the exchange rate is a rational option in most Latin American countries which want to diversify exports, there might be a case for combining crawling pegs with some exchange control on capital transactions. The situation may, admittedly, be different in Mexico and Uruguay, where exchange controls face particular difficulties. There must be a case-by-case approach.

Now a word about the responsibilities of the haven countries. First, serious study of the advantages of exchange controls must be carried out in the haven countries and at the multilateral financial institutions, so as to

---

1. Bela Balassa, Gerardo M. Bueno, Pedro-Pablo Kuczynski, and Mario Henrique Simonsen, *Toward Renewed Economic Growth in Latin America*. Mexico City: El Colegio de Mexico; Rio de Janeiro: Fundação Getúlio Vargas; Washington: Institute for International Economics.

make sure that the right advice is given and the appropriate conditions are established in future adjustment loans.

Second, tax exemption on time deposits of foreigners in the United States seems completely unjustified to me. It is a very clear distortion if capital income of most nationals is taxed. It clearly improves the rate of return of Latin American flight capital, and thus encourages it. In the present "crisis" environment, if this privilege is eliminated, the capital will not go to less safe "safe havens"—witness the decline of the financial sector in Panama. I would, therefore, recommend reinstating the 30 percent withholding tax on foreign bond holdings and introducing a similar tax on nonresident time deposits in the United States.

The alternative solution proposed, to eliminate capital taxation in source countries, is absurd from an equity point of view. Income distribution in Latin America is already very unequal, and eliminating capital taxation would make it more so.

Third, the donor governments and the international organizations should not allow private banks to force Third World governments to nationalize nonperforming private or nonguaranteed government debt. This has unfortunately happened in Chile, Colombia, and other countries.

Responsibility for the growing role of government in Latin America partly falls on the international banks. Sovereign guarantees mean less risk for foreigners than for nationals and make possible the simultaneous increase in both debt (of governments) and capital flight (of the private sector). Even if the flows compensate, in the source countries private investment is substituted by public investment.

Finally, it should be clear that eliminating capital flight cannot be a condition for implementing the Baker Initiative. On the contrary, a guaranteed flow of resources, of at least the size mentioned by Secretary James A. Baker III, is a necessary condition for the resumption of growth. Capital flight will continue or get worse if the Latin American economies do not start a sustained recovery, and this will not occur as long as they have to sacrifice investment and maintain underutilized capacity because they are using a large part of their foreign exchange and savings for debt-related transfers abroad.

Discussion

Many participants echoed Kindleberger's concluding words about the necessity of restoring confidence and the need that implies for "long-run macroeconomic stabilization that is seen to be politically supportable." William Hood lay out the priorities as, first, the persistent pursuit by the source countries of consistent national policies; second, the creation by the industrial countries of a healthy world environment with decreasing protection; very much third in order of importance, action in areas such as taxes and exchange controls.

The need to "fix" macroeconomic policies if capital flight is to be stemmed, let alone reversed, was about the extent of unanimity. And even the reality of this degree of consensus was questioned by Barbara Stallings, who pointed to the irony of the contrast between the economists' inability to agree on the proper definition of capital flight versus their unanimity in endorsing a prescription of "proper policies" as the prime remedy. She wondered whether such agreement would survive an attempt to spell out the content of "proper" policies.

One sharp difference of view concerned the question of whether developing countries should accept capital mobility as a fact of life and restrict taxation to immobile factors and consumption, advice dispensed by Harry Johnson back in the 1960s in the context of the debate on the "brain drain." In the words of Charles Kindleberger, the essential issue is whether a man belongs where he was born or where he can make the most money. Miguel Urrutia supported the claims of national origin and argued that the essential problem was the establishment of social cohesion. He objected strenuously that acquiescence in some of the most unequal income distributions on earth would amount to a basic corruption of the fiscal system. Michael Dooley suggested that it might suffice if developing countries avoided exceeding tax rates above the norm in industrial countries.

Latin American countries differ greatly in their attitude toward taxation of foreign-interest income. At one extreme is Argentina, which sticks strictly to the origin principle of taxation and whose law accordingly forbids the tax authority even to inquire about foreign assets. This in combination with a tax on the increment in net worth (held in Argentina) and tax relief on interest charges incurred within Argentina (on loans obtained from foreign banks using foreign deposits as collateral) creates a massive incentive to place funds abroad. In consequence, Conesa argued that the primary need was for the source countries to reform their fiscal systems.

In contrast, Venezuela permits the ownership of foreign assets but has recently passed a law requiring that interest earnings be declared as income for tax purposes. In the absence of enforcement help from foreign authorities, however, either in providing information on ownership of assets to the Venezuelan authorities or in collecting tax revenue, this law is effectively a dead letter.

A number of participants charged that US unwillingness to provide such help by information exchange amounted to turning the United States into a tax haven. The charge brought several vigorous counters. James Ammerman pointed out that the United States was willing to sign tax treaties with Latin countries, as it has with many others, which would obligate the US government to provide such information. It is the Latin attachment to the origin principle that has prevented them from accepting this offer. Edwin Truman, while accepting the potential value of foreign help in collecting tax revenue, pointed out that US banks were prohibited by law from providing information to a foreign government. Others asserted that US action alone would not suffice: common action with other major countries, notably Switzerland and Britain (with its authority over Bermuda and the Cayman Islands), would be the minimum necessary for any chance of effective action. Aloys Schwietert was one of those who raised the implications for personal freedom of compromising bank secrecy: his written comment constitutes the last section of this chapter.

Rudolph Hommes wondered aloud whether the traditional Latin objection to tax treaties was not being used as a cover for avoiding the practical (tax treaty) solution because too many members of the elite were benefiting personally from the tax-free ownership of foreign assets. To the extent that he is right, Urrutia's suggestion that the United States and other haven countries could at least impose withholding tax on foreign-interest income has particular force.

Rimmer de Vries's enthusiasm for debt-equity swaps was echoed by some other participants, but several who were less dismissive than Dornbusch felt that their role was unlikely to be more than marginal. For example, while Edwin Truman accepted the desirability of more equity and less debt, he pointed out that a debt-equity swap involved a potentially substantial subsidy for foreign investment that generates advanced amortization rather than a cash flow for the debtor country. Ingo Walter argued that sound microeconomic policies that would provide a hospitable climate for direct foreign investment offered greater potential gains than "frills" like debt-equity swaps.

James Henry took Rimmer de Vries to task for the role of Morgan Guaranty and other major banks in facilitating capital flight though the provision of "private banking" services to the residents of major debtor countries. In reply to Henry's allegation that Morgan Guaranty was the second largest provider of such services in Mexico, de Vries protested his ignorance of the actions of other parts of the bank and averred that Morgan would compete in whatever banking field it was legal to do so.

Views were also divided on the topic of exchange controls. No one confessed to believing that they could provide a substitute for sound policies, although David Bodner protested at what he saw as the willingness of many participants to substitute the provision of an international police system for the need to improve policy. In contrast, Carlos Massad argued that exchange controls make it easier to pursue sound policies by reducing the economy's exposure to every shift of the international wind. There seemed a strong tendency for Latin participants from countries with controls[1] to take a more optimistic view of their usefulness than those from countries without controls. For example, Miguel Urrutia wondered whether imposing controls might not be worthwhile if for no other reason than to prevent the major banks from seeking clients for their private banking activities and claiming that they were doing nothing illegal. Ernesto Zedillo, on the other hand, argued that any imposition of capital controls by Mexico would simply nullify the chance of continuing the repatriation of capital that had already started.

Not all participants accepted the premise that policy should be directed to securing the repatriation of capital. Dragoslav Avramovíc argued that, while it was feasible and important to stem further outflows of capital, there was little historical precedent for expecting a major reflow. He urged that bygones be accepted as bygones and cautioned against corrupting the fiscal system in a vain attempt to pursue the impossible, concluding that there was no escaping the need to resolve the debt crisis by debt relief provided at the initiative of the public authorities.

Comment on the Discussion
Aloys Schwietert

At several times during our discussions the question was raised whether the banks should not open their books and disclose the names of obvious depositors of flight capital. Aside from the simple fact that most Western banks are legally barred from such action, a more fundamental observation must be made.

---

1. With the exception of Miguel Rodriguez, but not of Rudiger Dornbusch, who demonstrated his honorary citizenship of Brazil by describing capitalists as having "the legs of hares and the hearts of rabbits."

Fighting against capital flight on this level, i.e., avoiding an assault on the real causes in the debtor country and instead trying to close down the "safe havens," would lead to an assault on basic human rights. It would, in fact, amount to curtailing individual property rights in favor of a "bonum commun," which would be very hard to define in practice.

The individual right to privacy is a basic concept that democratic countries recognize and reinforce with constitutional guarantees. Since this democratic principle is the cornerstone of all personal liberties, the erosion of privacy through government surveillance of citizens' activities and attitudes and, more recently, through the penetration of electronic data processing into various segments of private life, raises disturbing questions in any free society.

Under the Swiss Constitution, individual liberty and private property are considered indivisible human rights and therefore are given equal protection of the law extended to both Swiss and foreign citizens.

But secrecy, or discretion, in banking matters is not unique to Switzerland. In fact, it is practiced in various degrees in most countries. In Switzerland, however, it is protected by criminal penalties. Anonymous numbered accounts do not exist in Swiss banks, although numbers and passwords may be used to identify certain accounts. In those cases the identity of the customer is known only to a few senior bank officials. Bank secrecy is not absolute. In the case of prosecution of criminals, Swiss authorities do grant access to private banking records.

We should not forget that the Swiss Banking Law, enacted in 1934 to bolster the security of the banking system after the Great Depression and during the Nazi period and to ensure the safety of clients' deposits, represents a landmark in bank regulation. Its section dealing with banking secrecy put this concept, for the first time in history, under the official protection of penal law. The provisions of the Banking Law and the Criminal Code were "life preservers" for persons who escaped Nazi terror and for countless thousands of political refugees from states in Eastern Europe after World War II.

My reaction to the singling out of the "Swiss case" is that we definitely should avoid throwing out the baby with the bathwater. The only help banks can reasonably be expected to give is to insist that depositors identify themselves before opening an account and to inform account-holders that illegal deposits will not be protected by secrecy laws. This is exactly what the Swiss banks do—as already mentioned in Ingo Walter's paper.

9

The Problem and Policy Responses

Donald R. Lessard
John Williamson

The subject of capital flight arouses strong emotions. Some observers view it as a symptom of a sick society, a cause of Latin America's failure to recover from the debt problem, and a rational reason for foreign lenders to be leery of increasing their exposure. Others regard the very use of the term "capital flight" as a pejorative description of natural, economically rational responses to the portfolio choices that have confronted wealthy residents of some debtor countries in recent years.

The problem of capital flight is a difficult one because both these views of the issue are essentially correct. It is true that capital flight has been enormously damaging to the economies involved (see "Consequences," below), and that remains true, despite the modest reflow that some countries have experienced recently. In extreme cases it signals a breakdown in social cohesion, with implications that go far beyond its financial impact. But it is also true that it is the result of individual agents' reacting in the way that is posited as rational by economic theory and accepted as normal in industrial countries. This inevitably makes it difficult to resolve the chronic economic problems that the flight of capital has brought in its wake.

This chapter starts by considering the vexing question of how "capital flight" should be defined; proceeds to assess its magnitude, causes and consequences; and concludes with a discussion of the set of policies that might help to stop and reverse it. The analysis draws extensively (though not exclusively) on the conference that the Institute for International Economics held in October 1986, the proceedings of which are contained in the preceding chapters.

Definition

The question has often been posed: why do we refer approvingly to "foreign investment" by Americans, Japanese, and Kuwaitis and use the censorious

201

term "capital flight" to describe the same activity when undertaken by Latin Americans? Is capital flight in fact anything more than capital outflows of which we disapprove, or capital outflows that prove inconvenient to the government of the country losing the money? Must not a distinction between "normal" outflows of capital and "capital flight" be based on the legality of the outflow?

We believe that, as a matter of linguistic principle, terms should be used to mean what normal usage of the English language suggests they mean unless there is overwhelming precedent for a deviant technical usage. At the moment, the uses of the term capital flight are still so varied that there is certainly no overwhelming precedent for any particular usage, deviant or otherwise. Ingo Walter (ch. 5) points out that Webster defines "flight" as "an act or instance of running away." Kindleberger (1937, p. 158) defined capital flight as "abnormal" flows "propelled *from* a country. . . by. . . any one or more of a complex list of fears and suspicions." Accordingly, we believe there are both linguistic and economic precedents for defining capital flight as "money that runs away" or "flees."[1]

On this view, one refers to capital flight by Latin Americans but not by Japanese because of a belief that Latin investors are trying to escape the high risks they perceive at home while Japanese investors are responding to what they perceive to be better opportunities abroad. That formulation makes it very clear why many economists feel ill-at-ease with such a definition; we take it for granted that both groups of investors will base their decision on a *comparison* of the relative returns and risks involved in investment at home and abroad, and therefore tend to reject any distinction based on picking out just one of those factors. But this is to be excessively purist: it is like refusing to say that a current account deficit is due to overvaluation on the grounds that, at some sufficiently depressed income level, the deficit would vanish. The charge of overvaluation implies some judgment about normal or desirable income levels (for example, "full employment" or "internal balance"). Similarly, a diagnosis of capital flight implies some notion of normal risks and returns abroad, and reflects a judgment that the deviant factor propelling the outflow is the level of domestic risk perceived by some or all residents.

This definition implies that capital flight is not the same as an undesirable capital outflow. Indeed, it is not difficult to think of certain instances of "good" capital flight, such as that involving the French Huguenots in the

---

1. In another recent study, Michael Deppler and Martin Williamson (1987, p. 41) provided another precedent: ". . . capital flight may be defined as the acquisition. . . of a claim on nonresidents that is motivated by the owner's concern that the value of his asset would be subject to discrete losses if his claim continued to be held domestically."

late seventeenth century or German Jews in the 1930s. In other instances, capital flight may serve the social function of inducing desirable policy changes. Even if the normative perspective is that of the government rather than outside observers such as ourselves, capital flight can surely not be equated with undesirable capital outflow: as Miguel Rodriguez points out (ch. 6), the Venezuelan government actually welcomed the outflow of capital from Venezuela as late as 1981 on the ground that it would help combat inflation. Would we then want to say that there was no capital flight from Venezuela in 1981? And when the Venezuelan government changed its mind about the desirability of that outflow, would it be reclassified as an instance of capital flight after all? Conversely, can we not conceive of instances of capital outflow that the government finds inconvenient that we would not wish to describe as capital flight? Had a Labour government that deplored the British capital outflow of the early 1980s been elected in 1987, would we suddenly have declared Mrs. Thatcher's Britain to have been the victim of capital flight?

Our concept of flight capital as that which flees from the perception of abnormal risks at home implies that the question of the legality of the outflow is distinct from that of whether it is "normal" or "fleeing." As it happens, there were no exchange controls making the export of capital illegal when what are usually considered the major episodes of capital flight took place from Argentina, Mexico, and Venezuela. What our definition does suggest is that measurement of capital flight requires an attempt to measure the outflow of capital that may be considered "normal" and deduct this from the total outflow.

Dooley (1986) has made an explicit attempt to distinguish between capital outflows "motivated by normal portfolio decisions" and those "based on the desire to place assets beyond the control of domestic authorities." His technique, which involves taking as normal those outflows that generate a stream of income recorded in the balance of payments statistics, is subject to challenge (see "Magnitudes," below); but his concept of abnormal outflows as those motivated by an attempt to escape the control of the domestic authorities seems much the same as our concept of those fleeing abnormal risks at home.

Some participants in the conference, such as Miguel Rodriguez, would argue that the "normal" capital outflow from a capital-short developing country should be zero. To paraphrase Tobin (1977), "It takes a heap of Harberger triangles to fill a foreign exchange gap." Presumably, exceptions might be made for foreign investments that bring exceptionally high returns to the domestic economy, typically because of a benefit over and above the yield to the investor—such as direct investment that creates a demand for additional exports or assures a supply of raw materials, export credits that secure additional export orders, or bank claims that act as collateral to secure additional credits. But this is to revert to a normative definition, in which capital flight is defined to be that part of the outflow of capital owned by domestic residents that is by some criterion disadvantageous to the national economy.

In the end, we decided not to concentrate on measuring "normal outflows," or therefore "capital flight," but rather "resident capital outflow." We indeed argue below (see "Consequences") that the loss of savings and financial intermediation to the domestic economy resulting from resident capital outflow normally brings some loss to the national economy (and indeed to the world economy), except when it brings abnormally high returns, as instanced above, whether the outflow is normal portfolio diversification or abnormal flight. This is a good reason for concentrating on measuring resident capital outflow. As long as normal outflows for portfolio diversification remain small, the economic cost imposed by resident capital outflow will be modest. When normal outflows are reinforced by money fleeing abnormal risks, the cost will escalate. This is about as good a reason as seems to exist for continuing to use the emotive term capital flight to describe such episodes.

Magnitude

The discussion in this section will be illustrated by table 9.1, which shows a stylized set of balance of payments accounts. We are aiming to estimate

Table 9.1   Schematic balance of payments accounts

Exports of goods and nonfactor services	A
Imports of goods and nonfactor services	B
Investment income	C
Debt-service payments	D
Net remittances and transfers	E
Total current account balance $(A - B + C - D + E)$	F
Direct investment	G
Foreign loans, minus amortization	H
Increase in foreign assets of domestic banking system	I
Resident capital outflow: into long-term assets	J
Resident capital outflow: into short-term assets	K
Total capital account balance $(G + H - I - J - K)$	L
Errors and omissions $(N - F - L)$	M
Increase in reserves	N

resident capital outflow, items J and K in table 9.1, without much emphasis on identifying some part of the flow as "normal" and therefore deducting it to get a figure for capital flight. (It has sometimes been assumed that flows into long-term assets, J, are more likely to involve normal portfolio diversification, while those into short-term assets, K, are likely to involve flight capital.)

The basic reason that it is difficult to measure the size of capital flight, apart from the ambiguity of the concept, is that investors fleeing the perception of abnormal risks at home are unlikely to make a point of informing the compilers of balance of payments statistics of their actions. This means that item K, in particular, is usually very poorly measured.

In an attempt to circumvent this difficulty, three conceptually distinct approaches to the measurement of capital flight have been developed in the recent literature.

We start this section by describing these three approaches, proceed to examine a number of modifications that have been proposed, and conclude by looking at what is implied for estimates of resident capital outflow.

The Balance of Payments Accounts Approach

The obvious and traditional approach to measurement involves drawing on the balance of payments accounts. There has been a longstanding presumption that errors and omissions arise primarily because of a failure to measure many movements of private short-term capital, and therefore that it is appropriate to add them (M) to the recorded flows of short-term capital (K) in order to get an estimate of total flows. This approach was adopted by Cuddington (1986) in one of the pioneering studies of capital flight.

Table 9.2, row 1, shows estimates of the cumulative outflow of resident capital from six debtor countries over the period 1976–84 using this measurement technique. The definition used is that of Cuddington (1986), while the actual numbers come from the Cumby-Levich consistent data set (ch. 3).

The Residual Approach

Apparently spurred by a feeling that the relevant items in the balance of payments accounts were extremely tenuous, several recent analyses have broken away from this traditional approach to estimate capital outflow as a residual. The studies of Dooley et al. (1986), the World Bank (1985), Erbe (1985), and Morgan Guaranty (1986) took the increase in a country's recorded external debt over a period, added the inflow of capital on account

Table 9.2 Estimates of resident capital outflow and capital flight, 1976–84
(billion dollars)

	Argentina	Brazil	Korea	Mexico	Philippines	Venezuela	Total
1. Cuddington measure	16.0	−0.1	2.8	36.2	3.7	13.1	71.7
2. Morgan Guaranty measure	25.0	17.3	3.5	53.4	3.7	29.6	132.5
3. Bank deposits (end-1984)	8.2	8.8	0.4	15.1	1.0	12.2	45.7
4. Interest-compounding adjustment	4.9	0.0	n.a.	17.2[a]	n.a.	1.9	n.a.
5. Misinvoicing adjustment	−5.4	−2.1	−10.8	−18.4	n.a.	0.0	−36.7
6. Stock of "legitimate" resident external capital, end-1984	2.4	12.0	6.5	18.9	4.8	2.5	37.1
7. Zedillo's residual	n.a.	n.a.	n.a.	26.0	n.a.	n.a.	n.a.
8. Preferred measure	16	9	0	27	4	30	86

n.a. not available.
Source: Row 1, Cumby-Levich (ch. 3) estimate of Cuddington measure using consistent data set. Row 2, Cumby-Levich (ch. 3) estimate of Morgan-Guaranty measure using consistent data set. Row 3, *International Financial Statistics*. Row 4, Cuddington (ch. 3, table 3.2). Row 5, Gulati (ch. 3). Row 6, Cumby-Levich (ch. 3) estimate of Dooley measure. Row 7, Zedillo (ch. 7). Row 8, see text.
a. This estimate is an exaggeration inasmuch as the Mexican balance of payments figures already contain some allowance.

of direct investment (G), and subtracted the current account deficit (F) plus the increase in official reserves (N), and in some cases other elements, notably the increase in foreign lending by domestic banks (I). The logic of this was presumably that the recorded increase in foreign debt gave a better measure of net new foreign loans than the figure (H) in the balance of payments accounts, since otherwise this is just an indirect method of calculating J + K + M.

It turns out that, when measured on a consistent data set, resident capital outflow measured in this second way is almost invariably substantially greater than that measured in the first way (compare the first two rows of table 9.2 and also Cumby and Levich, ch. 3, tables 3.1–3.6 for annual comparisons). For example, Cuddington's measure of private resident capital outflow from Mexico over the period 1976–84 is $36.2 billion, as against $53.4 billion on Morgan Guaranty's measure; for all six countries for which figures were compiled from a consistent data set by Cumby and Levich, the difference was $71.7 billion versus $132.5 billion (table 9.2). These differences are far too large to be accounted for by *long-term* resident capital outflow (J), which is the only conceptual difference that would lead to a larger figure being yielded by the residual measure. It follows that at least one of these two measures must be subject to large and persistent measurement error: we discuss below which of the two is most at fault.

Bank Deposits

A third approach involves measurement of the increase in recorded foreign bank deposits owned by a country's residents. It is of course necessary to use a statistical source that distinguishes private from official holdings, which the older statistical series, those of the Bank for International Settlements (BIS), do not, but which the new series of the International Monetary Fund (IMF) do. The third row of table 9.2 shows the IMF figures for the stock of private bank deposits held abroad at the end of 1984.[2] In every case except that of Brazil, the recorded level of bank deposits is smaller than the estimates of cumulative resident capital outflow derived from either of the first two sources, even though presumably some of the bank deposits originate from prior to 1976.

This is not a surprise, since by no means all private funds held abroad get recorded in IMF statistics, for three reasons: some funds are held in bank deposits outside the major (reporting) financial centers; the nationality of the depositor is not always known or reported accurately; and substantial funds are held in assets other than bank deposits. Because the statistics for bank deposits underestimate the sums held abroad, the increase in those deposits will be an inaccurate (typically low) measure of capital outflow. This source can nevertheless be useful for certain purposes, for example, in forming an estimate of the minimum sum being held in liquid form abroad and therefore potentially available for repatriation (for which purpose those data are indeed used by Arellano and Ramos, ch. 7).

---

2. Because the IMF data series commence only in 1981, it is not possible to show the increase in bank deposits over the period 1976–84 to provide symmetry with the previous two measures.

Modifications

Several of the papers presented to the Institute's conference on capital flight, and discussion provoked by those papers, led us to conclude that none of the three measures of resident capital outflow presented above can be considered at all satisfactory. We proceed to describe and assess the several criticisms that came to light and, where possible, to suggest the modifications in the statistics that they call for.

Inadequacies in Debt Statistics

Zedillo (ch. 7) argues forcefully that, at least in the case of Mexico, the statistics used by Morgan Guaranty and others to estimate changes in external debt are egregiously misleading. The biggest problem, which appears to apply to some other countries as well, is that the coverage of debt statistics has improved markedly since 1982. Prior to the debt crisis, there was neither a legal requirement nor any motivation for the registration of Mexican private-sector external debt, and in consequence very little was registered. Since then, the statistical coverage has become much more complete, so that the recorded debt increased markedly in 1983–84 despite a modest level of actual new foreign borrowing. This leads to exaggerated estimates of capital flight over that period, although it suggests also that actual capital flight was larger in earlier years when debt accumulation was being underestimated. Incredible as it may seem, this elementary but important point has not been noted by the World Bank, which compiles the debt figures and used them to estimate capital flight (World Bank 1985, p. 64), or by other users such as Morgan Guaranty.

A second problem arises from exchange rate changes. When the dollar depreciates (appreciates), the dollar value of debt denominated in nondollar currencies increases (decreases), without any new borrowing taking place. This factor tended to depress the recorded increase in debt, and thus decrease estimates of capital flight, over the period from 1980 to February 1985, and has subsequently tended to exaggerate estimates. It is not a major factor in Mexico, where over 90 percent of the debt is dollar-denominated, but may be more significant elsewhere.[3]

Trade Credit

Ernesto Zedillo (ch.7) also points out that Mexico suffered a major loss of trade credit after 1982, including a decline in suppliers' credits, on account

---

3. See Cumby and Levich (ch. 3) for illustrative calculations of the importance of this factor.

of both the fall in imports and a reduction in the willingness of foreigners to extend such credits. He argues that estimates of this effect were available in the Mexican balance of payments statistics and should have been introduced in constructing estimates of capital flight.

Interest Income

Ernesto Zedillo, and also William R. Cline (ch. 3, discussion), argue that interest income earned on bank deposits (and other assets) already held abroad should not be counted as a part of capital flight. The Mexican authorities in fact estimate such interest earnings and include them as a credit in the current account statistics even though the money never enters the country. This reduces the current account deficit that is subtracted from the increase in foreign debt under the residual approach to estimating private resident capital outflow, and increases the "errors and omissions" item under the balance of payments accounts approach, in both cases increasing measured capital flight.

If the objective is to measure capital that is fleeing the country, a case can be made for arguing that, since this money was never in the country, it can hardly flee. But since we wish to measure resident capital outflow rather than capital flight, reinvested interest earnings can reasonably be included as a part of the outflow in view of the customary balance of payments accounting convention of including imputed foreign income as a credit item. Thus, we wish to include it in the measure on which we focus. As noted above, Mexico includes imputed interest on identified claims held abroad by Mexicans (and not just interest recorded as paid to Mexicans), but other countries do not make such estimates. Cuddington (ch. 4) has made estimates of imputed interest income for three of the countries shown in table 4.2; his estimates are presented in row 4.

Tourism

Cline also argues that, in the Mexican case, income from tourism and border transactions should be excluded from current account earnings, and therefore should not be included in capital flight even when Mexican residents use these earnings to increase their foreign bank deposits. His argument is that both tourist earnings and income from border transactions are traded in the free rather than the official market, and are therefore not available to the government (unless the authorities enter the free market as a buyer of dollars). He argues that it is misleading to treat earnings in the free market on a par with those in the official market when estimating the likelihood that future borrowing will seep out through capital flight by relating past flight to past borrowing. It is easy to agree with the last contention, which deals with the availability of cash flow for debt service, while still finding it natural to include all earnings used to increase Mexican private foreign assets as a part of capital flight. And resident capital outflow most certainly includes deposits financed by earnings on the free market.

Misinvoicing

As explained in depth by Gulati (ch. 3), capital flight can be effected by underinvoicing exports or overinvoicing imports. In the first case, exporters are not required to surrender to the authorities the full dollar value of their export receipts, and hence can build up holdings of foreign exchange. In the second case, importers receive more foreign exchange than they need to pay their foreign suppliers and can again use the balance to add to their foreign assets. In neither case is the extent of such operations detectable from the statistics, except those on foreign bank deposits, discussed up to now: errors and omissions (M in table 9.1) is not swelled when A falls or B rises to finance something that is not recorded under K.

In its influential article, Morgan Guaranty (1986) cited a number of cases where there was prima facie evidence that trade misinvoicing had been an important conduit of capital flight. The article implied that there was a presumption that capital flight was in general being underestimated by the failure to add in the effect of trade misinvoicing. It seems that Morgan Guaranty was wrong. In his detailed study in chapter 3, Gulati's systematic comparison of the bilateral trade data of nine debtor countries—Argentina, Brazil, Chile, Korea, Mexico, Peru, Philippines, Uruguay, and Venezuela—with the corresponding measures of the same trade flows by the industrial countries, finds that the underinvoicing of exports (which did occur in a majority of countries)[4] was in most cases outweighed by underinvoicing of imports. The motive was presumably to reduce customs charges or to circumvent import controls designed to limit the permissible value of imports. When an importer underinvoices imports for such motives, he does not qualify for official foreign exchange to cover the full value of his purchases, and hence has to draw down his foreign exchange holdings (or

---

4. However, Guzman and Alvarez (1987) show that, in the case of Mexico, the apparent underinvoicing of exports found by Gulati seems to be completely explicable by a series of adjustments in the Mexican figures, for example, to include the gross value of sales by the "in bond" assembly industries rather than just the Mexican value-added. Unless similar factors operate on the import side, this implies that the usual estimates of Mexican capital flight are even more exaggerated than Gulati claims.

else buy foreign exchange on the parallel market, which means that someone else has to draw on their holdings). The current account deficit is underestimated and the resident capital outflow is overestimated. According to Gulati's estimates, these effects are large for some countries, especially Mexico, Korea and Argentina (see table 9.2, row 5).

Normal Capital Exports

It was argued in the discussion on definitions that the concept of flight capital as that which flees demands that a deduction for the "normal" export of capital should be made from total resident capital outflow in order to end up with a measure of "capital flight." Such an adjustment has been proposed by Dooley (1986), based on the assumption that "normal" capital outflow can be identified with that which subsequently generates an interest return to the capital-exporting country identified in the balance of payments statistics. He suggests taking the recorded interest income of each debtor country and calculating the outstanding stock of foreign capital that would have been needed to generate that interest flow for each debtor country, given prevailing international interest rates. The Cumby-Levich estimates of this stock are shown in table 9.2, row 6.

It is not always true, however, that balance of payments figures are built up from transactions reported by those involved. For example, interest receipts in the US payments accounts are estimated on the basis of figures for various types of capital stock and the associated interest rates, rather than reports from recipients of interest. Similarly, the Mexican statisticians include in investment income an allowance for the imputed interest on foreign assets even when no income is remitted. In such instances, Dooley's method will underestimate the volume of capital that does not generate returns to the domestic economy. Another problem with his approach is that outflows that do not generate financial returns (such as investment in real estate for vacation homes) are ipso facto classified as flight capital.

Preferred Estimates

We are now in a position to express some views about the construction of preferred estimates of resident capital outflows.

First, since we believe it is more relevant to measure outflow than flight per se, we do not make any deduction on account of "normal" capital outflows.

Second, we treat the estimates of bank deposits in table 9.2, row 3, as minimum estimates of cumulative resident capital outflow, and ignore them when a preferred source yields a higher figure.

Third, we note Zedillo's estimate of the residual Mexican capital outflow, after adjusting for the increase in the coverage of registered debt, the rundown in trade credit extended to Mexico, and after deducting imputed interest on bank deposits held abroad by Mexicans. We regard the first two adjustments, but not the third, as appropriate from our perspective. The estimate of the interest-compounding (i.e., third) adjustment in table 9.2, row 4, is $17.2 billion; adding this to Zedillo's figure would give $43.2 billion. However, this is an overestimate inasmuch as the interest-compounding adjustment does not recognize that the Mexican balance of payments figures already make an allowance for interest income. The figure based on Cuddington's approach may therefore be the right order of magnitude.

Fourth, we have to take account of Gulati's estimates of the impact of misinvoicing. This is an effect that in principle should be added to any of the other estimates (apart from bank deposits), but in several cases its addition would lead to implausibly low estimates. We therefore treat it case by case, as discussed below.

For Argentina, it is known that there was substantial underinvoicing of imports, especially armaments, and we therefore deduct Gulati's estimate from the Cuddington measure, and add the interest-compounding adjustment, to get a preferred estimate of resident capital outflow of about $16 billion over the period 1976–84.

For Brazil, Cuddington's measure, even without Gulati's correction, gives a net inflow. This is not plausible in view of the size of external bank deposits owned by Brazilians. We therefore round up the latter to get $9 billion as our preferred measure.

Gulati's estimate of the misinvoicing adjustment for Korea dwarfs both estimates of resident capital outflow. Unlike most other countries, however, Korea shows large and persistent overinvoicing of exports. The only plausible explanation for this seems to be an attempt to qualify for large export subsidies, or possibly to establish property rights in anticipated future "voluntary export restraints." But it is scarcely conceivable that Korean firms actually draw on foreign bank deposits (which anyway they do not have, see table 9.2, row 3) in order to buy local currency equal to the value of the declared invoices. Thus, a good part of Gulati's misinvoicing figure is probably illusory. We assume that resident capital outflow was zero.

Gulati again has a very high estimate of the overestimation of capital outflow in the Mexican case. If that figure is deducted from Cuddington's measure, it leads to an estimate of capital outflow scarcely greater than the stock of identified Mexican-owned foreign bank deposits. We therefore deduct half of the misinvoicing estimate from Cuddington's figure, ending up with a figure close to Zedillo's.

The Philippines is easy: there is no estimate of misinvoicing, and no disagreement between the first two measures. (This does not, unfortunately, guarantee that $4 billion is the right figure!)

Gulati's estimate for Venezuela showed no net impact of misinvoicing. But in this case Cuddington's measure is hardly larger than the stock of Venezuelan-owned bank deposits, and this seems implausibly small. Indeed, in the Venezuelan case the capital inflows recorded in the balance of payments statistics are known to have been underestimated up to 1983, so that the Morgan Guaranty figure is preferable.

Clearly the above procedures are ad hoc. They reflect the considerable uncertainty that still surrounds the estimation of resident capital outflows. Nevertheless, we do believe that some facts are reasonably certain:

☐ that the scale of resident capital outflows has been very substantial in relation to, for example, the size of foreign debt

☐ that the scale of such outflows has, however, been exaggerated by some statistical methods, notably that adopted, inter alia, by Morgan Guaranty

☐ that the three principal countries involved are Argentina, Mexico, and Venezuela.

Other Countries

Besides the six countries analyzed at length, above, a number of others have been mentioned in one place or another (for example, Erbe 1985, Morgan Guaranty 1986) as having suffered significant capital flight at some time in the last few years. Unfortunately, there is in most cases no quantification of the scale of resident capital outflow that we consider to be at all reliable, and hence we merely list the countries we have seen mentioned:

Bolivia	Jordan
Cameroon	Malaysia
Chile	Nigeria
Colombia	Peru
Costa Rica	South Africa
Ecuador	Syria
Egypt	Tunisia
El Salvador	Turkey
Guatemala	Uruguay
India	Zambia
Indonesia	Zaire
Jamaica	

However, a recent study by Deppler and Williamson (1987) estimated both capital outflows and capital flight over the period 1975–85 for the aggregate of capital-importing developing countries. Of five different concepts that they measure, the one closest to our concept of resident capital outflow is what they call the "narrow measure of capital outflows." This is put at $153 billion from the end of 1974 to the end of 1985. This may be compared with our estimate of an outflow of $86 billion over 1976-84 from six countries that collectively have about 25 percent of the exports, 30 percent of the GDP and 50 percent of the bank loans of all capital-importing developing countries.

Time Profile of Outflows

Certain facts also seem to be fairly unambiguous about the time path of resident capital outflows from the major capital-flight countries (for details, see the lower part of the appendix tables in Cumby and Levich, ch. 3).

For Argentina, the outflow lasted from 1978–83, with a peak in 1981, and was followed by some repatriation. According to Morgan Guaranty (1987), this has totaled over $2 billion. However, newspaper reports as this goes to press speak of a renewed outflow following the Peronist election gains (September 1987).

In Brazil, the outflow was much more irregular, with most sources estimating some reflow in 1981. However, the outflow seems to have resumed afterwards and to be still continuing.

In the case of Mexico, the initial flight of 1973–77 peaked in 1976, was followed by a respite or even modest repatriation in the late 1970s, until the truly massive outflow of the early 1980s got under way around 1980 (the precise date differs between one source and another, from 1979 to 1981). The outflow eased after its peak in the first half of 1982, but estimates differ drastically by how much; Zedillo's estimate that it declined to a relatively modest level in 1984–85 appears plausible. There was a sizable reflow in 1986, estimated by Guzman and Alvarez (1987) to have amounted to $1.2 billion. This seems to have increased further in 1987, reportedly to over $2 billion in the first five months of the year.

In Venezuela, major capital flight got under way in 1979 and an outflow has continued to the present day. The period of massive outflows was from 1981 until February 1983.

The estimates of Deppler and Williamson (1987) for all capital-importing developing countries confirm the picture of peak outflows—at an annual rate of over $22 billion—in 1979–82. In 1975–78 they estimate that outflows averaged almost $7 billion per year, while in 1983–85 they were just over $9 billion per year. Morgan Guaranty (1987) estimates that for 10 countries (our six except Korea, plus Chile, Colombia, Ecuador, Nigeria, and Peru) the outflow declined from almost $19 billion in 1983 to $8 billion in 1984, $5 billion in 1985, and changed sign to a reflow of almost $2 billion in 1986.

Causes

At the most general level, resident capital outflow results from a difference in perceived, risk-adjusted returns in source and haven countries. Most discussion and research has focused on source-country circumstances, which is hardly surprising since the very concept of capital flight is "that which flees." In view of our own interest in resident capital outflow rather than capital flight per se, we investigate causes in the rest of the world as well as in source countries. In fact, however, we see little reason to doubt that major capital outflows are associated primarily with source-country policies: episodes of capital flight in various countries have not coincided closely.[5]

Even if one concentrates on the source-country side of the equation, many factors help explain international capital flows. These factors may operate at two different levels. Factors such as natural resource discoveries, changes in terms of trade or technologies that alter the value of national endowments, effective industrial policies, or demographic shifts may cause the economic return on capital in a particular country to tend to diverge from the world level.

In addition to these "fundamental" factors, national macroeconomic and regulatory policies may cause the financial return—the return realized by a private investor—to diverge from the underlying economic returns to a greater extent than in the world economy at large.[6] Higher tax rates will cause such a divergence. So does financial repression—ceilings on deposit rates, required reserves that bear less than the market rate of interest, and directed investment or lending at less than market rates. Price controls and bureaucratic restrictions can also drive a wedge between economic and financial returns.

While all these factors affect expected financial returns and risks—the determinants of private capital flows—some of them have different impacts

---

5. The average of the rank order correlation of episodes in terms of severity among Argentina, Mexico, and Venezuela is 0.57; adding Brazil reduces the coefficient to 0.22; adding Korea and the Philippines as well reduces the coefficient to only 0.11.

6. We use the terms economic and financial returns in the way they are normally defined in the public finance and development literatures. Economic returns (and risks) refer to the total returns to the society of a particular activity, adjusted for price distortions and externalities. Financial returns refer to total returns to private investors, calculated at market prices, net of explicit and implicit taxes. (These concepts have sometimes been described by the terms "social" and "private" returns respectively.)

Table 9.3 Taxonomy of factors explaining international capital flows

	One-way flows	Two-way flows
Economic risks and returns	Natural resource endowments Terms of trade Technological changes Demographic shifts General economic management	Differences in absolute riskiness of economies Low correlation of risky outcomes across countries Differences in investor risk preferences
Financial risks and returns, relative to economic	Taxes (deviations from world levels) Inflation Default on government obligations Devaluation Financial repression Taxes on financial intermediation Political instability, potential confiscation	Differences in taxes and their incidence between residents and nonresidents Differences in nature and incidence of country risk Asymmetric application of guarantees Different interest ceilings for residents and nonresidents Different access to foreign-exchange denominated claims

on the risk-adjusted financial returns to certain classes of investors, particularly residents versus nonresidents. There are two reasons for this. First, many taxes, constraints, and other political or fiscal risks do not apply equally to all investors. Second, some investors have a comparative advantage in bearing particular risks because of differing risk preferences, abilities to diversify the risks in question, and abilities to mitigate these risks. If nonresidents are less exposed to the risk of their claims' losing value in the event of a financial crisis (because, for example, they are denominated in foreign exchange), an increase in the likelihood of such a crisis will cause nonresident capital to replace resident capital. Similarly, if interest-rate ceilings apply to resident deposits, but not to loans from nonresidents, foreign funds will replace resident deposits, effectively arbitraging the interest ceiling.

Table 9.3 presents a taxonomy of various factors that give rise to international capital flows. The upper left quadrant identifies those factors that explain "normal" one-way, aggregate capital movements on the basis of differences in (risk-adjusted) economic returns across countries. These are the factors that give rise to a balance of investment opportunities relative to investible resources that is out of step with the world, the classic determinants of international capital flows that are typically viewed as being reflected in differences in real interest rates.[7] The upper right quadrant includes those additional factors that give rise to two-way flows—"normal" portfolio diversification—again on the basis of economic returns. These include differences in risk preferences and the ability to diversify particular risks across, as opposed to within, national boundaries.[8] The lower left quadrant captures government interventions that create wedges between economic and financial risk-adjusted returns, and give rise to one-way capital flows *incremental* to those that would take place on the basis of the underlying economic returns. The lower right quadrant identifies those interventions that cause two-way, round-trip capital flows, again incremental to those that would take place on the basis of the underlying economic risks and returns.

Most theoretical and empirical studies of capital flight have interpreted it as that subset of capital outflows that are propelled by source-country policies and that are, somehow, abnormal. Therefore, they have typically emphasized those factors that drive a wedge between economic and financial returns, whether they operate across the board or asymmetrically among residents and nonresidents—those captured in the lower half of table 9.3. Some studies have also included a subset of those factors that explain differences in aggregate economic returns as well, on the premise that "underlying" and "policy-based" factors can never be completely separated.

Given the complexity of the phenomenon, most studies take partial perspectives that fall into one of two groups. Some economists, including Cuddington (1986 and ch. 4), Conesa (1987), and Dornbusch (1985), focus on the *overall investment climate,* stressing those factors like overvaluation, fiscal deficits, and inflation that influence the financial attractiveness of source-country assets relative to the world standard regardless of who holds them, and thus explain one-way private flows—those included in the left half of table 9.3. Others, including Dooley (1986 and discussion, ch. 3), Khan and Ul Haque (1985), Eaton (1987), and Ize and Ortiz (1987), point to *discriminatory treatment* of resident capital in the form of differential taxation, financial repression, different currency of denomination, or investment guarantees and their subordination to nonresident claims in the

---

7. Of course, in a frictionless capital market, differences in interest rates would never materialize since capital flows would serve to equate them. Further, actual observed differences in rates often reflect the types of barriers and distortions captured in the lower two quadrants.

8. For a discussion of these risk-return factors in determining international capital flows, see Williamson (1983, section 9.3).

event of financial crisis, and thus explain resident capital outflows that coincide with nonresident inflows. Each approach can be relevant in a particular context.

Much of the accumulation of foreign assets by the domestic private sector in Latin America in recent years has coincided with external borrowing by the sovereign. Thus, the pattern of net capital flows has been much different, typically smaller and often of the opposite sign, than that of resident capital flows. The investment climate approach does not explain this phenomenon of capital simultaneously leaving and entering the country. The discriminatory treatment approach, though, does provide an answer: resident claims are in effect subordinated to foreign claims since these involve a contractual obligation subject to commercial sanctions, which the claims of residents do not. Eaton (1987), for example, stresses the fact that, by explicitly or implicitly guaranteeing external but not internal borrowings, governments create a differential between expected returns to domestic and foreign claimants, generating round-trip flows.

A critical element in both perspectives is that capital flight is typically a reaction to risks associated with domestic assets rather than merely differences in promised rates of interest or return in the two markets. Quoted interest rates in the source country, in fact, may be higher than those elsewhere, but the set of investments offering expected, risk-adjusted returns that match the world standard may be limited or nonexistent.

The risks to which domestic assets are exposed include, among others, inflation, devaluation in excess of the anticipations reflected in domestic interest rates, limits on convertibility of local claims, confiscatory taxation or even confiscation. All are "country risks" in that they involve some element of policy choice on the part of the sovereign.[9] While country risk is typically associated with claims against a country held by outsiders, for example, commercial banks, it also extends to domestic holders of money or other financial assets. In fact, in many cases it is more severe for these claims than for the outside claims. The critical characteristic of such risks is that they derive at least in part from the possibility of sovereign acts in response to circumstances under which either the ability or willingness of the sovereign to meet its total commitments is impaired.

While there is no question that country risk in the form of actual or threatened default is a major risk to lenders to developing countries, the response of these governments to financial crises often generates risks of even greater magnitude to resident asset holders. Consider the "Mexican rescue" of 1982.[10] In the process of stepping back from the brink of default

9. For a definitive review of the theory of country risk as it applies to sovereign borrowing, see Eaton, Gersovitz, and Stiglitz (1986). Lessard (1987) discusses its implications for a wider set of claims.

10. See Kraft (1984) for a discussion of the rescue of Mexico's external obligations.

on its external obligations, Mexico underwent a major spiral of devaluation and inflation which almost totally wiped out the value of obligations denominated in Mexican pesos, assets that were held predominantly by Mexican residents. It also imposed exchange controls, effectively halving the value of obligations such as Mex-dollar deposits and petrobonds that were denominated in dollars but payable only within Mexico. These claims, too, were predominantly held by Mexican investors. Finally, it imposed drastic austerity measures coupled with radical structural changes on the domestic economy, again reducing the value of many existing businesses and the direct and indirect claims against them held by both local and foreign investors, at least in the short run.

As a general rule, the consequences of fiscal crises are most severe for a government's implicit obligations to residents, such as assets denominated in the local currency, and risky private-to-private, cross-border claims, such as portfolio and direct foreign investment, and less severe for external sovereign obligations, which are explicit in that they are denominated in a currency other than that of the borrower (Lessard 1987, Magee and Brock 1986). The reason for this is that the enforceability of any particular claim depends on the trade-off between the benefits of default and the sanctions that it would trigger. A default on foreign obligations might induce collective action imposing a partial or total cutoff of international trade and finance, while a default on implicit domestic obligations will typically involve fewer immediate sanctions, although it will result in a further stimulus to capital flight, higher domestic real interest rates, a consequent reduction in capital formation, and perhaps a loss of domestic political support.

The result of this greater exposure of implicit domestic claims is that up to a point an increase in country risk is likely to induce capital flight, as cross-border sovereign claims that represent explicit, general obligations of the state are substituted for implicit domestic claims.[11] This substitution is triggered by residents' recognition that these domestic claims are effectively subordinated to the external sovereign obligations.[12] But private local and

---

11. Implicit domestic claims include assets denominated in the local currency, assets redeemable only in the local jurisdiction regardless of their currency of denomination, and equity and quasi-equity claims on local firms whose value depends on implicit claims on the sovereign. For an excellent discussion of the relative risk of a sovereign's explicit foreign obligations and its implicit domestic obligations, see Protopapadakis (1985).

12. For a rigorous development of this argument, see Ize and Ortiz (1987) and Eaton (1987). Gennotte, Kharas, and Sadeq (1987) demonstrate some of the implications of the resulting conflicts among senior and junior claimants, although their primary focus is on the conflict between first-tier creditors, including the IMF and the World Bank, and second-tier commercial bank creditors, rather than between these two taken together and domestic claimants.

foreign investment is discouraged by the uncertainty over macroeconomic and regulatory policies precipitated inter alia by concerns over a growing external debt burden. At some point, all claims become extremely risky and voluntary flows cease.

With hindsight, severe debt problems and capital flight in developing countries have often involved a slippery slope. To increase or maintain domestic consumption in the face of external shocks, or to increase the power of the state in allocating resources,[13] the sovereign borrowed abroad, increasing its future fiscal and foreign-exchange requirements. In some cases the borrowing was used to finance productive investment that would generate returns to pay the debt service, but in other cases it was not. In reaction to an internal or external shock, and in some instances in response to external pressure, the state absorbed a significant proportion of the external obligations of the private sector to prevent failures that would have reduced domestic confidence or violated its implicit or explicit guarantees to foreign lenders, thus increasing its fiscal and foreign-exchange burden. Then private claimants, recognizing their subordination to increased foreign claims on the sovereign, often as a result of the violation of some implicit contract by the increasingly pressed sovereign, seek to transfer assets to other jurisdictions. In the absence of a securities market where such attempted transfers depress asset prices and, hence, face an implicit penalty, these attempted transfers create a run on foreign exchange reserves, forcing either further foreign borrowing (and subordination of private claims) or some form of default on existing claims. Variations on this theme have occurred in most Latin American countries.

The likelihood and severity of such crises are increased by opportunistic behavior on the part of source-country residents, who arrange their financial affairs so as to reduce their exposure to these policy responses as well as to exploit arbitrage opportunities resulting from government interventions that are typical in such crisis periods. This behavior involves shifting funds abroad and simultaneously increasing the proportion of domestic undertakings financed by external credit, which are likely to be "socialized" when the going gets rough. Therefore, capital flight is both a cause and an effect of fiscal instability, creating a vicious circle that is extremely hard to break.

Empirical Findings

Cuddington (ch. 4) estimates the causes of capital flight for four major flight countries—Argentina, Mexico, Uruguay, and Venezuela. His model, like

---

13. Frieden (1981) has argued compellingly that many developing countries used external finance to increase the state's sphere of influence in the domestic economy.

most others of the investment-climate variety, is a portfolio model—where a representative investor allocates his wealth among various assets based on their relative returns and risks. Using nine annual observations, he estimates the extent to which resident capital outflow is statistically explained by several variables: the expected rate of depreciation (the difference between the current real exchange rate and its long-run average) plus the foreign interest rate, the domestic interest rate, expected domestic inflation, and disbursement of public and publicly guaranteed loans.

In the case of Mexico, Cuddington finds a significant correlation between capital flight and overvaluation, disbursements of public debt, and lagged capital flight. He interprets these results as suggesting that the fear of devaluation is a major "driver" of flight in this case and that foreign lending did provide liquidity to support the flight. His estimate of the "propensity to flee" with respect to additional sovereign external borrowing is 0.31. In other words, 31 cents out of a dollar lent by foreign creditors leave the country in the form of capital flight! Foreign interest rates did not enter his final equation, but he argues that this could be due to their relatively high correlation with disbursements.

In the case of Argentina, the only variables remaining in his final fitted model are the lagged real effective exchange rate and the error of the model in prior periods.[14] This he interprets as suggesting that exchange rate expectations are the primary drivers of capital flight in Argentina, and that disbursements and foreign interest rates played no significant role. The results for Uruguay are very similar. In the case of Venezuela, overvaluation and foreign interest rates both enter into the explanation.

Conesa (1987) estimated a similar model with 16 data points.[15] While his findings also vary from country to country, he identifies six major causes of capital flight: lack of economic growth in the source country; an overvalued exchange rate; a high US (nominal) interest rate; local inflation; an excessive fiscal deficit; and (with ambiguous results) the real local interest rate. In theory, the association between (a lack of) growth and capital flight could go in either direction. A lack of growth could signal a lack of attractive

---

14. This model was estimated using annual data. Cuddington notes that in his other work, using quarterly data, the current exchange rate enters as well.

15. A major limitation with the empirical estimates reported here and elsewhere is the very small number of observations available if one relies on balance of payments figures. In an attempt to overcome this limitation, Conesa related capital flight to each of the six factors one by one, and decided which factors were important on the basis of the results of each bivariate regression. Unfortunately this procedure has serious statistical difficulties, which make the results unreliable. Several conference participants suggested that greater attention be given to time series, such as foreign bank deposits in the United States which, although incomplete in scope, are reported with greater frequency. Another suggestion for future work was the use of pooled cross-section, time-series data.

investment opportunities, while capital flight, whatever its motivation, can be expected to reduce growth. Conesa argues convincingly that the causation runs from growth to flight. In contrast with Cuddington, Conesa does not attempt to estimate overvaluation relative to some equilibrium exchange rate. Rather, he uses the level of government external borrowings and reserves as proxies for overvaluation, arguing that they permit overvaluation to occur. Further, he claims that the real exchange rate by itself has limited explanatory power.

Studies of the discriminatory-treatment variety emphasize those factors that cause expected asset returns to residents to diverge from the underlying social returns and from expected returns offered nonresidents. Dooley, for example, does not seek to model residents' full portfolio choice. Rather, he focuses on ways that source countries explicitly or implicitly impose discriminatory "taxes" on domestic asset holders, where the taxes are interpreted broadly to include not only outright taxes, but also takings through inflation, interest ceilings, or multiple exchange rates. He estimates capital flight as a function of three independent variables: inflation—capturing the "inflation tax" on domestic noninterest-bearing monetary assets; financial repression—a measure of the degree to which domestic yields are held below "market-clearing" levels; and a country-risk variable that attempts to measure the riskiness of a country's obligations to the rest of the world relative to that of its claims on the rest of the world. He finds that all three are significantly related to capital flight.

Cuddington's results taken as a whole, supplemented by Conesa's similar results, tell a story of capital flight that is in large part the result of macroeconomic mismanagement—especially exchange rate overvaluation, but also at least by implication high inflation and fiscal deficits. Dooley's more narrowly focused results also point to macroeconomic errors, albeit in the form of inflation, financial repression, and a general measure of country risk.

One notable omission from all the studies are estimates of the impact of exchange controls on capital flight. While Brazil and Colombia, which maintained such controls, experienced proportionately less flight than the other major Latin countries, this could be attributed either to the controls themselves, the macroeconomic policies made possible because of the controls, or factors totally unrelated to the controls. Cuddington's approach of estimating separate equations for each country could not have picked up the effect of controls remaining in force throughout the period studied. Further, he did not include these two countries. Dooley, in contrast, employed a cross-sectional approach, but he did not include capital controls as a factor.

The results described above are not as dissimilar as the contrast between the investment climate and discriminatory treatment hypotheses might have led one to expect. As noted by Khan and Ul Haque (1985), all of these phenomena—overvaluation, inflation, and financial repression—are often symptoms of a country that is fiscally overextended, although Venezuela provides an exception. In reviewing the Argentine case, Dornbusch (1985) states that the

source of capital flight was a combination of currency overvaluation, the threat of devaluation, and ongoing and increasing financial instability. The domestic instability derives from an inability to bring deficits under control and [to] stop the inflationary process in a decisive way.

Eaton (1987) reinterprets this in terms of a tax on resident claims, stressing that

The [Argentine] government's inability to finance expenditure, including debt service obligations, led to inflationary finance, a form of taxation of domestic capital. As a consequence, capital fled.

Perhaps the greatest difference between the two perspectives lies in their interpretation of the role of loan disbursements. In the investment-climate hypothesis, new loans permit a relaxation in policy that allows residents to satisfy their desire to place funds abroad. In the discriminatory treatment hypothesis, in contrast, a vicious circle can be triggered either by an increased desire of residents to place funds abroad or by an increase in external borrowings, with larger outflows stimulating additional borrowing and extra borrowing increasing the concern of residents about the probability of an impending crisis.

Viewed in that light, one surely has to conclude that both perspectives can help to explain events of recent years. The most rapid resident accumulation of foreign assets occurred while countries were getting themselves into trouble, but still faced an elastic supply of foreign exchange through sovereign borrowing since the risks to external creditors appeared appreciably less than those to domestic residents. But capital outflows persisted after voluntary external lending had ceased, in response to an increase in country-risk levels to the point where even sovereign claims were jeopardized, which can hardly be explained by the discriminatory treatment hypothesis.

Consequences

In the case of a country without exchange controls, where capital flight takes place through the official market, its immediate consequence is to reduce the level of foreign-exchange reserves or to require increased foreign borrowing. When any excess reserves and unused borrowing capacity have been used up so that the foreign-exchange constraint starts to bite, the country will be obliged to initiate balance of payments adjustment. At best, this will involve devaluation (or equivalent measures) to switch purchases of tradables from foreign to domestic sources, thus absorbing resources that would otherwise have been available for domestic investment into the generation of a current account surplus to pay for the capital flight. At worst, adjustment will take place not by expenditure switching but by expenditure reduction—by reducing demand, and with it output, to whatever point is needed to cut the demand for imports enough to transform capital outflow into current account surplus.

Thus, the best case involves a reduction in the savings to finance domestic investment, of a magnitude essentially[16] equal to the size of the capital flight. Future growth will in consequence be lower. The worst case involves a reduction not just in future growth possibilities but also in the current level of output, by some *multiple*[17] of the size of capital flight. This decline in output will typically have a high component of investment, either because the government finds cuts in public investment the easiest to make, or because it deliberately seeks to squeeze import-intensive activities, or because of the adverse effects of recession on business confidence. Thus, future growth potential is likely to decline, as well as current output, by even more than in the "best case." In the best case, the savings constraint is tightened and reduces future growth possibilities; in the worst case, the foreign exchange constraint imposes both a larger cutback in future growth and a loss in current output.[18] The typical case is presumably intermediate, with some expenditure switching (hopefully in increasing proportion) limiting the necessary short-run decline in output, but a cut in investment at least as large as the magnitude of capital outflow.

To set against those losses, one must weigh the foreign interest income earned by those who placed capital abroad. In the best case, where the loss of future domestic income is equal to the marginal product of capital (times the capital outflow), society as a whole will gain if the rate of return on foreign assets exceeds the marginal product of domestic investment, and lose in the converse case. A simple-minded neoclassical view would be that this implies that foreign investment will occur if and only if it is socially

---

16. If devaluation has an adverse impact on the terms of trade, the decline in resource availability and therefore in the potential level of investment will be somewhat larger. But the difference is likely to be extremely modest in developing countries, which rarely have much monopoly (let alone monopsony) power in international trade in the medium term.

17. The foreign-trade multiplier analysis shows that the necessary decline in income is $(1/m)$ times the needed improvement in the trade balance, where m is the marginal propensity to import, a fraction. See Williamson (1983, section 8.2).

18. The analysis is that of the two-gap model. See Williamson (1983, section 12.3).

advantageous, for why would investors place their funds abroad if they did not anticipate a higher rate of return?

In fact, however, there are strong reasons for expecting the economic return on domestic investment to exceed the economic rate of return to the source country on foreign assets, especially in the context of capital flight. In the first place, capital is relatively scarce in developing countries, and hence there is a presumption that, unless policies cause extreme distortions, its marginal product will be higher there. Second, the rate of return on real capital typically exceeds that on financial assets, since it includes returns to managers and entrepreneurs to compensate for the trouble and risk of undertaking real investment. Third, some part of the return to domestic capital formation accrues to workers (in the form of higher wages) and consumers (in the form of better and cheaper products) rather than to the investors. Fourth, investors normally pay taxes on interest and profits generated at home, whereas that earned abroad is usually de facto tax-free (of foreign as well as domestic taxes). Finally, when output is constrained by the shortage of foreign exchange, the economic cost of the loss of a dollar of foreign exchange is much greater than the cost of one less dollar of investment, as explained above by the two-gap analysis.[19]

Thus, there are strong reasons for expecting the economic return on the displaced domestic investment to exceed the return earned on the foreign investments bought by the funds that flee. This does not contradict the expectation that private investors will shift funds abroad only if they perceive the risk-adjusted return to be higher there, because all of the above factors except the first involve a wedge between the economic return on investment and the financial return to the investor, and it is, of course, the latter that drives private investment decisions. Indeed, there is yet another reason why foreign investment may appear more attractive to individual wealth-owners than it does to their society, namely that many of the risks they are seeking to escape—such as expropriation or devaluation—involve a redistribution of income at the expense of the wealth-owners rather than a net loss to the society.

The conclusion that developing countries are harmed by capital flight does not imply that developed countries could expect to benefit by restricting

---

19. We are, however, somewhat dubious of the argument that the returns on foreign investments can be dismissed because the funds "never come back." If those investments proved extremely lucrative and their owners spent all the profits abroad, it is not obvious that this is worse from a national perspective than to have the wealth-owners make equally profitable investments with zero spillover benefits at home and then take the proceeds abroad to spend. An egalitarian may not regard the outcome as contributing much to national welfare, but this is because the income accrues to the rich (we would feel differently if the proceeds were used to give educational foreign trips to orphans) rather than because it is "lost to the country."

capital outflows. For example, capital is typically not a scarce factor in developed countries. Neither do developed countries typically suffer from a foreign-exchange constraint, any more than they do from acute fears of expropriation or massive devaluation. Furthermore, the existence of double taxation treaties, with their provisions for information exchange, makes it somewhat less likely that taxes can be avoided by holding funds abroad. It is still true that real domestic investment is to be preferred to foreign financial investment inasmuch as real investment produces returns that accrue to other agents besides the owners of capital, but most developed countries probably gain practically as much from those benefits yielded by inward direct investment as they lose from the outward investment they permit. In sum, capital mobility seems a sensible enough policy for the typical developed country, but this does not imply that the same is true for a natural capital importer.

The preceding analysis is based on the "two-gap model," the classic tool for analyzing the impact of a change in foreign-exchange availability on a developing country.[20] It has been argued that the standard conclusions of that model—namely, that a loss of foreign exchange is disadvantageous, and that this is particularly true when it creates a foreign-exchange constraint independent of the savings constraint—apply as much to losses caused by capital flight as to any others. But, in a provocative paper, Rodriguez (ch. 6) argues that the effects of capital flight are far more corrosive than this.

He points out that it is the wealthy who had, and exploited, the opportunity to place funds abroad during the years when capital flight was motivated by discriminatory treatment. Those dollars were bought at subsidized rates (in the days of overvalued exchange rates). In some cases the state was simultaneously subsidizing domestic investments undertaken by those same individuals, while state enterprises were then pushed into foreign borrowing in order to satisfy the public-sector budget constraint. In other cases the private sector borrowed abroad on behalf of its productive enterprises at the same time that it was building up dollar bank deposits in its private

---

20. The analysis assumed that capital outflows were legal and therefore took place through the official foreign exchange market. It is interesting to ask what difference it makes when exchange controls prohibit the placement of funds abroad and therefore capital flight has to take place through a parallel or black market. The proximate effect will be to increase the premium on the dollar in the black market. This will divert some sales of foreign exchange from the official to the black market, for example, by promoting misinvoicing (Gulati, ch. 3), or by encouraging smuggling; to that extent, the effects will be the same as if there were no black market. It is also likely to stimulate some export sales that would not otherwise have taken place and whose proceeds can be realized in the black market. This will preempt resources as in the analysis of the savings-constrained case when the economy is fully employed, but when there is unemployment it will promote additional output. The distributional and other effects discussed below will be absent or much attenuated.

capacity. In both cases, even before any of the problems discussed above that result from a shortage of savings or foreign exchange had materialized, the local economy had begun to suffer from a shift of financial intermediation offshore and consequent stultification of the development of the local capital market.

However, matters worsened dramatically when the debt crisis cut off access to new foreign borrowing. Since the foreign assets held by the private sector did not generate any dollar income for the source country but the foreign debts had to be serviced in dollars, balance of payments adjustment became necessary. This involved large real devaluations, which enriched holders of dollar assets and impoverished those with dollar liabilities. Even where those liabilities had originally been incurred by the private sector, they were soon de facto nationalized, either directly or indirectly (via the provision of foreign exchange to make interest payments at privileged rates), in some cases under foreign pressure but in many cases apparently without any serious consideration of the alternative of allowing the indebted enterprises to go bankrupt. This might well have induced the return of some of the flight capital (to keep the enterprises solvent), while in other cases it would have reduced the foreign debt and permitted reorganization under new management, public or private, domestic or foreign. In fact, government help in servicing foreign debt, by the provision of foreign exchange at a special exchange rate, on occasion tended to deter repatriation, inasmuch as the owners might have feared that repatriation would provoke offsetting claims. The one country to flirt with the straightforward capitalist solution of allowing bankruptcy was Chile, which was quickly forced to nationalize its foreign debts by its commercial bank creditors, on pain of withdrawal of trade credit. Rumor has it that oil tankers bound for Chile turned around, and the government capitulated within 24 hours (Arellano and Ramos, ch. 7, n. 4).

The process everywhere ended up with the public sector owing the dollar debts and the wealthy owning private dollar assets. The public sector's enlarged obligations pushed it into structural deficit, from which all the efforts toward fiscal austerity have not yet rescued it. The burden of fiscal austerity is borne by the less wealthy segments of society, who did not have the resources to place their funds abroad beyond the reach of taxation. The fiscal gap is filled by the inflation tax. The net impact is a regressive redistribution of income and wealth on a massive scale.

Hence the consequences of capital flight include not just the macroeconomic costs of lost output and curtailed future growth opportunities, but also the exportation of financial intermediation, perverse redistribution of income, structural budget deficits, and inflation. But Rodriguez argues that even this is not the end of the story. Domestic capitalists who find themselves with a large part of their wealth abroad for a lengthy period are tempted to start looking for more challenging investment opportunities than passive ownership of financial assets and real estate. They start taking over corporations in the developed countries, and before long not just their wealth but their entrepreneurial energies and their economic stake in national policies are lost to their native societies. In this vision the whole future of the development process is jeopardized by capital flight.

Source-Country Policies

The principal responsibility for stemming resident capital outflows inevitably falls on the source countries, since there is no question but that their own inadequate policies were the primary source of the problem. To defend their interests, the wealthy reacted to those policy failings, but this merely emphasizes that policy should always be designed on the assumption that that is how those with the ability to do so will behave. The present section examines what countries need to do to "set their house in order" so as to ensure that capital flight does not recur.

Macroeconomic Fundamentals

In the final paragraph of his historical survey of capital flight, Charles Kindleberger (ch. 2) recalled a 1937 memo of his which:

... laid heavy emphasis on the restoration of confidence. Such restoration, it was thought, might precede or follow renewed domestic investment and economic recovery ... but excluded further depreciation. ... This essentially means that short-run measures in the foreign exchange market, such as a stabilization or a squeeze, must be buttressed by long-run macroeconomic stabilization that is seen to be politically supportable. It is quite an order.

The conclusion that, however difficult the task, macroeconomic policy needs to be firmly set on a sustainable course, if there is to be any chance of containing capital outflows, was one of the few propositions to win general consent during the Institute's conference. Confidence in the sustainability of macroeconomic policy is unlikely in the absence of a realistic exchange rate, a positive but moderate real interest rate, robust economic growth, and a medium-run resolution of the debt problem.

Cuddington (ch. 4) provides strong evidence that an overvalued exchange rate is a prime cause of capital flight, a result that confirms intuition and much anecdotal evidence.[21] If a government wishes to control capital flight,

---

21. This is not to say that an overvalued exchange rate is always associated with capital flight. On the contrary, misplaced confidence may well cause or sustain overvaluation for a time—as happened in Britain in 1980–81, in the United States in 1982–85, and in Chile in 1981 (an episode explored by Arellano and Ramos, ch. 7).

it must break with the bad habit of allowing its currency to become overvalued. This may be accomplished either by allowing the currency to float or by setting it at a realistic level and then making sure that the real exchange rate is not appreciated by high domestic inflation. It is vital to gain public confidence that this policy will be maintained, even in the event of political change. Without this certainty, exporters will lack the incentive to invest, and hence the trade adjustments needed to sustain the policy are unlikely to materialize.

A sensible interest-rate policy is also of key importance, although for technical reasons (namely, the problem of reverse causation) Cuddington was unable to provide econometric evidence to buttress this claim. The aim should be a dependably positive real interest rate that is somewhat above the international rate even after allowing for any depreciation of the domestic currency needed to preserve competitiveness. But it is important that the interest rate not be too high as well as that it not be too low. An excessively high interest rate discourages productive investment and can even jeopardize the financial viability of existing productive enterprises. It also raises the problem of adverse selection: that is, only entrepreneurs with speculative projects in mind are prepared to borrow, comforted by the thought that the lender will bear a part of the cost if the project fails. An economy where the financial markets have been reduced to gambling casinos is all too prone to generate capital flight, as shown by Argentine experience in the early 1980s.

It is also plausible that economic growth will help to reduce capital flight, by generating confidence in the domestic economy, opening up attractive investment opportunities, and allowing the economy to pay remunerative interest and profit returns without cutting real wages to a point that would generate social unrest. Indeed, Conesa (1986) reports evidence of such an effect: according to his analysis, growth is actually the most important single deterrent to capital flight. Of course, growth is not a policy variable in the direct way that exchange and interest rates are, but the conclusion that growth helps deter capital flight nevertheless provides another reason for welcoming the pro-growth bias of official policy since the conception of the Baker Plan, and for avoiding excessive austerity in IMF programs. Likewise, this conclusion provides another reason for supporting supply-oriented adjustment measures—including market liberalization, fiscal reform, debu-reaucratization, and outward orientation, as Balassa et al. (1986) urge—as well as the longer term approach to debt rescheduling that at last seems on the road to implementation.

The proposition that realistic exchange rates, positive but reasonable real interest rates, and a resumption of growth are necessary to master capital flight seems to be rather uncontroversial. Where controversy still rages is on whether "getting the fundamentals right" is just a necessary or is also a sufficient condition for dealing with capital flight.

This question deserves a qualified answer. It may well be that a full restoration of confidence, including confidence in the permanence of the new policy stance in the face of possible political change as well as establishment of realistic exchange and interest rates and a resumption of growth, would suffice to induce a return of flight capital.

The problem with this conclusion is that it does not explain how to break out of the vicious circle of low growth, capital flight, foreign-exchange constraint, and thus continued low growth. Mere changes in macroeconomic policy may not permit the restoration of growth until the foreign-exchange constraint is broken, while capital flight will not go into reverse and help break the foreign-exchange constraint until growth resumes. Very tight credit policies may help bring capital back, as in Mexico recently, but they are hardly calculated to restore growth. Moreover, confidence in the future may be very hard for a government to engineer, no matter how well-intentioned it may be, if only because that confidence depends also on perceptions of the likely actions of its political opponents. In an intermediate situation where current policies merit confidence but the long-term outlook remains problematic, the array of other policies discussed below can be of especial importance.

Corruption

In many countries it may not be just a change in macroeconomic policy that is needed to master capital flight but also a change in the ethics of those involved in public life. No matter how attractive domestic economic prospects, anyone who derives illicit income from bribes on public-sector contracts or from the award of import licenses is likely to wish to place at least some of the resulting assets abroad (see Walter, ch. 5). And a correction of the tax distortions that currently provide an incentive to place funds abroad (see below) is hardly likely if the officials who would have to negotiate a tax treaty attach greater importance to their private interest in retaining tax-exempt, foreign nest-eggs than to the social interest in achieving tax neutrality. A society that lacks the social cohesion to ensure that its leaders place public duties ahead of personal gain may well be condemned to repeated bouts of capital flight.

Of course, policy changes can significantly reduce the incentives for corruption. Ending the rationing of underpriced foreign exchange or credit would remove some of the major sources of gain from such behavior. However, such policies are not always mere miscalculations. They are major sources of state power, and they are unlikely to be definitively changed until there is both a public awareness of their distorting, demoralizing effects and a political commitment to honest government.

This is a delicate subject, on which foreign preaching is unlikely to achieve much. Indeed, if preaching is not to be counterproductive, it is important that the preachers not pose as more self-righteous than their own actions justify. At the same time, neither the delicacy of the subject nor the lack of reliable estimates of the social cost of corruption should deter one from recognizing the pervasiveness of the problem and the urgency of those societies' coming to terms with it. Perhaps the most useful thing that outsiders can do is to support the efforts of countries (like the Philippines) that show signs of trying to escape from the debilitating grip of pervasive corruption.

Domestic Financial Markets

As well as establishing credible, consistent macroeconomic policies, source countries need to undertake major changes in their treatment of domestic financial intermediation in order to avoid an excessive gap between the economic returns provided by the underlying economic prospects and the returns that private investors can reasonably expect to earn. At the same time, they must limit their fiscal exposure to private losses in order to increase their ability to maintain consistent policies.

Source-country governments have to recognize that they are engaged in international competition for capital. Hence, they must avoid viewing domestic savings as captive resources that can be taxed and allocated at will. As noted in our discussion of the causes of capital flight, source-country residents face numerous explicit and implicit taxes and fiscal risks when investing in domestic securities and business activities. Passive income from wealth is often (though by no means always) taxed at high rates relative to world average levels, both because of high statutory rates and the increase in effective rates that results from inflation. Further, the rate payable on formal savings instruments, especially bank deposits, is often limited by law to nominal levels that result in low or negative real returns. This financial repression is an implicit tax on savings that is typically passed on to the government or to government-favored sectors through reserve requirements and direct lending at controlled rates. Even where interest rates are not controlled, noninterest-bearing reserve requirements coupled with inflation act as a tax on domestic financial intermediation. In order not to erode the "tax base," these taxes have to be coupled with limits on currency convertibility (which can be avoided only through illegal capital flight).

Potential changes in explicit and implicit taxes on financial intermediation are also a major source of financial risk. In periods of overall financial crisis, these are often the only mechanisms through which governments can increase revenues in the short run, either by tightening restrictions or simply by printing money and imposing an inflation tax that falls primarily on financial intermediation. Thus, even though a government may have a policy goal of providing residents with internationally competitive returns on savings, this policy will not be credible if there is a significant chance of an overall fiscal crisis.

While fiscal crises threaten domestic financial intermediation, the structure of that intermediation often contributes to the potential for such crises, creating a vicious circle. Governments are often compelled to intervene to maintain the viability of both public and private enterprises and, particularly, financial institutions that incur significant losses.[22] This problem is exacerbated in many developing countries, including most of the major sources of capital flight, by their heavy reliance on bank or nonbank intermediaries that issue primarily liquid, supposedly default-free, securities. *A la par y a la vista,* at par on sight, are the terms not only for bank deposits but also for the liabilities of nonbank intermediaries such as *financieras,* which represent the bulk of financial assets held by households in many Latin American countries. Government intervention to maintain these terms has played key roles in recent internal financial crises in Argentina, Chile, Mexico, and Venezuela, among others.

With such "house of cards" structures, any significant asset loss can trigger a collapse of the financial sector with the attendant social costs. The fact that the government is committed to intervene in the case of major losses encourages opportunistic behavior in the financial sector, since the value of the implicit call on government resources is an increasing function of the potential variability of the assets it holds.[23] This tendency is typically exacerbated by lax controls over self-dealing by private financial institutions, allowing scoundrels to borrow from banks they control directly or indirectly at (excessively low) rates that reflect depositors' faith that the government will make good on the claims in the case of private failure.

Any event that increases the perceived risk of a financial crisis is likely to trigger a run on the domestic financial system since the value of deposits remains fixed in the short run. This, in turn, will reduce tax revenues, further weakening the fiscal situation. If exchange rates are also stabilized in the short run, this run on the system takes the form of capital flight.

The negative consequences of these financial dynamics are readily apparent. Because of the distortions introduced by present and possible future

---

22. See Gillis, Lessard, and Jenkins (1982) for further development of this point in the case of state-owned enterprises, whose growth was promoted by foreign borrowing in many developing countries.

23. Merton (1977) provides the pioneering analysis of this phenomenon.

interventions, the system fails to allocate resources properly. It is crisis prone, and crises, and even expectations of crises, are likely to trigger capital flight.

In the light of these complex interactions, removing financial repression is a necessary but not a sufficient condition for restoring stable, viable patterns of domestic intermediation in developing countries. Financial markets need to be broadened and deepened so that a much larger proportion of the risks implicit in real investments are passed through to investors in the form of securities whose price can vary in line with the perceived value of the underlying assets. This requires strengthening the capital base of the financial sector to allow it to absorb greater fluctuations in asset values; improving bank regulation to ensure that bank shareholders rather than society bear these residual risks; and increasing the role of bond and equity financing.

Such reforms are difficult to accomplish, although a number of countries are now looking at the question very seriously. Improving bank regulation involves a difficult balancing act. On the one hand, the government must signal its commitment to maintaining the value of deposits and the solvency of the system. On the other hand, it must do so in a way that does not encourage opportunistic behavior that increases the state's risk exposure.

Deepening financial markets requires a coherent and appropriate body of corporate and securities law. In many cases, it also requires reforms in tax statutes and improvement in tax enforcement, since, in practice, most developing-country tax systems discriminate against formal financial intermediation, whether through banks or through equity markets. Effective reforms will typically include a reduction of taxes on capital gains or, at a minimum, price-level indexing to determine gains, and the elimination of special wealth taxes on securities.

Exchange Control

Among the Latin American countries, at least, there is an exact correspondence between the countries that had no exchange control at the turn of the decade and those that suffered capital flight on a massive scale. Argentina, Mexico, Uruguay, and Venezuela all experienced massive outflows; in all of them the outflows were perfectly legal. In contrast, outflows were relatively modest from Brazil, Chile, Colombia, and Peru, all of which maintained restrictions on capital outflows that made the accumulation of foreign assets illegal. (One cannot, however, be sure that the outflows were quite as modest as the figures suggest, since the very fact that capital transfers are illegal tends to ensure that capital flight takes forms that are harder to trace.) Korea and the Philippines, which both maintained exchange controls and experienced minimal and modest outflows, respectively, also fit the pattern.

This contrast makes it difficult to justify policy advice to debtor countries to dismantle an existing system of exchange controls. Moreover, the welfare gain from allowing private citizens unimpeded access to world capital markets comes primarily from the opportunity this gives *creditors* to choose a portfolio that suits their preferences in terms of rewards and risks. But for a *debtor* country, allowing citizens to invest abroad means either increasing its financial exposure by borrowing more or curtailing its absorption of real resources. In either event, the social loss has to be weighed against the private gain of the investor. Admittedly, some libertarians argue that the freedom to invest is a right that should not be circumscribed by "nationalistic" conceptions of the impact on social welfare, but an egalitarian can retort that the gainers from free capital movements are virtually certain to be richer than the losers.

In addition, a more concrete objection exists to a policy of preventing capital outflows, assuming this to be feasible. Especially in countries with exposure to a few commodities or industries, constraining residents to hold only domestic assets will impose on them large but potentially diversifiable risks. If the opening of markets to capital flows would result in inflows to offset the outflows, the country would gain relative to being closed. However, there is little evidence that the cross flows for diversification actually take place, except in the past in the form of bank debt which placed excessive risk on the debtor. The interest now being shown in "emerging market" equities by investors in developed countries is, however, a hopeful sign that things may be changing.

In view of these conflicting considerations, the decision as to whether to maintain exchange controls surely falls within the area of legitimate national discretion, provided that a country that decides to maintain controls also makes a credible commitment to resist the potential for increased opportunism on the part of the government. It would certainly be an error to imagine that exchange controls offer some sort of panacea. Many countries have imposed exchange controls but have failed to make them work, including Mexico (not to mention France) in 1982. And the reason that some countries managed to avoid massive capital flight is not merely because they made it illegal. Brazil offered attractive indexed domestic assets and kept the exchange rate competitive; Chile liberalized its trade account to a point where it was easier to shift into durable goods than into foreign financial assets; Colombia had a stream of illegal foreign earnings that permitted accumulation of foreign financial assets without anything that showed up as capital flight in the statistics; and Peru provided domestic dollar-denominated assets. Absent those factors, it is entirely possible that these countries would have experienced major capital flight even with exchange control. Indeed, Brazil appears to have developed a nonnegligible volume of capital flight after 1982.

Moreover, exchange controls cannot be used to induce a return of flight capital. On the contrary, experience shows that imposition of exchange controls deters a reflux of capital and that their removal encourages such a return. This is not surprising, since an important motive for shifting funds abroad is to ensure their ready availability in terms of foreign exchange.

Perhaps the most sensible attitude is that of Miguel Urrutia (ch. 8) in his defense of Colombian practice. He pointed out that Colombia has maintained capital controls over the years while being careful to ensure that they were not used as a *substitute* for sound policies. Thus, the dollar has sometimes been at a premium and sometimes at a discount on the black market: capital controls have helped to minimize fluctuations in the real exchange rate facing exporters as well as to reduce flows of hot money that might otherwise have destabilized the economy. On average these controls may also have helped to maintain somewhat lower interest rates than would otherwise have been necessary, but they have not been asked to override any major incentive to shift funds abroad.

Provided that not too much is asked of exchange controls, they may be a useful element in the policy arsenal. Capital-importing countries that have a functioning exchange-control system should certainly not be pressed to abolish it. Even countries that have already lost much resident capital may need to ponder the trade-off between reduced chances of attracting it back if exchange controls are imposed versus increased dangers of losing new savings if they are not. Nevertheless, exchange controls will do more harm than good if they are treated as a panacea that can substitute for adequate policies.

Taxation

Capital outflows can be encouraged or discouraged by taxation arrangements in both source and haven countries. We defer until the next section a consideration of the responsibilities of haven countries, and concentrate here on the actions that the source countries need to take in order to remove the tax incentive to place funds abroad.

A distortion encouraging capital outflow arises when the effective rate of taxation on either investment income or wealth is lower on assets held abroad than on those held domestically. This can arise either because the statutory tax liabilities are lower on investment income generated (or wealth held) abroad, or because enforcement of legal obligations is less effective.

As described below, in practice many tax-exempt assets are available to nonresidents in the haven countries. Thus the legal tax obligation faced by a developing-country investor depends primarily on the laws of his home country. These vary enormously, depending on the country's attitude toward the "origin principle" versus the "residence principle" of taxation.[24] Argentina is the extreme case of a country that follows the origin principle. This means that it does not attempt to tax Argentine residents' investment income generated, nor wealth held, outside Argentina. But since it does tax the increase in wealth held in Argentina as well as investment income earned in Argentina, Argentine residents face a strong tax incentive to place funds abroad (especially when this enables them to avoid showing an increase in wealth held in Argentina on their tax returns). These incentives are actually stronger the more scrupulous a taxpayer is in fulfilling his legal obligation to declare the increase in his Argentine-held wealth.

Venezuela provides a good example of a country that has recently embraced the residence principle of taxation. While it still permits the ownership of foreign assets, it has passed a law requiring the registration of foreign investments and the declaration of income on them for tax purposes (taxable at the rather modest rate of 14 percent). If all taxpayers were completely honest and the tax rate were the same on domestic and foreign income, the tax incentive to hold assets abroad rather than at home would be eliminated.

Since, however, many taxpayers declare income only when they believe the tax authority can police their compliance, the tax incentive would in fact be eliminated only if enforcement were equally effective with respect to interest income earned abroad rather than at home. This is by no means the case. Among the developing countries of the Western Hemisphere, only a few small Caribbean countries[25] have tax treaties with the United States that entitle them to information-sharing with the US tax authorities. Without an information-sharing agreement with the major haven countries, foremost the United States, the possibility of effective enforcement of taxes on investment income earned abroad is virtually nonexistent.

Two distinct policy initiatives are therefore called for if the developing countries are to eliminate the tax incentive to place funds abroad.

First, for the reasons analyzed above, many developing countries need to reform their own tax laws so as to replace the origin principle (which used

---

24. The "origin principle" (or "source basis") of taxation, referred to by tax lawyers as an exclusively territorial concept of taxation, involves an attempt to tax exclusively the income generated within a certain country (the components of GDP). The "residence principle" involves an attempt to tax the income generated anywhere in the world that accrues to the residents of a particular country (i.e., the components of GNP), referred to by tax lawyers as an extraterritorial or global concept of taxation.

25. The United States has encouraged countries to conclude tax treaties within the context of the Caribbean Basin Initiative, prior to which it had a treaty only with the Netherlands Antilles. (In July 1987 the United States announced its intention of terminating this treaty because of an inability to agree on the restrictions that should apply to residents of third countries, but subsequently found that this raised more complex problems than it realized.) Tax treaties with Barbados, Jamaica, and Trinidad and Tobago are now operational, while one with Costa Rica is under negotiation.

to be in their national self-interest, for reasons noted below) by the residence principle. This may not accomplish much alone, but without this step all else is futile.

Second, they need to establish information-sharing agreements with the principal haven countries. This has traditionally been done as a part of tax treaties. Latin countries have, however, held back from signing tax treaties with the United States. Honduras signed a treaty in 1956, but it was abrogated long ago. Brazil commenced negotiations in 1967 that dragged on until 1981, in which year the US Senate ratified the resulting treaty (and a similar treaty with Argentina). Both Argentina and Brazil refused to reciprocate the ratification, however, in view of changes made by the Senate.

At least two factors underlie this failure. The immediate cause of the refusal of Argentina and Brazil to ratify the tax treaties so laboriously negotiated was the Senate's deletion of "tax-sparing" provisions. Tax sparing involves an agreement by one party that a tax concession made by the other (normally to attract investment) will be treated as a tax credit rather than an increase in taxable income. France, Germany, Japan, and Sweden have all concluded tax treaties with Argentina and Brazil that allow tax sparing for the incentives provided to attract direct investment. Without a similar feature in the tax treaty with the United States, both countries felt that the arrangement they were being offered was unacceptably one-sided.[26]

A more general factor that has militated against the conclusion of tax treaties is the Latin attachment to the origin principle. This principle used to be very clearly in the self-interest of the Latins: as large net foreign debtors on private account (with GDP exceeding GNP), they could gain revenue by taxing the profits earned by multinationals. Indeed, they used the principle to justify (or rationalize, some might claim) a practice of combining corporate and withholding taxes at rates that ensured that virtually all the tax revenues extracted from multinationals operating in Latin America accrued to the local tax authority rather than to the Treasury of the multinationals' home country. The US attempt, as a part of each tax treaty, to regain some of the tax revenue was one stumbling block to the negotiation of treaties. Naturally, a country committed to the origin principle of taxation sees little advantage in a tax treaty that would help it do what it does not desire to do, namely tax the foreign income of its residents.

Whatever may have been the rights and wrongs of these matters in the past, it seems clear that the Latins are now paying a high price for their refusal to negotiate tax treaties. The avoidance of double taxation that a tax

---

26. The issue of tax sparing has become less important as a result of reductions in marginal tax rates in the United States in recent years. Most firms with foreign operations will now have excess foreign tax credits, and hence will benefit from lower local tax rates.

treaty ensures could be expected to help revive direct investment. And, following the big cuts in US tax rates, the benefit of being able to tax foreign corporations has been severely eroded. This means that the incidence of the high tax rates still in force in many Latin countries will fall on the multinational rather than on the US Treasury, limiting the much needed expansion of direct foreign investment despite the otherwise improved investment climate of many countries in the region and their more competitive exchange rates. In contrast, the vast sums now held by Latins in US bank deposits and other instruments have much increased the Latin interest in information sharing. Latin self-interest therefore demands a reappraisal of their traditional hostility to signing tax treaties.

Some participants at the Institute's conference argued that developing countries should concede their inability to tax investment income (just as, in one view, they should refrain from attempting to hold the post-tax real income of the technocracy below international levels, for fear of provoking a brain drain). But this contention was strongly disputed by participants alarmed at the highly concentrated distribution of income and wealth in many debtor countries, which could only be worsened by abandoning the effort to tax investment income. This would imply even greater pressure on immobile factors of production, especially unskilled labor. Moveover, while such a step would eliminate one motive for capital outflows, it would also reduce the source countries' fiscal strength and thus could actually increase the prospects for crisis-related episodes of capital flight.

In our view, source countries need to be realistic in recognizing that high tax rates on wealth (including inheritance taxes) or investment income will tend to motivate citizens to place funds abroad and seek out tax-exempt assets, but they also need to avoid the defeatism of ceasing even to try to tax income from wealth. Opportunities for emigration and tax evasion are sufficiently important to justify the avoidance of tax rates much above the international norm, but not so ubiquitous as to dictate abandoning the attempt to collect revenues comparable to those levied in the major industrial countries. Countries like Argentina need thoroughgoing tax reform designed to reduce the present very high marginal tax rates and compensate for the effect of this on revenue by widening the tax base.

Haven-Country Policies

While the primary responsibility for curbing capital flight falls on the source countries, increasing interdependence implies that the attractiveness of placing funds abroad is also importantly influenced by policies pursued in the countries to which money can flee. We designate these the "haven countries," though without implying that they have deliberately sought to attract funds (in the way that the term "tax haven" implies a conscious attempt to attract clients).

Wealthy individuals throughout the world face a broad array of offshore investment alternatives. As recounted by Walter (ch. 5), such individuals, whether located in Latin America, Europe, or the Middle East, are called on at home by private bankers from the world's premiere institutions and are welcomed in major world financial centers. Some of these are offshore financial centers, such as Geneva, Luxembourg, or Panama, which effectively rent their local jurisdiction as a place through which to invest directly or indirectly in other countries. Others, including New York, London, and now Tokyo, are centers for investment as well as intermediation that compete with the offshore centers at least in terms of taxation, though typically not secrecy.

Each magnet location offers a slightly different mix of advantages, and therefore attracts flight capital of a particular type. The United States, for example, offers substantial tax exemption and, while it does not offer secrecy, it does offer deposit insurance and deep capital markets. Hence a middle-class Mexican or Venezuelan, for example, who holds foreign assets as a hedge against domestic crises but has little or no reason to fear being prosecuted, is likely to find a US bank account as attractive as a Swiss one. An investor more interested in hiding overseas holdings, perhaps because capital transfers are restricted by law or because the wealth was gained illicitly, will find Switzerland or Panama more attractive. A Panama does not offer the same government backing of deposits or depth of capital markets as the United States, but this competitive disadvantage may not hold for branches of European banks that can compete on their own financial strength.

While this shifting of funds conjures up images of drug smugglers moving suitcases of cash, most capital flight seems to take place through normal channels. Latin Americans, in particular, are often in effect dual citizens because of their heritage and extensive international travel for business and pleasure. Maintaining a bank account in Miami or San Diego is common-place, and often completely legal. Even when exchange controls exist, under normal circumstances foreign bank deposits are readily available through relatives or acquaintances.

Policies in the haven countries influence the incentive for residents of developing countries to place their funds abroad through at least three important channels: through the system of taxation, through deposit-seeking activities by the banks, and through the level of world interest rates. These are discussed in turn, starting with taxation, to continue the analysis initiated above with respect to the policies of the source countries.

The taxation of investment income is perhaps the most important way policies of the haven countries may help to suck capital out of developing countries. These policies involve both the taxes the haven countries impose on the investment income of nonresidents and the help they provide developing countries to collect taxes the latter impose on the investment income earned by their residents in the haven countries.

Most developed countries, including the United States, have now abandoned taxation of most nonresident investment income. For example, the United States has long exempted from taxation interest on bank deposits owned by nonresidents: it does not even impose a refundable withholding tax. In 1984, it exempted interest on Treasury securities held by nonresidents from withholding as well—a move swifty followed by France, Germany, and Japan. Thus, withholding tax is now levied only on nonresident income from sources such as dividends, interest on corporate securities, real estate, and royalties.[27]

The waning of the effort to tax nonresident income seems to have arisen as a joint result of two factors. One is sympathy in most developed countries for the residence principle of taxation, which implies that it is proper to exempt nonresident income. The other is international competition for funds: it is argued that internationally mobile investment funds have so many tax-exempt alternatives that any attempt to impose taxes either raises the return the borrower must pay or squeezes the borrower out of the market.

Many participants in the Institute's conference were extremely critical of the implicit policy of most industrial countries—to allow or even solicit offshore funds for tax-free investment with no questions asked. This erosion of the "global fiscal commons," through beggar-my-neighbor competition among industrial countries, is intensified by the competition from tax havens. The time has surely come to try to reverse this trend. It is doubtful if this can be done piecemeal, given the incentive that each country has to ensure that its tax treatment of nonresident income is at least as favorable as the international norm. Rather, one needs to think in terms of a treaty within the Organization for Economic Cooperation and Development (OECD) that would commit all the industrial countries to imposing a substantial withholding tax, which would be refundable on presentation of evidence that the recipient had reported any investment income to his national tax authority.

---

27. In addition, nonresidents are subject to income tax on income effectively connected with a US trade or business and to capital gains tax on real estate.

Such a proposal naturally raises a number of questions. Perhaps the most obvious is whether such an agreement would not inevitably be undermined by the existence of tax havens. Provided that all the industrial countries subscribe to the OECD treaty, this fear is exaggerated. The reason is that the tax havens act as intermediaries and need to place abroad virtually all the funds deposited with them. Interest earned on sums lent to the industrial countries could itself be made subject to withholding (since a tax haven cannot sign a tax treaty without ceasing to be a tax haven). In this event a tax haven could afford to pay only a rate of interest equal to the post-withholding-tax rate of return in the industrial countries.

Another question is whether withholding tax should be refundable to residents of countries that had not signed a tax treaty with the country where the interest was earned. Presumably this would not be possible since, in the absence of a tax treaty, there would be no mechanism for ensuring the authenticity of tax returns.

However, a related proposal deserves consideration. Diaz-Alejandro (1984) proposed that the United States should turn over the tax revenue from a withholding tax on the interest paid on the deposits of Latin Americans to the Inter-American Development Bank. While such revenue-sharing may sound visionary, the United States has already accepted the principle in one particular context: the proceeds of assets seized in the course of narcotics control from nationals of countries with which the United States has concluded Mutual Legal Assistance Treaties are shared between the United States and the country whose subjects are involved. This precedent deserves to be built on.

The United States has traditionally favored the conclusion of tax treaties. It and the other haven countries should maintain this positive attitude, inter alia, to permit an exchange of information with the source countries to help them enforce their tax laws. In the past, the main obstacle to the negotiation of such treaties has come from the Latin side, as noted in the previous section. But, now that tax reform has reduced the size of the sums at stake, it might be opportune to reconsider the traditional US hostility to the principle of tax sparing, which would encourage Latin willingness to sign tax treaties.

In conclusion, we wish to stress two further points. The first is that the proposals advanced above do not threaten to compromise the personal freedom of Latin investors, but only to promote fairness by bringing their earnings within the tax net. A resident of a country without a tax treaty would have the option of paying withholding tax and retaining anonymity. A resident of a country that does have a tax treaty would not have that option (assuming his home country bases its taxation on the residence principle), but tax treaties include clauses ensuring that information supplied can be used only by the tax authorities and is not transferable to other government agencies, notably the exchange-control authorities. Any violation of this undertaking could result in suspension of the tax treaty. Indeed, it would seem appropriate to maintain tax treaty relationships only with countries whose governments have a record of respecting civil rights—a group now much larger than a few years ago, as a result of the trend toward democracy in many debtor countries. And, of course, anyone who genuinely fears political persecution always has the option of holding assets that do not generate interest income. Thus, our proposals should be exempt from charges that they could facilitate political persecution such as are directed at proposals for indiscriminate disclosure of asset ownership to the governments of source countries.

The second point worth emphasizing is that reversing the erosion of the global fiscal commons is very much in the interest of the major industrial countries as well as developing countries that have suffered capital flight. Their acceptance of this assessment is evidenced by the efforts currently under way within the OECD to negotiate a treaty providing for mutual exchange of information among tax authorities with a view to curbing tax evasion (the Draft Convention on Mutual Administrative Assistance in Tax Matters). The OECD countries owe it to the Third World to make available to them the same opportunities that they are providing among themselves: one wonders whether they should not open this treaty to developing countries.

Deposit Seeking by Banks

Many of the major commercial banks have a second relationship to the debtor countries besides that of creditor to their governments: namely, they have accepted substantial deposits from their citizens. At the same time that their research departments and public spokesmen have been explaining that they can hardly be expected to lend more while the citizens of the debtor countries are showing their lack of confidence by moving money out, the private banking departments of some of those same banks have been actively wooing the fleeing dollars. The pioneering article of Glynn and Koenig (1984) on capital flight recounted the recollection of one rueful New York banker:

When I saw my colleagues in the private banking division at the airport and they said they were making a lot of money. . . I knew the countries the money was coming from were in trouble. When people "vote" with their cash that way, you know the end is nigh. . .

Before condemning the role of the banks in welcoming deposits of flight capital, one should contemplate the defense offered by one thoughtful banker. Schwietert (ch. 8) points out that Swiss secrecy laws were initially designed to protect Jewish depositors moving their assets out of Nazi Germany. Switzerland does not provide secrecy for criminals, or at least for crimes that are recognized as such in Switzerland (which include tax fraud but not tax evasion or the violation of exchange controls). A bank decision to reveal deposits of private citizens to suit the convenience of their governments would represent a massive extension of the coercive power of the state.

These arguments surely deserve respect, even if the Swiss concept of illegality will strike some as restrictive. Yet these arguments do not excuse the provision of "pouch services" to move money out of a country illegally, or the deliberate solicitation of new clients (activities that are indeed already prohibited by the banks' own code of conduct). It is one thing to accept the deposit of a rich foreigner on the same basis as of a poor native. It is quite another to seek private profit by encouraging practices that impoverish the bulk of the population in the source countries. Such activities are no more ethical than the corruption that sometimes provides the source of flight capital. The commercial banks have a responsibility to show decent restraint, and abandon the excuse that some other bank will inevitably do it even if they do not, as their contribution to resolution of the problem of capital flight. One advantage of imposing exchange control, incidentally, is that it prevents the banks from claiming that solicitation of flight capital involves no illegal act and that they are merely matching their competitors.

World Interest Rates

Cuddington (ch. 4) produced statistical support for the proposition that high world interest rates helped to suck funds out of the debtor countries. This provides yet another reason, in addition to the help that lower interest rates would give to the fiscal position in virtually all countries, the stimulus they would give to investment, and the balance of payments relief they would give directly to the debtor countries, for desiring lower real interest rates in the major industrial countries.

To recognize that high international interest rates intensified the exit of capital from debtor countries is to acknowledge that the industrial countries contributed to the problem of resident capital outflow. They need to play their part in ending the problem. A contribution they should make is to reduce real interest rates to historically normal levels.

No one should want to see central banks return to a policy of trying to push interest rates down regardless of the consequences. If markets react to a cut in short-term rates by marking bond prices down, prudence dictates that the effort to reduce rates be called off for the time being. Nonetheless, over time, central banks do have some power to lead interest rates down. Given the current state of the world economy, they should be aiming to use that power unless very strong special circumstances dictate otherwise (for example, a country with an undervalued exchange rate may be justified in maintaining relatively high interest rates to defend its currency). They should most certainly not resist market pressures to lower interest rates in strong-currency countries.

Capital Repatriation: Caboose or Locomotive?

Morgan Guaranty (1986) has argued:

LDC capital outflows have to be tackled as part of the solution to the debt problem, not as something that need be addressed only later. If capital flight is given a free ride in the caboose of the LDC debt train, the train has little hope of making the station. It is both necessary and feasible to deal forthrightly with issues affecting capital flight. It is necessary for quantitative and psychological reasons; it is feasible because the causes of capital flight are fairly well understood, and the means exist to stem and reverse it.

Rimmer de Vries repeats this position in chapter 8. He criticizes Dornbusch for stating that the return of flight capital is like the last car of the train, and asserts that he wants to put the caboose up front.

Is it possible to make the repatriation of flight capital the locomotive that would pull the debtor countries out of the debt crisis? The causes do indeed seem reasonably clear, even if econometric problems (notably the limited number of observations) have prevented them from being established as definitively as one would wish. But the policy recommendations to which we have been led—the restoration and maintenance of responsible macro-economic policies, far-reaching reforms of domestic financial systems, and a switch from the origin to the residence principle of taxation coupled with major efforts to improve tax enforcement involving a willingness to sign tax treaties—are quite demanding, even without adding the restoration of social cohesion and the elimination of corruption. Yet doubt must remain as to whether even the most determined action to "put the house in order" will always guarantee prompt and substantial repatriation of the capital already held abroad, rather than simply prevent further capital flight.

The principal reason for questioning whether capital will return as soon as the reasons that initially caused it to flee have been remedied is the fear that repatriation will expose the investor to penalties for taxes that were unpaid or exchange control regulations that were violated. This fear will be less in countries that lacked exchange controls when the capital fled and which do not attempt to tax investment income earned abroad. This may explain why Argentina and Mexico were the first countries to experience a substantial reflux of flight capital. But, even then, the holders of flight capital may fear that they will be viewed as having unfairly benefited from financial chaos or as having avoided their "fair share" of the adjustment borne by their compatriots. Such perceptions may create political pressures for after-the-fact settlements. This is especially true if the source-country government has been forced to bail out banks or enterprises controlled by individuals or groups with substantial foreign-asset holdings in the wake of withdrawals of funds or borrowings by these individuals.

History abounds with such cases. Kindleberger (ch. 2) chronicles the problems of speculators who profited from the Mississippi bubble in 1718–20:

Keeping profits in notes was risky because they were depreciating, and even buying real property in France—though many including John Law did—was dangerous since most financial troubles in France, and ends of reigns, had been followed by *Chambres de Justice* in which excess profits— what we would perhaps call today "undue enrichment"—were examined and fined or confiscated.

Suggestions for similar ex post settlements have been aired in the press of some of the debtor countries in recent years. Glynn and Koenig (1984) documented the concern of the Venezuelan authorities that those with dollar assets should not profit from cheap foreign exchange to service their dollar debts:

In Venezuela, for example—where capital flight was a national pastime until the government finally threw in the towel and devalued the boli-var—a government agency, Recadi, reviews all requests for low-cost dollars. Applicants must first pass through the "department of rejections," where Recadi attempts to uncover hidden dollar assets in subsidiaries or related firms. "A lot of people have tried to get us to pay for their condos in Miami," says Recadi's director, Francisco Maldonado.[28]

These factors create a significant threshold that must be overcome in order to induce the repatriation of funds held abroad. This threshold may be greater than that required to attract funds from nonresidents, despite the relative lack of information and expertise of the latter regarding source-country prospects as well as their greater difficulty in becoming directly involved (due to cultural, social, and linguistic differences as well as explicit barriers to direct foreign investment). It may, in other words, be simpler to live with offshore intermediation than to attract funds back.

---

28. Miguel Rodriguez comments that a lot succeeded.

What Can Countries Do?

The challenge of recovering flight capital is not a new one, nor is it limited to developing countries. Numerous programs have been proposed and many have been tried. Programs currently in place include France's amnesty with regard to exchange-control violations for residents who repatriate funds held abroad; Chile's debt-for-equity swap program that includes special provisions for residents (ch. 7), which has to date resulted in a reflow of nearly $1 billion, some 5 percent of Chile's debt; and Colombia's "repatriation bonds" (also described in ch. 7). Mexico, in contrast, reports a significant reflow of capital with no program aimed explicitly at recovering flight capital—it has tightened credit to the point where real interest rates rose enormously and simultaneously created major private-sector investment opportunities by realigning its exchange rate and commercial policy.

In general, these programs involve one or more of the following elements:

☐ an amnesty with regard to past taxes and sanctions for the violation of exchange controls

☐ favored exchange rates in purchasing domestic assets

☐ special guarantees against particular fiscal risks.

Each of these has its benefits and costs. One possible cost is the crowding out of new private investment unless the entrepreneur has flight capital at his disposal! It is not clear that this is a desirable basis for selecting new investments.

Amnesty programs, if credible, overcome the "threshold" problem, but they also undercut national authority and may create expectations that tax or other regulations can be violated with impunity in future. Therefore, the decision as to whether to employ an amnesty involves a trade-off between the benefits associated with the recapture of funds and the costs of reduced future enforceability of tax and exchange rate rules.

Favored exchange rates involve transfers to residents holding funds abroad. Thus, they implicitly reward capital flight and tax the capital and immobile factors that remained behind. This too can lead to undesirable and unsustainable expectations over time, increasing the potential danger that residents' financial holdings will become "hot money" in periods of crisis. In extreme cases, the creation of an arbitrage potential between rates of return available to residents with funds outside the country and those with only domestic assets will lead to "round tripping" where capital will flow out in order to take advantage of the inward arbitrage. This is a primary concern in the design and management of debt-for-equity swap programs (Zedillo, ch. 7). If such programs are perceived as inequitable, they will undermine the legitimacy of government policy.

In those cases where residents with foreign holdings place a high value on preserving their anonymity to avoid economic or political reprisals, credibility is even more difficult to obtain. So called whitener bonds, bearer bonds sold offshore that can be converted for domestic use, have been employed in some cases. A limitation of these schemes is that the anonymity is retained only as long as residents are content to invest locally on a passive, arms-length basis. One can add the option of converting to local currency to permit holders to invest in directly controlled operations, but anonymity inevitably ends when that option is exercised.

Special guarantees, such as allowing dollar-denominated bank accounts for residents bringing foreign exchange or guaranteeing the convertibility of "registered" inflows will, if credible, reduce the fiscal risks faced. However, such special treatment of returning resident capital implicitly subordinates other domestic claims, increasing their exposure to risk. Thus, they could exacerbate "arbitrage" capital flight in periods of crisis. Further, given the track record of many countries with respect to such guarantees, for example, Mexico's treatment of Mex-dollar accounts, it is unlikely that they will be fully credible, especially in cases where there is a large overhang of external sovereign debt with even more senior status.

Offshore Intermediation

In his survey of history, Kindleberger (ch. 2) pointed out that Argentines were important buyers of Argentine bonds floated on the London capital market in the late nineteenth century. Similarly, India has recently created a mutual fund to allow Indian expatriates to invest in Indian industry, Mexicans are known to be significant purchasers of Mexican securities in US markets, and Latin businessmen are understood to borrow from Miami banks using their deposits in the same banks as collateral.[29]

The existence of such offshore intermediation casts doubt on the proposition that foreign placement of funds can be explained in terms of portfolio diversification, since most of the risks to which the investor chooses to expose himself are those of his domestic economy. Indeed, the fact that the investor chooses to expose himself to those risks despite having taken his funds abroad suggests that he feels more comfortable with the economic risks of the economy that he knows. What he must be seeking is either a more liquid medium (perhaps assuring convertibility into foreign exchange)

---

29. The advantages of this procedure are that, in his capacity as foreign borrower, the businessman gets access to official exchange to service his debt while, if things go wrong at home, he would retain a foreign asset provided that he could get the debt taken off his hands when he sold the company.

for his assets than offered by local markets, the chance to change the currency denomination of his claim so as to evade the risk of devaluation of the local currency, the opportunity of evading taxation, or else protection through anonymity and the leverage provided by the foreign jurisdiction vis-à-vis those country risks that weigh more heavily on resident than on nonresident capital.

With regard to anonymity, offshore intermediation can provide an effective laundering of funds to reduce the risk of ex post claims or sanctions. Further, it provides residents with nonresident bedfellows which may provide some protection against attempts to impose reprisals.

To the extent that offshore intermediation can be relied on to recycle funds back to the local economy, capital flight would not have some of the damaging effects analyzed above ("Consequences"). In particular, it would not aggravate the foreign-exchange or savings shortage. It would still, of course, impede the development of local financial markets. If it involves acquisition of a claim denominated in foreign exchange, it would increase the social cost of devaluation. And it would still leave the perverse redistribution of income and wealth and attendant fiscal problem.

The main problem with offshore intermediation, however, would appear to be that it is not a reliable form of recycling. Domestic residents may be willing to recycle their funds, or some part of their funds, under normal circumstances, but the moments of acute national emergency, when the need to conserve foreign exchange is greatest, are precisely those when newly fleeing money is least likely to be recycled and previously recycled money is most likely to flee. Thus, in most cases, offshore intermediation would not seem an attractive long-run solution. Its most useful role may be as a first stage in the return of flight capital.

Should Countries Seek to Recapture Flight Capital?

While one might be tempted to take it as axiomatic that countries should seek to recapture flight capital, the issue is at what cost and to what end. How much better terms should a country be willing to offer residents with funds abroad than those without or than nonresidents? What special benefits will such recapture bring? While it will improve the image of a source country in world financial circles, there is no assurance that this would lead to more favorable terms on outstanding debt. Further, there is no reason to expect recaptured funds to be less footloose in case of future crises than either foreign funds or new resident savings. However, to the extent that such funds are more likely to be combined effectively with local management and entrepreneurship, they might be considerably more valuable than inflows of foreign capital.

Some countries may find it impossible to translate policy reforms into renewed growth without an initial injection of foreign exchange provided by the repatriation of flight capital. The obverse problem is that the amnesties necessary to secure a rapid repatriation of capital may undermine the rule of law and hence respect for the policy reforms. It does not seem possible to offer a general conclusion as to which of these dangers is greatest, but two criteria are highly relevant:

☐ the magnitude of the sums currently held abroad by residents relative to the alternative sources of foreign exchange available to the country

☐ the feasibility of convincing the public that any amnesty is once-and-for-all.

Countries with relatively adequate foreign exchange availability are probably well-advised to learn to live with offshore intermediation until funds seep back of their own accord. But countries that have suffered massive outflows and have little alternative prospect of restoring growth should examine whether they cannot make a credible commitment to a once-and-for-all amnesty. The worst of all worlds would be to allow policy to be paralyzed between these two solutions.

Summary and Conclusions

We defined capital flight as resident capital that flees from the perception of abnormal risks at home. We argued, however, that a more interesting concept to measure than capital flight was *total* outflows of resident capital, including "normal" portfolio diversification, because a loss of domestic savings to a savings-short economy has the same ill consequences whether or not it is "normal." In practice, of course, resident capital outflow is a serious problem only when normal outflows are reinforced by capital flight.

Our concern with outflows of capital from developing countries is not a rejection of the desirability of international integration of financial markets. Rather it reflects the view that poor countries can and should be able to retain their domestic savings at home, as well as draw on foreign savings. Ideally this might be achieved with domestic holding of foreign assets for security and diversification purposes being offset by foreign holdings of (risky) domestic assets, but in the absence of suitable offsetting investments it is necessary to be concerned if outward flows become sizable.

Despite the effort that has recently been invested in estimating resident capital outflow, there remains a great margin of uncertainty about the statistics. It is nevertheless clear that a great deal of money—probably approaching $100 billion from just five of the principal countries involved (Argentina, Brazil, Mexico, the Philippines, and Venezuela)—did flee. Argentina, Mexico, and Venezuela were particularly heavily affected. Significant sums have started to return to some countries in the past 18 months or so.

Two general theories have been advanced to explain capital flight. One points to a deficient overall investment climate resulting from macroeconomic mismanagement that raises fears of currency devaluation, inflation, fiscal deficits, low growth, and a debt overhang. The other focuses on discriminatory treatment of resident capital in the form of taxes, financial repression, and the nonavailability of foreign-exchange denomination of claims, and subordination to nonresident claims in the event of financial crisis. Unlike the overall investment-climate theory, the discriminatory-treatment theory can explain resident capital outflows that coincide with nonresident inflows. It is therefore the natural explanation for the capital flight that antedated the debt crisis. Conversely, the discriminatory-treatment theory cannot explain the persistence of resident capital outflows after voluntary lending to the debtor countries dried up in 1982: the natural explanation is inadequacy of the overall investment climate. Empirical studies seem to point particularly clearly to the role of currency overvaluation. Presumably the recent repatriation of capital to Argentina and Mexico reflects some improvement in the investment climate as well as high real interest rates.

Resident capital outflow is generally bad for the country involved and bad for the world as a whole. This is not to deny that it results from rational and perfectly understandable behavior on the part of wealth-owners, nor indeed that it may at times serve to induce desirable policy changes. Nevertheless, resident capital outflow from a country that is a natural net capital importer necessarily implies either that investment, and therefore growth, is lower than it need be, or that the country is a bigger gross borrower from the world capital market, with the attendant financial exposure. In the former case, a loss of domestic capital may intensify the foreign-exchange constraint as well as the savings constraint, and thus dictate a cutback in current output as well as future growth. In either case, resident capital outflow means the exportation of financial intermediation and therefore stultification of the growth of domestic financial markets. It may also lead to a fiscal crisis, and hence inflation, and a massive perverse redistribution of income and wealth. In the worst case, domestic capitalists may start looking for more challenging foreign investment opportunities than liquid assets and real estate, leading their native societies to lose not just their capital but also their entrepreneurial energies and their economic stake in national policies.

The primary responsibility for stemming resident capital outflows rests on the source countries, for it is their inadequate policies that turned the minor problem of normal outflow into the major problem of capital flight. Our four key policy recommendations may be summarized as follows:

- restoration and maintenance of responsible macroeconomic policies involving competitive exchange rates, positive but nonprohibitive real interest rates, and fiscal probity, hopefully leading to the restoration of economic growth

- reform of the domestic financial system to make it less dependent on government intervention and more resilient to shocks

- a pragmatic attitude to exchange controls that avoids regarding them as a substitute for sound policies and recognizes that they cannot attract back money that has already fled, while using them in appropriate circumstances to limit the exodus of new savings

- a decision to base the tax system on the residence principle and a major effort to improve tax enforcement, involving in particular a willingness to sign tax treaties so as to secure an exchange of information with the principal haven countries that will permit the collection of taxes due on foreign investment income.

Capital outflows from debtor countries are also importantly influenced by policies in the haven countries, however, as the significant coefficient on US interest rates in some estimates of the causes of resident capital outflows has confirmed. The haven countries have a duty to help resolve this problem, in the following ways:

- by imposing a substantial withholding tax on all nonresident investment income, which would be refundable on evidence that the recipient had reported the income to his national tax authority, coupled with a continued or an enhanced willingness to sign tax treaties so as to enable the source countries to tax the foreign investment income of their residents

- by the private banking departments of commercial banks ending the deliberate solicitation of new clients in developing countries and the provision of "pouch services"

- by continuing efforts to reduce real interest rates to historically normal levels.

The most important priority is to stop the hemorrhage of new capital outflow rather than to attract back the money that has already fled. Whether special efforts (tax amnesties or "whitener bonds") are worth making to attract capital back depends on the size of the stock held abroad and the possibilities of securing adequate finance from other sources, and also the feasibility of carrying credibility with a commitment that these are once-and-for-all measures.

Although some capital returned to two of the three principal source countries in the past 18 months, it would be wrong to think that the problem of capital flight has already been resolved. The price of that repatriation has been extremely high interest rates—far higher than are consistent with an investment boom and hence the restoration of growth prospects. Moreover, recent reports indicate renewed capital flight from Argentina. While much progress has been made toward the institution of responsible macroeconomic policies and several countries are getting to grips with needed reforms of their domestic financial systems, there has as yet been no action on the needed fiscal reforms. Moreover, resolution of the problem will require confidence that these changes will be maintained over the long haul and not allowed to slip once the money returns. The challenge remains, in Kindleberger's words, "quite an order."

References

Balassa, Bela, Gerardo M. Bueno, Pedro-Pablo Kuczynski, and Mario Henrique Simonsen. 1986. *Toward Renewed Economic Growth in Latin America*. Mexico City: El Colegio de Mexico; Rio de Janeiro: Fundação Getúlio Vargas; Washington: Institute for International Economics.

Conesa, Eduardo R. 1987. *The Causes of Capital Flight from Latin America*. Washington: Inter-American Development Bank.

Cuddington, John T. 1986. *Capital Flight: Estimates, Issues, and Explanations*, Princeton Studies in International Finance, no. 58. Princeton, NJ:International Finance Section, Department of Economics, Princeton University.

Deppler, Michael, and Martin Williamson. 1987. "Capital Flight: Concepts, Measurement, and Issues." In *Staff Studies for the World Economic Outlook*. Washington: International Monetary Fund, August, pp. 39–58.

Diaz Alejandro, Carlos. 1984. "Latin American Debt: I Don't Think We Are in Kansas Anymore." *Brookings Papers on Economic Activity*, no. 2.

Dooley, Michael, William Helkie, Ralph Tryon and John Underwood. 1986. "An Analysis of External Debt Positions of Eight Developing Countries Through 1990." *Journal of Development Economics*, vol. 21, no 2, pp. 283–318.

Dooley, Michael. 1986. "Country-Specific Risk Premiums, Capital Flight and Net Investment Income Payments in Selected Developing Countries," DM 86/17. Washington: International Monetary Fund.

Dornbusch, Rudiger. 1985. "External Debt, Budget Deficits and Disequilibrium Exchange Rates." In *International Debt and the Developing Countries*, edited by Gordon W. Smith and John T. Cuddington. Washington: World Bank.

Eaton, Jonathan. 1987. "Public Debt Guarantees and Private Capital Flight." *World Bank Economic Review*, vol. 1, no. 3 (May), pp. 377–95.

Eaton, Jonathan; Mark Gersovitz; and Joseph E. Stiglitz. 1986. "The Pure Theory of Country Risk." *European Economic Review*, vol. 4, no. 30, pp. 481–513.

Erbe, Susanne. 1985. "The Flight of Capital from Developing Countries." *Intereconomics*, (November/December).

Frieden, Jeff. 1981. "Third World Indebted Industrialization: International Finance and State Capitalism in Mexico, Brazil, Algeria, and South Korea." *International Organization*, vol. 35, no. 3, pp. 407–32.

Gennotte, Gerard; Homi Kharas; and Sayeed Sadeq. 1987. "A Valuation Model for LDC Debt with Endogenous Reschedulings." *World Bank Economic Review*, vol. 1, no. 2, pp. 237–72.

Gillis, Malcolm; Donald Lessard; and Glenn Jenkins. 1982. "Public Enterprise Finance: Toward a Synthesis." In *Public Enterprise in Less Developed Countries*, edited by Leroy P. Jones et al. Cambridge: Cambridge University Press.

Glynn, Lenny, and Peter Koenig. 1984. "The Capital Flight Crisis." *Institutional Investor*, international edition. (November), pp. 109–19.

Guzman Calafell, Javier, and Jesus Alvarez Gutierrez. 1987. *Las Fugas de Capital en Mexico: Un Analisis Critico de los Planteamientos Recientes*. Mexico City: Banco de Mexico.

Ize, Alain, and Guillermo Ortiz. 1987. "Fiscal Rigidities, Public Debt, and Capital Flight," IMF *Staff Papers*, vol. 34, no. 2 (June), pp. 311–33.

Khan, Mohsin S., and Nadeem Ul Haque. 1985. "Foreign Borrowing and Capital Flight: A Formal Analysis." IMF *Staff Papers*, vol. 32, no. 4 (December), pp. 606–28.

———. 1987. "Capital Flight from Developing Countries," *Finance and Development* (March).

Kindleberger, Charles P. 1937. *International Short-Term Capital Movements*. New York, NY: Augustus Kelley.

Kraft, Joseph. 1984. *The Mexican Rescue*. New York, NY: Group of Thirty.

Lessard, Donald R. 1987. "Country Risk and the Structure of International Financial Intermediation." Federal Reserve Bank of St. Louis, Conference on Financial Risk, forthcoming.

Lessard, Donald R., and John Williamson. 1987. *Capital Flight and Third World Debt*. Washington: Institute for International Economics.

Magee, Stephen P., and William A. Brock. 1986. "Third World Debt and International Capital Market Failure as a Consequence of Redistributive Political Risk Sharing." In *World Debt Crisis: International Lending on Trial*, edited by Michael P. Claudon. Cambridge, Mass.: Ballinger.

Merton, Robert C. 1977. "An Analytic Derivation of the Cost of Loan Guarantees and Deposit Insurance: An Application of Modern Option Pricing Theory." *Journal of Banking and Finance*, no. 1, pp 3–11.

Morgan Guaranty. 1986. "LDC Capital Flight." *World Financial Markets* (March).

——— 1987. "LDC Debt Realities," *World Financial Markets* (June–July).

Protopapadakis, Aris. 1985. "An Analysis of Government Credit 'Crises.'" Federal Reserve Bank of Philadelphia, Working Paper, no. 85–14.

Tobin, James. 1977. "How Dead is Keynes?" *Economic Inquiry* (October).

Williamson, John. 1983. *The Open Economy and the World Economy*. New York, NY: Basic Books.

World Bank. 1985. *World Development Report—1985*. Washington.

Appendix

Participants, Conference on Capital Flight, Institute for International Economics, Washington, October 2–4, 1986

Osvaldo R. Agatiello
Banco Central de la Republica Argentina
Buenos Aires

James E. Ammerman
Department of the Treasury
Washington

Dragoslav Avramovíc
Bank of Credit and Commerce International
Washington

George B. N. Ayittey
Bloomsburg University
Bloomsburg, Pa.

Norman A. Bailey
Colby, Bailey and Associates
Washington

Bela Balassa
Institute for International Economics
Washington

C. Fred Bergsten
Institute for International Economics
Washington

Jagdish Bhagwati
World Bank
Washington

David R. Bock
World Bank
Washington

David E. Bodner
Bank Julius Baer
New York, NY

Eduardo R. Conesa
Inter-American Development Bank
Washington

Hugh W. Conway
Federal Deposit Insurance Corporation
Washington

Vittorio Corbo
World Bank
Washington

John T. Cuddington
Georgetown University
Washington

Robert E. Cumby
New York University
New York, NY

Jorge Daly
AFL-CIO
Washington

David T. Devlin
Citibank
New York, NY

Robert Devlin
United Nations Economic Commission
    for Latin America and the Caribbean
Santiago

José A. Diaz-Asper
ATC Consortium
Washington

Michael P. Dooley
International Monetary Fund
Washington

Rudiger Dornbusch
Massachusetts Institute of Technology
Cambridge, Mass.

Vance van Dyne
Morgan Stanley International
New York, NY

Jorge Espinosa-Carranza
Inter-American Development Bank
Washington

Thomas L. Farmer
Prather, Seeger, Doolittle & Farmer
Washington

Richard E. Feinberg
Overseas Development Council
Washington

Ava S. Feiner
IBM
Washington

C. David Finch
International Monetary Fund
Washington

Isaiah Frank
Johns Hopkins University
Washington

Erhard Fürst
Creditanstalt
Vienna

Sunil Gulati
Columbia University
New York, NY

José Angel Gurria
Ministry of Finance
Mexico City

Efraim Gutkino
Trade Development Bank
Geneva, Switzerland

Carleton R. Haswell
Chemical Bank
New York, NY

H. Robert Heller
Federal Reserve Board
Washington

C. Randall Henning
Institute for International Economics
Washington

Richard J. Herring
University of Pennsylvania
Philadelphia, Pa.

James S. Henry
New York, NY

Rudolf Hommes
Estrategia Económica
Bogotá

William C. Hood
International Monetary Fund
Washington

Shafiqul Islam
Institute for International Economics
Washington

Alain Ize
International Monetary Fund
Washington

Fred Z. Jaspersen
World Bank
Washington

Alexandre Kafka
International Monetary Fund
Washington

Suhas L. Ketkar
Marine Midland Bank
New York, NY

G. Russell Kincaid
International Monetary Fund
Washington

Charles P. Kindleberger
Massachusetts Institute of Technology
Cambridge, Mass.

Linda P. Kinney
Department of State
Washington

Norman R. Klath
Morgan Guaranty Trust Company
New York, NY

Charles Kovacs
Chase Manhattan Bank
New York, NY

Pedro-Pablo Kuczynski
First Boston International
New York, NY

Donald R. Lessard
Massachusetts Institute of Technology
Cambridge, Mass.

Richard M. Levich
New York University
New York, NY

Frank E. Loy
German Marshall Fund
Washington

Richard T. McCormack
Organization of American States
Washington

William J. McFadden
Department of the Treasury
Washington

Carlos A. Massad
United Nations Economic Commission
  for Latin America and the Caribbean
  and University of Santiago
Santiago

Hyman P. Minsky
Washington University
St. Louis, Mo.

Jeremiah L. Murphy
Siemens Capital Corporation
Washington

Marcus Noland
Institute for International Economics
Washington

Richard R. O'Brien
American Express Bank
London

Barbara N. Opper
World Bank
Washington

Carlos Paredes
Brookings Institution
Washington

Guy Pierre Pfeffermann
World Bank
Washington

Jorge Pinto
Embassy of Mexico
Washington

Rafael Pozas
Embassy of Mexico
Washington

Peter J. Quirk
International Monetary Fund
Washington

Joseph R. Ramos
United Nations Economic Commission for
  Latin America and the Caribbean
Santiago

John G. Rehak
Siemens Capital Corporation
Washington

Alfred Reifman
Congressional Research Service
Washington

Eli M. Remolona
Federal Reserve Bank of New York

Wolfgang Rieke
Deutsche Bundesbank
Frankfurt, Germany

Rhys Robinson
Institute for International Economics
Washington

Miguel Rodriguez F.
Instituto de Estudios Superiores
  de Administración
Caracas

Riordan Roett
Johns Hopkins University
Washington

John B. Ross
Institute of International Finance
Washington

Robert Samuelson
Newsweek
Washington

Horst Schulman
Institute of International Finance
Washington

Aloys Schwietert
Swiss Bank Corporation
Basel, Switzerland

Michael R. Sesit
Wall Street Journal
New York, NY

Barbara B. Stallings
University of Wisconsin
Madison, Wis.

Leon S. Tarrant
Comptroller of the Currency
Washington

Jane L. Barber Thery
Institute for International Economics
Washington

Edwin M. Truman
Federal Reserve Board
Washington

Miguel Urrutia
Inter-American Development Bank
Washington

Philip K. Verleger Jr.
Institute for International Economics
Washington

Rimmer de Vries
Morgan Guaranty Trust
New York, NY

Ingo Walter
New York University
New York, NY

Richard G. Ware
Bank of England
London

Alfred J. Watkins
Joint Economic Committee
Washington

Richard C. Webb
Universidad Católica
Lima

Peter J. West
Institute of International Finance
Washington

Howard Wiarda
American Enterprise Institute
Washington

John Williamson
Institute for International Economics
Washington

Martin C. Williamson
International Monetary Fund
Washington

Paul Wonnacott
Institute for International Economics
Washington

Ernesto Zedillo
Banco de Mexico
Mexico City

Other Publications from the Institute

POLICY ANALYSES IN INTERNATIONAL ECONOMICS SERIES

SPECIAL REPORTS

FORTHCOMING